MW01089402

Loren,

Best wishes

Bob

Bob Kabel

Inside *and* Out

The Odyssey of a Gay Conservative

Print ISBN: 978-1-09831-664-8

eBook ISBN: 978-1-09831-665-5

This book is dedicated to my parents, whose support and encouragement have been invaluable to my growth and success over the years.

ACKNOWLEDGMENTS

SEVERAL INDIVIDUALS WERE HELPFUL IN CONCEIVING AND WRITing this book, but two stand out. *Inside and Out* has been the product of more than five years of work, starting with more than 50 hours of taped interviews with Michael Williams. Michael developed first drafts for most chapters of the final manuscript. He helped organize the book and kept us on track as it developed. Michael is a professional writer and long-time friend.

More recently, Patrick Sammon has provided invaluable insights that have improved the manuscript, including extensive editing. Patrick helped pull together the final manuscript and photographs for publication. Patrick is a documentary filmmaker, former president of Log Cabin Republicans, and long-time friend.

TABLE OF CONTENTS

CHAPTER 1

Trump Time

MY LIFE STARTED JUST AFTER WORLD WAR II AS AMERICA EMERGED as the most dominant power in the world. I have lived during a time of unprecedented economic, social, and political change in the United States. My life has been impacted by two of our nation's biggest post-war political movements: the push for LGBT civil rights and the political dominance of the conservative movement. Both of these battles have been integral to my life: helping define where I worked, how I lived, who I loved, and the person I became.

As a young man, my fascination with politics and the Republican Party helped propel me toward a career in the upper echelons of American government. Over more than 40 years observing and working in national politics, I have been fortunate to have worked for some remarkable political leaders from whom I learned much about integrity, hard work, and the importance of fighting for causes greater than myself.

One movement that has been important to me during much of my adult life is the struggle for LGBT civil rights. From 1946 when I was born through my childhood and into adulthood, gays and lesbians endured punishing laws and hostile societal attitudes. Those laws and attitudes have changed in remarkable ways. I have worked hard, doing what I can in the Republican Party to push for freedom and fairness for LGBT Americans. Some people might wonder how I could be a proud, openly gay man while also remaining a loyal and dedicated Republican. The answer is simple. The Republican Party's basic principles have always matched mine: personal liberty, individual responsibility, economic freedom, limited government, and a strong national defense. It hasn't always been easy walking the tightrope of life as a gay Republican, but I have tried to live with integrity and honor, standing up for my beliefs, taking arrows from some Republicans and even more from members of the LGBT community.

In my long life, nothing has been more surprising to me than the rise of Donald Trump to the presidency of the United States. Historians will write about this period for generations to come. His presidency may be the most unlikely in our nation's history. And I've had a front row seat for all of it.

As a member of the Republican National Committee (RNC), I attended the first debate for Republican Presidential candidates in Cleveland in early August of 2015. I remember entering the debate hall with anticipation and excitement. As a political junkie, I was like a kid at Christmas anxious to see what Santa left me under the tree. Candidate Trump ran an unconventional campaign from start to finish. His announcement at Trump Tower in New York City on June 16, 2015 was a harbinger of things to come. His tirade against illegal immigrants, especially undocumented Mexican immigrants, produced headlines around the world. *The Guardian* reported, "The 69-year-old businessman best known for his 'You're fired' catchphrase on *The Apprentice*, announced he was running for president on Tuesday with an eccentric speech attacking Mexican immigrants and promising to build a great wall along the U.S. southern border." Trump directed most of his ire at Mexico. "They're sending us not the right people," he said. "The U.S. has become a dumping ground for everyone else's problems."

Two months later by the time he reached Cleveland for the first debate, the so-called experts, including yours truly, doubted that he would be able to continue his early momentum. I thought his inflated poll numbers in the GOP primary were based largely on his high name recognition and unconventional style. Would his momentum hold up under the hot lights when his opponents aired his dirty laundry which included a less-than-stellar business record, a closet full of personal scandals, and a list of policy positions that veered from GOP orthodoxy on a range of issues?

On that late summer Cleveland night, candidate Trump was in attack mode from beginning to end. He didn't care about conventional wisdom or business as usual. In one particularly memorable exchange, Megyn Kelly, then at Fox News, asked him to defend his descriptions of women he disagreed with as "fat pigs, dogs, slobs and disgusting animals." After interrupting with "only Rosie O'Donnell," Trump offered a more detailed reply: "I've been challenged by so many people, and I don't frankly have time for total political correctness. And to be honest with you, this country doesn't have time either."

To describe him as a bull in a China shop is a bit of an understatement. And that was his style in all 11 of the subsequent Republican Presidential debates. Like many other Republicans, I left the Cleveland debate hall that first night thinking that a man with his background and temperament could not become the party's standard bearer. Much to my amazement, the polls immediately declared him the winner of the first debate. He was off and running. Still, my innate political sense and decades of experience would not allow me to believe this man could win my party's nomination, much less be elected President of the United States. Not for the first time in my life and not for the last, I was dead wrong.

So how did Trump do it? How did he win what may be the most surprising presidential victory in American history? I see six main reasons for Trump's victory: his ability to garner the media spotlight, his unorthodox style, his ability to read and tap into the country's political mood, voter fatigue with the Obama administration, the weakness of Democratic nominee Hillary Clinton, and the Republican Party ground game. Let's take these in order:

Trump was a marketing genius as a businessman and TV personality, and he used that talent to maximum effect in his presidential campaign, grabbing round-the-clock media attention. No one in the GOP field could match his aggressive "take-no-prisoners" approach. He regularly called into cable television news shows, in particular *Morning Joe* to discuss the race with Joe Scarborough and Mika Brzezinski. Years of successfully marketing himself in his businesses and his exposure on *The Apprentice* paid off. The cable networks would regularly cover his speeches and news conferences. GOP voters loved how he regularly sparred with news reporters. He didn't need to be handled. His message didn't need to be crafted by his advisors. He didn't need to be kept on script. That's because he was writing the script and the American public couldn't get enough of him. He was a ratings winner. His supporters tuned in because they loved every second of it. His opponents tuned in to see what outrageous thing he would say next. That interest translated into hundreds of millions of dollars of free publicity. The value of that spotlight can't be understated.

The second reason Trump won was because of his ability to read the mood of the country in 2016. He capitalized on the underlying dissatisfaction many Americans had with status quo politics and politicians from both parties who had ignored the needs of middle and lower-middle class voters. Both Trump and Bernie Sanders focused on the forgotten Americans in small towns and cities who were upset because their lives had been upended by globalization and automation that left behind a depleted manufacturing base. Trump supporters were tired of business as usual, especially the gridlock that has defined Washington for most of the past 20 years. Add to that the weariness of two long, expensive wars and the residual trauma from the 2008 financial crisis and you had a recipe for political revolution if a candidate could tap into the discontent. Voters wanted change and Trump offered it. While Trump caught many of us by surprise, his campaign succeeded because, better than any other GOP candidate, he understood the country's mood. Trump won the presidency as a populist opposed to many of the GOP's basic tenets such as free trade, an aggressive foreign policy, restrained federal spending, and limited government. Growing frustration by voters of all political stripes with big business, the media, and public elites opened the door in 2016 for populist candidates;Trump for the GOP and Sanders for the Democrats (though he fell just short of winning his party's nomination).

The third reason for Trump's success comes down to one word: authenticity. Love him or hate him, he is who he is. American voters have become weary of blow-dried candidates who speak in perfect talking points and never veer from the script. They never say anything controversial. Trump was the opposite and voters ate it up. They had grown weary of overdone political correctness where people and groups were constantly taking offense at even the most minor slight. His controversial statements resulted in a brighter spotlight. At one point, he famously said, "I could stand in the middle of 5th Avenue and shoot somebody, and I wouldn't lose voters." The rules of political gravity didn't apply to him in 2016. One controversial statement after another defined his campaign. Stories that would have destroyed other presidential candidates had little if any effect on his numbers. Voters don't always agree with him, but they appreciate that he is the real deal.

The fourth reason for Trump's victory boils down to one man: President Barack Obama. In hindsight, he seems more popular than he was in fact. He likely would have lost re-election in 2012 had Republicans nominated a stronger candidate. People forget that Obama's economic recovery was quite anemic. Plus, Obamacare was incredibly unpopular. Also, for the last 75 years, American voters have almost always turned out the incumbent party after eight years in the White House. Since the Eisenhower administration, voters have been ready for change after a two-term president. Not only different policies but also different personality types. The only exception to this rule was the election of George H.W. Bush to succeed President Ronald Reagan's two terms. The two-term rule helped elect Donald Trump as President. President Obama's presidency had further polarized the country and many voters were ready for a change.

The fifth reason for Trump's victory comes down to one person: Hillary Clinton. She was a weak candidate who failed to excite her own base while energizing Trump's base by calling them a "basket of deplorables…they are racist, sexist, homophobic, xenophobic." That comment persuaded me Trump might actually win. Clinton also had a baffling political strategy. After the Democratic Convention, she never visited Wisconsin once. She barely made it to Michigan. She and her team took Pennsylvania for granted. They assumed because voters in those states had supported every Democratic presidential candidate for six straight elections, they would do so again. She and her team had too much faith that the so-called "blue wall" would propel her to victory. The first rule of politics is you have to show up. Unbelievably, Clinton didn't do that. It's political malpractice.

The final reason for Trump's victory comes down to good old-fashioned campaign strategy. First, Trump's campaign wisely invested its comparably limited resources in digital advertising. As head of the campaign's digital strategy, Brad Parscale rolled out a sophisticated under-the-radar plan to connect online with Trump supporters. Using sophisticated data analytics and micro-targeting, Trump's team found his supporters and motivated them to vote. Many of his supporters had never before voted for a Republican or they hadn't voted in many years.

The second key campaign strategy came from the Republican National Committee. After emerging as the GOP nominee, it became clear Trump didn't have a ground game mapped out anywhere. However, to the Trump campaign's advantage, the Republican National Committee had developed its own ground game along with strong technological capabilities. After the 2012 election defeat when candidate Mitt Romney's election day get-out-the-vote effort flopped because of technology glitches, the RNC was determined not to allow that to happen again. The party created a nationwide infrastructure that would be turned over to the 2016 nominee at the end of the primary season.

These initiatives were launched by then-RNC Chairman Reince Priebus who raised millions of dollars for two voter contact programs. This effort was recommended by the so-called 2012 autopsy report that was put together following Romney's defeat. The first initiative placed full-time RNC staff on the ground earlier than ever before in target states, especially focused on diverse demographic groups including Latinos, Asians, African Americans, and others. The second part of the RNC's plan involved developing the most sophisticated technological capability any political party had ever possessed. By 2016, the RNC's technology capabilities far surpassed the much-touted Obama 2012 campaign in that area. The GOP's ground game and the technology edge helped the Trump campaign enormously as it would have done to whoever the party nominated.

On Election Day of 2016, I rose early to try to avoid the crowds at my voting precinct a few blocks from my home. The line was already long when I arrived around 8 a.m. just as the polls opened. It was a foregone conclusion that Hillary Clinton would win the District's three electoral votes. Clinton won D.C. with 91% of the vote. Candidate Trump received just 4%, little more than half the registered Republicans in Washington. For much of the rest of the day, I checked to see how the voting was going in other parts of the city and watched the reports of turnout around the country.This wasn't the typical election and I wouldn't watch election results like I usually did. In the past, I attended large gatherings in hotel ballrooms hosted by one of the key GOP political organizations. In 2016, the RNC was holding its election night watch party at the W Hotel, and as a national committeeman I was invited to attend. I opted for a quieter evening than what I knew would be the raucous atmosphere at such a large event. I invited a few friends to join me watching the results from the comfort and serenity of the Metropolitan Club. I was anticipating a fairly short evening that would result in a clear victory for Hillary Clinton. As Trump began taking a lead in toss-up states and then even in states favored by Clinton, the mood in the room began to change. Ohio was called for Trump at 10:39 p.m., then Florida 15 minutes later. By that point, attendees, including me, decided to head home to watch the remaining results. At 2:30 a.m., the news outlets declared Trump the winner of Wisconsin. The state's ten Electoral College votes pushed Trump past the 270 electoral votes required to be president-elect. Hillary Clinton called Trump at 2:35 a.m. to congratulate him. Candidate Trump was now President-Elect Trump. Even nearly four years later, the whole thing seems unbelievable.

Love him or hate him, President Trump is a transformational political figure. Some people in the media predicted and certainly hoped that candidate Trump would give way to a different President Trump. They thought he would evolve his style and his beliefs. That was never going to happen; a fact that became clear minutes after he was inaugurated.

On January 20, 2017, Trump's Inaugural Address mirrored the tone of his campaign. It was the angriest presidential speech I can remember. As I sat in the section for RNC members, I was stunned by his rhetoric, especially his dark characterization of the state of the country and his pointed criticism of many current and former leaders who were seated around him. Most presidents use their inaugural address to unite the American people and bind the wounds of a nation divided by a long campaign. Not Trump. Instead, his address sounded more like a campaign speech with lots of harsh rhetoric and dark images about the state of the nation. "We must protect our borders from the ravages of other countries making our products, stealing our companies, and destroying our jobs," said Trump. "Protection will lead to great prosperity and strength. I will fight for you with every breath in my body and I will never ever let you down."

It was a cold, damp day, and I had arrived with other RNC members several hours before the swearing-in to get through security and find my seat. I was delighted when it was over, so I could go someplace warm. Since 9/11, intense security has made it difficult to enjoy Inauguration Day. I tried to take a friend to an inaugural ball that evening but gave up after discovering we had misread the ticket and were in the wrong line. I felt sorry for the many Trump supporters from out of town who didn't know what to expect and were trying to make the most of it. Recognizing we probably had at least another hour's wait, my friend and I gave up and had a quiet dinner before walking home.

With Trump's first term nearly over, here's where I think the nation stands. Until the COVID-19 pandemic brought the U.S. and world economies to a standstill earlier this year, President Trump's domestic policies had resulted in a dramatic economic boom. There was record low unemployment and rising wages. And the rising tide was lifting all boats as economic statistics showed unemployment rates reaching historically low rates among African Americans and Latinos. The financial markets, a reliable indicator of economic well-being and projected growth, reached record levels, and consumer confidence reached levels not seen in many years. The shutdown of the American economy and the resulting layoffs make all of that good news seem like a distant memory. The question is whether President Trump will get blamed for the sagging economy. By November, the economy may have turned a corner, providing the president with a much-needed boost. Or we may be mired in a deep recession that serves as an anchor around Trump's re-election chances.

During his term, President Trump's economic policies have consisted primarily of a dramatic reduction in federal regulations especially in the area of the environment and financial services. The 2017 tax reform bill included a cut in corporate tax rates, making our country more competitive with the rest of the world. The tax cuts also brought broad-based relief to average Americans. Soon after the cuts, many big companies announced employee bonuses. The then House Minority Leader Nancy Pelosi absurdly dismissed the good news by describing them as "crumbs." That's easy to say for a San Francisco millionaire. However, most average hard-working Americans appreciated the extra money in their wallet. Talk about out of touch!

Aside from deregulation and tax cuts, President Trump renegotiated NAFTA and embarked on a painful trade war with China. A new deal with China is now in place. However, if Trump wins re-election, it seems like that war could resume in 2021. Trump has been committed to encouraging American manufacturing to return to the U.S. The COVID-19 crisis is likely to speed up the trend to return manufacturing to this country. It's now a national security and public health imperative. The American business community has responded enthusiastically to Trump's business friendly policies. For the first time in memory, an experienced businessman sits in the White House. He understands the needs of the business world and has acted to improve the regulatory environment for small and big businesses.

The chaotic, tumultuous atmosphere of the 2016 Trump campaign has continued into his presidency. It became clear to American voters that candidate Trump relied primarily on his personal experiences and instincts during his campaign and it should come as no surprise that he has conducted his presidency much the same way. The first several months were especially chaotic. Symbolic of his management style, President Trump is on his fourth chief of staff, having fired or in some fashion moved on from the first three. His entire administration has been a revolving door. Frequent vacancies and firings have at times created chaos in the White House and throughout the government. Meanwhile, Trump continues to hold the spotlight daily and continues to spar with the news media. Of course, he also relentlessly tweets. Through it all, many Americans, including me, have learned to tune this out and focus on the bigger picture. We support most of President Trump's policies even if we don't always like his style.

In foreign affairs, President Trump has shaken up the global establishment much like he has done on the domestic stage. The United States continues to be the major financial contributor to many international organizations. President Trump has used this as leverage to question the role and impact of many of these organizations. As a result of his consistent criticism, NATO member countries have increased their annual defense budgets and contribution to NATO's funding. He has gotten other results including winding down our involvement in Iraq and Afghanistan and opening a dialogue with North Korea. He also took the United States out of the Iran nuclear deal and the Paris climate agreements. Both of these deals had major flaws and Trump was right to pull our nation out of these agreements, especially since neither had been approved by the U.S. Senate.

No matter what happens in November, Trump's presidency will leave a lasting mark on the U.S. The GOP-controlled Senate has confirmed more federal judges, including two Supreme Court justices, than any previous president. Following the lead of a previous Democratic Senate, the GOP modified the filibuster to allow a simple majority vote on Supreme Court justices. The Brett Kavanaugh confirmation was especially contentious with Judiciary Committee Democrats trying to use a decades-old sexual assault allegation to sidetrack his nomination. Former Senate Majority Leader Harry Reid (D-NV) changed the filibuster rule in 2013 to confirm Obama-nominated District and Circuit

Court judges by majority vote; Senate Majority Leader Mitch McConnell (R-KY) took that one step further to Supreme Court nominees.

Many Democrats continue to question the legitimacy of the Trump presidency and have worked tirelessly to bring him down, starting the effort even before he was inaugurated. The initial effort was a more than two-year inquiry into allegations of Russian interference in the 2016 election and collusion in the Russian effort by Trump's campaign. The Mueller Report outlined a litany of examples of Russian interference, but it found no collusion from the Trump campaign. He made no finding on the question of whether President Trump obstructed justice in an effort to derail the inquiry. Just months after the release of the Mueller Report, in the summer of 2019, a whistle-blower allegation against President Trump regarding a phone call he had with the president of Ukraine turned into an impeachment inquiry. House Speaker Nancy Pelosi (D-CA) resisted calls for an impeachment inquiry but after several months caved to the most radical wing of her caucus and agreed to proceed. After the House voted in mid-December on party lines to impeach President Trump, Pelosi delayed sending the paperwork to the Senate in an effort to pressure Senate Republicans to call witnesses in the Senate impeachment trial. Republicans held firm and Trump was acquitted on February 5, 2020. Astonishingly, the evening before the impeachment vote in the Senate, Speaker Pelosi tore up President Trump's State of the Union speech just as he finished delivering it. Publicly tearing up the president's speech as millions of viewers watched speaks volumes about the state of partisanship in our country.

Democrats are running former Vice President Joe Biden as their candidate against President Trump in November. After a contentious primary season with more than twenty candidates in the race, Biden won the Democratic nomination but only after he was forced to move far to the left by the progressives that have taken over the Democratic Party. Senator Bernie Sanders (I-VT), a socialist who ran in the Democratic primary, had the most impact on the party's dash to the left.

As a Republican who chafed at candidate Trump during much of 2016 for his demeanor and often outrageous behavior, I have grown to admire President Trump for his policies and the results he has gotten for the country. With the Democratic Party lurching to the left and the way Democrats have treated him from Election Day 2016 to the present, I have an easy choice in 2020. It remains to be seen whether voters will agree with me and decide to give President Trump a second term. Ultimately, he'll win or lose based on how voters judge his response to the COVID-19 pandemic. The jury is still out.

White House Christmas reception with President and Mrs. Trump and Marya Pickering, treasurer of the DC Republican Party.

CHAPTER 2

Members Only

BEING A GAY REPUBLICAN, ESPECIALLY SOMEONE INVOLVED IN politics, is a tightrope act. No event better summarizes this reality than a meeting of the Republican National Committee (RNC) in the spring of 2013. It was a defining moment in my personal and professional life.

As the RNC meeting was getting underway, LGBT Americans had made considerable progress toward equality, in both public opinion and the law. At the end of 2010, Congress repealed the odious Clinton-era "Don't Ask Don't Tell" policy; so now gay men and lesbians could serve openly in the U.S. military. Many states and localities had adopted anti-discrimination laws protecting the LGBT community. The freedom to marry was now legal in several states and the District of Columbia. Plus, the Supreme Court was considering two important cases involving marriage rights for gay and lesbian Americans.

The RNC's April meeting was held in the heart of Hollywood, at a hotel adjacent to the theatre that annually hosts the Academy Awards. Meeting in L.A. was part of a strategy developed after the 2012 election defeat — called the Growth and Opportunity Project and commissioned by RNC Chairman Reince Priebus — to, among a lengthy list of action items, "reach out" to the liberal-leaning blue states and especially to certain minority constituencies. I have enjoyed these meetings. We all share a love of our country and a desire to serve it by promoting the Republican Party's core policies and principles. One of my favorite events during this three-day meeting was an awards luncheon for Asian-American Republicans. It was heartwarming to see so many deserving senior Asian-Americans receiving awards for service to their country and party. It was also gratifying to hear their eloquent comments, filled with wisdom derived from a long life and a culture that reveres its seniors. President Ronald Reagan's son Michael also spoke at this luncheon; he was terrific in warning of the dangers of being overly harsh on social issues. It was a harbinger of things to come.

A few weeks before the spring meeting, I had learned there would be two resolutions addressing the freedom to marry. One resolution highlighted the GOP's socially conservative principles as stated in the party's 2012 platform, including the definition of marriage as being between one man and one woman. The other resolution specifically outlined the party's opposition to gay marriage. From my perspective, and that of many other RNC members, these resolutions were unnecessary, if for no other reason than the 2012 GOP platform that had been adopted the previous August already included those items. There was no need to accentuate them. Let me be clear: I opposed having these references in the party platform at all, but I understood they were there to placate social conservatives. I also knew the Herculean effort that would be required to remove them. Proposing these two resolutions was a combination of power play and publicity stunt by the party's far-right wing to bring extra attention to the issue ahead of the Supreme Court's pending decision on gay marriage. As a gay man and a committed member of the Republican Party, I could not just let these two resolutions pass without some effort to stop them. It was unlikely I could stop them because resolutions, even those offensive or embarrassing to certain constituency groups, are typically passed without much debate by the RNC Resolutions Committee and then brought up as a package to be considered during a voice vote at the general session, which is open to the public. So, I decided to raise my concerns at the members-only session, which is held at every RNC meeting. As the name suggests, this session was for RNC members only. No staff or journalists allowed, so I knew I could say what was in my heart and on my mind, and not be accused of public grandstanding. The Republican National Committee has 168 members; three members from each U.S. state, territory, and the District of Columbia. The three members include a state party chairman, a national committeeman, and a national committeewoman.

The members-only session was scheduled for breakfast on Thursday morning. I told Reince Priebus, the RNC Chairman, the evening before that I was going to do two things at the breakfast. First, I would come out as a gay man. Second, I would express my concerns about the two marriage resolutions. I considered Reince a friend with a very difficult job, so I owed him a heads-up. He urged me to get to the microphone early in the meeting so there would be time for discussion. That night, I wrote and re-wrote the talking points for my statement. To be effective I had to make my points as thoroughly and as succinctly as possible. My training as an attorney and advocate served me well as I crafted my "case." This work helped keep my mind off the potential ramifications of my speech. Eventually, I settled on the appropriate phrases and tone I would use. Then I had some red wine before going to bed for some much-needed sleep.

The next morning at the members-only session, I followed Reince's advice. As soon as he was finished speaking, I quickly stood up to speak, but I was beat to the microphone by Dr. Ada Fisher, a retired medical doctor who was the Republican national committeewoman from North Carolina. Ada is one of a handful of African American members in the party's national leadership. A larger-than-life figure in every sense of the word, she always makes very pointed, challenging comments but with a down-home sense of humor that usually gets a laugh from her audience.

As Ada was speaking, I had extra time to think more about what I was going to say, and how my comments would be received. The room was filled with men and women from all over the country, some of whom I had known for years and other newer members I was just getting to know. I had built a career, a reputation, and a life with service to the GOP as its foundation. I had always lived my life with a sense of dignity and with an eye on earning other's respect. I had no doubt I had earned the respect of many people in that room. Some of them knew I was gay, but many more didn't. I hadn't made a special effort to hide my sexual orientation, but I didn't need to. Nothing about my manner suggested the stereotypical "tells" of a gay man. I had always been rather quiet and reserved, and not given to talking about my personal life with professional colleagues in any setting. But I knew that once I broke the seal and talked about my sexuality and placed it in the arena of politics, my standing in that community would be permanently impacted. I didn't know if the reaction would be positive or negative. But I was committed, in that place and at that moment, to step outside my comfort zone to stand up for my beliefs.

After Ada Fisher finished speaking, I walked to the microphone. My hand had a slight tremor that belied my nervousness, but my voice was steady. I told the assembled RNC members that while many of them knew me others did not, so I asked for their indulgence to give them some of my background. I told them that I had grown up in the 1960s in Ohio when being a Republican meant being a fiscal conservative, strong on defense and foreign affairs. People's personal lives were considered private and the GOP stayed out of that sphere until some years later. I scanned the room, looking at the faces watching me speak, knowing that what I was about to say would change the expressions on many of those faces. I described myself as a "hard-wired"

Republican and a "hard-wired" gay man. A few jaws dropped; I also noted a few smiles.

I went on to say I had been elected four times as Chairman of the DCGOP as an openly gay man and city wide in Washington, D.C. as the Republican national committeeman. I felt I had some standing to discuss LGBT issues. I raised my concerns about the two resolutions on marriage that had been voted on the previous day by the Resolutions Committee, noting that the resolutions had been drafted by social conservative members and backed by a large group of social conservative organizations led by ultra-conservative Phyllis Schlafly in response to the Supreme Court cases on gay marriage. I discussed recent polls showing most younger voters in support of same-sex marriage. And I mentioned other polls dispelling the assumption that African Americans and Hispanics strongly opposed the freedom to marry. I added that the margin by which voters aged 18 to 29 supported Barack Obama (60% for Obama versus 36% for Republican candidate Mitt Romney) was the largest advantage for the President of any voting group other than African Americans. I concluded by saying that if we lost them again in the 2016 Presidential contest, we would probably lose them forever. I then sat down and waited for reactions to my speech.

I didn't have to wait long. The reactions rolled across the room like a like a summer storm. There are certain states where the election process for Republican national committeeman and Republican national committeewoman is structured in such a way that social conservatives almost always win; the representatives from those states had the most visceral reaction to my speech. The member who was waiting his turn behind me at the microphone was one of the most socially conservative members in the entire GOP, a somewhat bitter man with a countenance that made me think of someone who had eaten nails for breakfast. After hearing me say "hard-wired gay man," he moaned. After I sat down, he took the microphone and proceeded to ask in a very angry tone why the RNC was reaching out to homosexuals; that they were an infinitesimal percentage of the population who didn't count. I was prepared to respond to his remarks, but before I could someone else joined the fray. Glenn McCall, the committeeman from South Carolina who also happened to be African American and a member of the GOP panel appointed earlier in the year by Chairman Priebus to study the 2012 election results, responded that the RNC had a long history of working with the Log Cabin Republicans, a conservative gay organization that I have been involved with personally for years. He pointed out that all gay Republicans wanted was what every living person wanted, to be treated with respect.

What he said about gay and lesbian Republicans is true but it's hardly the whole story. Whether someone agreed with me or not that there is a moral imperative to support LGBT equality, there was a political imperative for the GOP to change its tone on these issues. That's because the next generation was turning its back on the GOP as were many other fair-minded Americans who just won't abide the angry treatment the hard right imposes upon LGBT Americans. Period, end of story. To lose the nation's next generation of voters over an issue as resolvable as same-sex marriage is political suicide. It is an obvious fact to all but those who are blinded by ideology and prejudice. To be clear, my opposition to the resolutions was based on my ethical and moral views regarding equal treatment for LGBT Americans as well as my views on the political and strategic imperative for the Republican Party.

I was braced for a long and acrimonious debate, but something else happened instead. Within a few minutes, what had threatened to become an ugly room turned reasonable, even benevolent. I was so zoned out from the emotion of having said my piece that the meeting could have gone on for hours and I probably wouldn't have noticed. As it turned out, the meeting ended shortly after the comments made by the "nail eater." Several members quickly came up to me to thank me for my comments and for raising this important issue. Shawn Steele the Republican national committeeman from California was the first to tap me on the shoulder to tell me that my comments were the highlight of the meeting for him. That evening, a major party fundraiser told me that big donors time and time again raised concerns about the GOP's obsession with social issues. Over the next few days, more than a dozen RNC members made similarly positive comments to me. It would be disingenuous to say that I wasn't relieved by the supportive reaction. I am a risk-averse person and I had risked a lot in that room. But the payoff was well worth it. I was now not only out; I was out in front.

Unsurprisingly, the anti-gay resolutions passed the committee as a package and were brought to a voice vote in the general session. There was a chorus of affirmative votes on the question, a seemingly unanimous vote in favor. But when the call came for those opposed, there was at least one "Nay!" vote...mine. As the meeting ended, I was approached by reporters who wanted to know why I hadn't voted against the resolutions; of course, I had voted against them, but the reporters hadn't heard me. I guess they expected a full-on, fire-breathing, rainbow-flag waving demonstration. I told the reporters that I had cast my dissenting vote, but that I wasn't very loud about it. "It's not my style," I said. "I prefer to do it one-on-one as opposed to grandstanding. I'm not into grandstanding." To me the real art of politics is making a difference without making a show. I would rather have reasonable people resolve their differences with a discussion than a demonstration or a lawsuit. Whether that comes from nature or nurture is unclear; like with most people, it's probably a bit of both.

From my high school years when I began to recognize and build on my interest in politics, my life developed to this moment where I stood up in defense of my values and dignity. Since shaking hands with Richard Nixon the day I represented my high school at Cincinnati City Council Day and attending a Barry Goldwater rally with my uncle in the fall of 1964, politics has been an integral part of my life. Recognizing my sexual orientation stood me apart from many of my friends and colleagues, I have endeavored to open the Republican Party to people who are different. These forces combined to give me the personal background, determination, and confidence to speak openly and honestly to my fellow GOP leaders. A lot had led up to this event. I had come a long way from humble beginnings in America's heartland.

My story begins in Cincinnati where I developed an interest in Republican politics. It continues in Nashville, Tennessee where I landed my first political job with the newly elected Republican governor, on to Washington, D.C. where I worked for two Republican United States Senators and President Ronald Reagan. I served as an early board chairman of Log Cabin Republicans and became involved in the D.C. GOP in leadership roles which brought me to this RNC meeting in Los Angeles. The GOP has changed dramatically over these decades as has the Democratic Party. My story discusses some of the changes I have witnessed, my views on them and my efforts to change hearts and minds on LGBT issues. Despite misgivings from time to time about my party, Washington has taught me the value of picking a side and sticking with it. Being a political independent in Washington doesn't work. Over the post-World War II decades, the Democratic Party has had its own LGBT members fighting for equality within their ranks. I joined with other LGBT Republicans to do the same in the Republican Party where it was so clearly needed. It has been a long, interesting, and challenging journey.

As a Republican national committeeman, I worked closely with Reince Priebus. He helped rebuild the GOP after Mitt Romney's 2012 loss to President Obama.

CHAPTER 3

Nature vs. Nurture

MY CHILDHOOD AND YOUNG ADULTHOOD SPANNED 1946 through the 1960s. During that period, the atmosphere for gay and lesbian people was intolerable. Homosexuality was illegal in most states, and it was the basis for being denied employment or being fired from the federal workforce and many other places. After World War II, tens of thousands of gay men and lesbians finished their military service, arriving back in the U.S. to major port cities such as New York City, San Francisco, and Los Angeles. These military veterans helped develop vibrant gay communities in these cities. In 1952, when I was six, the American Psychiatric Association (APA) listed homosexuality as a sociopathic disorder in its "Bible" of psychiatry. This mental illness label was not removed from the Diagnostic and Statistical Manual for more than 20 years, in 1973, the year after I graduated from law school. The APA's designation encouraged many states to enact laws criminalizing homosexuality and, in some cases, provided for the incarceration of homosexuals and/or the castration of gay men and hysterectomies for lesbians. Great Britain also had strict anti-homosexuality laws resulting in the 1953 chemical castration of Alan Turing, the genius mathematician who broke Germany's Naval Enigma Code that was pivotal in ending World War II, just because he happened to be gay. After his castration, Turing committed suicide in 1954 at the age of 41.

The free world lost a brilliant man who was a war hero and the father of computer science due solely to his homosexuality. The British government only recently posthumously pardoned Turing for his "crime." His treatment as a "criminal" speaks louder than any other single event to the stupidity and cruelty of this era towards gay and lesbian people.

The early 1950s featured McCarthy hearings which exposed Communists and "deviants" (homosexuals) who were allegedly "infiltrating" the federal government and Hollywood. The hysteria led President Dwight Eisenhower to issue an Executive Order in 1953 that, among other things, prohibited homosexuals and other "security risks" from being part of the federal workforce. The Lavender Scare, as it became known, had a catastrophic effect on gay and lesbian federal employees. Tens of thousands were fired from their jobs across the federal government. Even the hint of "deviant" behavior was enough for someone's life to be destroyed. Additionally, thousands of service members were kicked out the military for being homosexual.

In 1958 when I was 12, the U.S. Supreme Court issued a mostly forgotten, but hugely important free speech case impacting homosexuals in America. The U.S. Postal Service tried to censor ONE, the nation's first gay focused magazine, which started in 1953. A year after its founding, the Post Office prohibited the magazine's distribution through the mail even though it wasn't pornographic. Four years later, the Supreme Court, in an unsigned one-sentence decision, issued even before oral arguments happened, reversed two lower court rulings and established First Amendment protections for speech that advocated in favor of gay rights. It might seem like a minor point now, but the early homophile movement, as it was then called, would have been severely limited in its ability to help create change if not for this high court ruling.

On June 28, 1969, a month after I graduated from college, the Stonewall Inn located in Greenwich Village was raided by the New

York Police Department. Patrons were arrested and carried off to jail. Such raids and arrests were commonplace during that era not just in New York City, but all over the nation in cities big and small. The uprising and intense protests by gays and lesbians in New York after that particular raid has been recognized as the beginning of the modern LGBT civil rights movement in the U.S. The gay pride parades and related events that occur annually in hundreds of cities in the U.S. and around the world are typically held in June to commemorate the Stonewall rebellion.

But I'm getting ahead of myself. Like any story, this one starts at the beginning. I was born Robert James Kabel on November 30, 1946 in "beautiful downtown" Burbank, California, as Johnny Carson liked to say on *The Tonight Show*, across the street from the Walt Disney cartoon studios. Both my parents were born and raised in Cincinnati and had moved to California with my maternal grandparents after World War II. Shortly after I was born, they returned to their native Ohio - for good. Dad had a job waiting for him back in Cincinnati and they were building their first house. What would become the booming California economy was still a few years away, so they moved back as soon as I was old enough to travel. But the clincher for my mother was when she was pregnant with me, her doctor, who considered himself a kind of "Obstetrician to the Stars" and knew Mom was not a starlet, treated her badly. She has never forgotten it and it colored her view of Los Angeles. She still talks about how much she hated living there. After I was born, she wanted out of L.A. as soon as possible. My parents were young with two kids in tow: my brother, Rodger, who was two and me. It's hard to imagine driving across country in the winter with two babies and two-lane highways all the way. But then driving cross-country was the only way to go since affordable air travel for most people was decades away.

My father was Herman James Kabel, the quintessential self-made man. After starting as a salesman, he worked his way up and eventually became the owner and president of Wallingford Coffee Mills, which under his leadership became one of the best-known brands in the Midwest. Dad's company specialized in supplying coffee to hotels, institutions, and restaurants, including some of the largest and most successful chains. If you've ever had a cup of coffee at a White Castle or any Bob Evans Farms restaurants in the Midwest, you've had a cup of Wallingford coffee.

He became the sole owner when I was in my final semester of law school and built the most modern coffee roasting plant in the nation. He sold the business many years ago to the employees through an Employee Stock Ownership Plan. They continued to operate the business. Recently Wallingford's was sold to a large national beverage company. Soon after COVID-19 shut down much of the U.S., the roasting plant was closed, and the employees were laid off or fired. A sad end to a once thriving business.

Other than living for less than a year in California and serving in the Army Air Corps in WWII in India where he contracted a type of malaria, he always lived in Cincinnati. In their late 50s my parents bought a condo in Naples, Florida where he eventually became a resident and died in March 2006. Dad was a survivor. In his late forties, he had a life-threatening case of colon cancer, followed by occasional heart issues and a recurrence of colon cancer in his early 80s. He lived to 88. As successful as he was, he never graduated from high school.

My mother was born Margaret Elizabeth Doyle in the summer of 1920 in Cincinnati. She turns 100 this year and still lives in Naples, Florida where she moved permanently after Dad died. Because of her outgoing nature, she has several friends, all female and mostly widows, who look after each other and try to make each other happy. She has always been my most supportive fan and my partner in so many activities while I was growing up in Cincinnati. I owe much to both of my parents, but especially to my mother.

My maternal grandparents bought a combination bar and skating rink in nearby Elizabethtown, Indiana called Winter Gardens, complete with live country western entertainment on the weekends and a beautiful, classic jukebox to entertain customers the rest of the week. I absolutely loved the place as a kid, especially liked the smell of the wood floors and the sound of the beer kegs being unloaded from trucks and moved to the cellar for storage.

The classic psychology question is, "Who are you more like, your father or your mother?" I'm not sure if there is a definite answer for me. I certainly get a lot of drive and determination from my father. As wonderful as my mother is, her attitude was more along the lines of "it's perfectly OK if you're average." Having said that, I think intellectually I am more her child. Dad became a successful businessman. He was more street smart than anything, but Mom was intellectually brighter. She was the one who managed the family finances and did an excellent job of it. She juggled taking care of housework, family, and community and made it look easy.

My early years could be described as typical midwestern, which translates to predictable and relatively uneventful. My father was the breadwinner and my mother was the homemaker. Mom was always involved in the Pleasant Ridge Elementary School PTA (as well as the PTAs of my subsequent schools) and in church activities. She was always at home when we arrived from school, usually with a snack waiting for us as she was starting to prepare dinner.

My earliest memories of my father are from when we moved into a house in the Pleasant Ridge area of Cincinnati when I was five years old, the house where I lived until going away to college. My first memory was Dad helping me plant an oak tree seedling I had received in kindergarten for Arbor Day. On a recent nostalgia trip around Cincinnati, that tree, now more than 60 years old, is the most imposing one on the street, almost overwhelmingly so. I have earlier memories of my mother but not of Dad. My earliest memory of her was when she helped me pack a suitcase and put me on the front porch of the house we rented in an area called Deer Park. I was three or four and determined to leave home over some issue, but of course never made it beyond the front porch.

Dad worked a lot, so we spent most of our time with Mom. He would come home tired but doing his best to connect to the home front. He had nicknames for us kids; to my chagrin, I was not Sport or Scooter or even Skipper. I was affectionately known as "Punkin." I guess it was because of my round face. All the women in my family called me "Bobby," which I liked better.

The point is, he had a name for each of us, which was an expression of his affection for us. Like most men of his generation, he was not especially emotive in his interactions with his children. But he would show us his love in ways other than hugging and kissing. I enjoyed the comfort that my father had with my brothers and me as we became older. It felt good to have adult conversations and to feel his attention and respect. That feeling of connection was missing when I was younger, in my late teens and early twenties. We were quite good on a man-to-man basis, but man-to-boy was a wreck, always arguing over something of little consequence.

We didn't go to movies together or play catch. It was practically a newsworthy event on those rare occasions when he did try to organize some common activity for us. One Sunday, he came to Rodger and me and said, "Hey, let's go bowling." I couldn't have been more surprised, but I was delighted at the prospect of spending an afternoon with Dad. We went to a popular local bowling alley. We bowled a couple of games, mostly in silence, and came back home. I was talking with Mom about the day and how Dad had taken us bowling but hadn't really seemed to enjoy it much. She looked at me and said, "I told him that he needed to spend more time with his boys."

My instincts had been correct. He didn't really want to do it. It wasn't even his idea.

His favorite thing to do on a winter Sunday was to lie on the couch and watch a ball game or nap, something for which I now have greater empathy. Later in life he regularly apologized for what he called "ignoring" us as kids. I don't know why he started expressing that sentiment in his early 70s. But clearly he felt guilty for not spending more time with us. It seemed unnecessary to me; Greg and I had turned out fine and Rodger's problems would probably not have been solved by extended father-son fishing trips. I don't think he was apologizing for taking something from us; it was more that he was sorry for what he had missed out on himself.

He did miss out, but it wasn't really his fault. My parents had typical parenting roles of the times. The man turned the children over to his wife to be raised and then went out into the world to provide for the family. Almost all my friends had the same situation at home. It was rare for a mother with children to work outside the home. Today the roles of nurturer and provider are shared and blurred, and in that game of parenting it sometimes comes to pass that neither parent plays either role with an acceptable level of competence. My parents weren't perfect, but they knew what they were doing, and they trusted each other to do what the other could not. I always knew they loved us even though that word was seldom uttered. Parents and partners; the words are similar, aren't they?

Like I said, the most precious thing that I could get from my father was his time. Sometimes on Saturdays when I was very young, he would take me with him in his truck to make coffee deliveries to his customers. It was a joy to ride around to the different locations and watch how well he connected with people. He was by nature an introvert, but he could sell anything to anybody. He was a very determined man, impatient with others but also with himself. He was very entrepreneurial.

He figured out how to make money in the coffee business by putting himself under the tutelage of an older gentleman who was the sole coffee roaster and wholesaler in Cincinnati. He provided roasted coffee to the several small coffee distributors in Cincinnati, including my father's business. This man who had no children of his own must have loved the fact that a young man like Dad was interested enough in the business to spend Saturdays with him being educated on the coffee business. Dad quickly learned that to make real money he had to stop selling somebody else's product and begin importing and roasting his own. So he leased an old warehouse near the University of Cincinnati that had a coffee roaster and a single packing line that had been sitting idle. He developed business relationships with coffee brokers in New York and New Orleans. He brought the roaster and packing line into production, and that was the beginning of the family business, Wallingford Coffee. Dad had bought into the business a few years earlier, but he made it a profitable one through his entrepreneurial drive and pure determination. Once it got going, it became a fixture on the Cincinnati landscape. You could smell the roasting coffee beans for miles around.

I worked there when I first graduated from high school; within weeks of graduation I was working as a packer on the line. I worked with two great men: an older African American gentleman named Paul and Dennis, a slightly disabled man who lived in a facility for the blind. Dennis did his job so well that Dad always said he was his most reliable employee. During college summers, I was a salesman for the company. I'd take one week to go around with a different salesman to meet the customers on one of the routes, and then for the next two weeks I would handle the route on my own. I would take and fill orders from the restaurants and cafés and various institutions. My first stop when I was working the downtown Cincinnati route was a bar in the Over the Rhine neighborhood. It has become somewhat gentrified in recent years, but back then it was the city's most down and out area. It was a hardscrabble area where men would be knocking back a shot of whiskey with a beer chaser at 8 a.m. before going to work.

That was one of several eye-opening experiences I gained working at Wallingford. Other than the fact that there was no air conditioning in the truck and Cincinnati in summer is as hot and humid as anywhere I have ever lived, the job was interesting and an amazingly educational experience as I look back on it. I liked being out of the office and the roasting plant, and I liked meeting people. I especially got a kick out of it when people would say, "Oh, you must be Herm's son!"

Like most people, Dad had a lot of contradictions. He was a respected guy in the community, and yet he was a guy who lost the respect of some people because he swore like a longshoreman and was not discreet about when and where he expressed himself. He was a man who had a lot of professional drive and personal initiative. I believe I was the one who inherited that drive the most; I believe he recognized that, and he was as proud of that shared strand of DNA as he would have been of any physical feature in me that bore his resemblance. Greg also inherited some of Dad's drive and, intellectually, is the brightest of us all.

Our older brother, Rodger, also was a hard worker for several years in the family business, but his mental illness limited his options and outcomes. I got a measure of both gifts; I was smart like Mom, I had the entrepreneurial spark that defined my father, and I was a hard worker like both of them. Of those character traits, the entrepreneurial streak probably turned out to be the biggest advantage, if not a necessity, for success in the political world. In politics, you must be able to look at a situation and think "Well, I could do that" or "I can do that better than that guy" or "That organization would be well-served having me at or near the top." You must be able to see a need, pitch your tent, and start producing. That is the nature of an entrepreneur.

Dad was not a particularly religious man; I was never aware that he went to church. But he wanted us kids to go, so we did. Dad was raised Catholic and Mom was raised Methodist, but on Sundays she took us to the Presbyterian church up the street, Pleasant Ridge Presbyterian Church, directly across the street from the elementary school my brothers and I attended. Like almost every choice they made in their lives, my Mom chose that church for practical reasons. It was close to home and she liked the minister; I know of crazier ways to choose a house of worship. It was a very comfortable place to be, with just the right combination of spiritual and social. I loved the simplicity of the sanctuary with its clean lines and white woodwork. I agreed with Mom: the minister, Clyde O. York, gave great sermons full of positive thoughts and energy. He had a wonderful Scottish brogue I can still hear in my head. Never once do I recall hearing the term homosexual expressed in the church or Sunday school, which I attended for many years. I was involved for several years in the church youth group that met Sunday evenings for a potluck dinner and program.

While we went to church almost every Sunday and I was involved in the youth church, I was not taught a rigid religion. Many religions teach strict "right from wrong" and homosexuality was invariably on the "wrong" list. Both Catholicism and Evangelical denominations traditionally taught that homosexuality was evil and a sin. Somehow, I was saved from that, not only because of the church we attended, but also because in the 1950s and early 1960s, conservative Cincinnati didn't talk about sex, gay or straight. It was not drilled into me in church or elsewhere that homosexuality was evil. The silence around the subject effectively allowed me to think of it in my own way, with no burden of guilt about my sexuality. That was not to say I didn't recognize the social stigma attached to being gay, but that was easier to deal with than to believe I was a sinner and going to hell just because of my sexual orientation. Many gay men I have known from strict religious backgrounds had a more difficult time than I did coming to terms with their sexuality. Some never have.

My parents had their disagreements, but they never played one against the other. They never tore each other down or criticized each other to the kids. I appreciate that now, as I see many couples do it differently. They had a good relationship; maybe not as good as some but better than most. Of course, there were periods of strain, just like any marriage. One of their ongoing issues was my father being inconsiderate of her time. Sometimes he wouldn't show up until quite late. She'd have dinner ready and waiting, but he just wouldn't show and also didn't call. He wasn't having an affair or anything like that; it wasn't in his nature to introduce that level of complication into his life. He was just working late, completely absorbed by the task in front of him and talking shop with his employees over drinks. Those instances would launch them into some of the worst arguments they ever had. It was scary to me, as it would be to any child. We never even saw the arguments because they happened after we had gone to bed. But we could hear every syllable clearly enough in our small house.

On the other side of the coin, I am hesitant but tickled to report that the passion in their relationship was not limited to their arguments; they had a quite healthy physical relationship. My mother, being a "cover your bases" kind of gal, did not take Dad's attentions for granted and took appropriate measures to ensure their continuance. My mother didn't have to work too hard at that because she was quite beautiful. Both my parents were always attentive to their looks, not to the point of being vain or self-centered but certainly to the level of wanting to be appealing to others and each other. When my mother was in her early 50s, Greg graduated from high school and left the house leaving our parents as empty nesters. She figured that if Dad was going to go play golf every weekend, she might as well join him, so she took up golf. Funny thing, Dad was already a devoted golfer, but she ended up loving the game even more than he did. She played during the week with her lady golfer friends and on Sundays with Dad and usually another couple. It was a smart thing to do; rather than moping about being a golf widow, she turned golf into a positive thing for both of them.

This is my favorite photo from childhood. My brother Rodger (left) and I were so happy to be dressed in cowboy outfits that we were all smiles for the camera.

Here is another picture with my brother Rodger (right). The cute little girl in the middle must have been someone from the neighborhood.

This is a picture of my parents from the late 1990s. They had a big influence in the person I am today.

CHAPTER 4

And Baby Makes Three

FOR A LONG TIME, IT WAS JUST MY PARENTS, MY OLDER BROTHER Rodger and me. Rodger was two years older than me. Although we shared the same parents and the same upbringing including a bedroom, we could not have been more different. Rodger was more of a dark, brooding type than I was. As he got older, the tendency to be a malcontent fermented into a streak of full-blown '50s-style teenage rebellion. The most striking example of our differences was our friends. My friends were the standard buttoned-down, college-bound crowd and his were best described as the school troublemakers with uncertain futures. I think Rodger felt a sense of dread or even doom about his future, and the anxiety of those feelings could sometimes cause him to lash out verbally or physically. From early on I learned how to tell when Rodger was in one of his moods and to give him a wide berth. Although our lives were quite predictable, Rodger's wildcard personality added a measure of stress to the family dynamic that was manageable, but always palpable.

It was a tense time around the Kabel household in the late '50s. I was 11 and firmly in my own world. Rodger was 13 and just beginning his stint as a troubled teenager. It was a period of relative joylessness for us. We had our routines, activities, chores, and responsibilities that keep people busy. And then, suddenly, everything changed.

I often tell my younger brother Greg, to his never-ending embarrassment, that the best thing that ever happened to our family was his being born because it gave all of us something new and special on which to focus. Greg brought joy into our lives, the kind that only a baby can bring. He was cute and funny, and he didn't cry too much. He was the youngest in our family and the youngest grandchild. Had my parents had their druthers there would have been more of us. Greg was meant to be the first of a second wave of Kabel kids, but the pregnancy had proved difficult for my mother. She was 38, which at that time was considered quite an advanced age to have a baby. The doctors strongly advised her against another pregnancy, so that left Greg as a second wave only child.

As I said, my brother Greg is the brightest mind in the family. Since my older brother proved very early in our lives to be something other than an ideal role model, I felt a responsibility to play that role for Greg. Like me, he went to Denison University, where he graduated Phi Beta Kappa. Like me, he went to law school, getting his law degree from the University of Chicago Law School and an MBA from its business school. And like me, he is gay, although I can't really claim any influence on that. We both suspect homosexuality runs in our family on our mother's side.

Greg practiced law in Chicago for several years at two prestigious firms but grew tired of the monotony, especially for a mind with his creativity. So he left law firm life to become an interior designer. It wasn't as drastic a change for Greg as it sounds. He had done such a spectacular job on his own condominium in Chicago while he was still practicing law that it was chosen for the cover in an issue of *Traditional Home*. Greg had to go back to school to earn an associate's degree in design, to qualify under Illinois law to be considered an interior designer. So, after a bachelors, law, and MBA degrees from prestigious universities, he had to return to school to earn an associate degree in design. Eventually, after one too many cold Chicago winters, he moved to Ft. Lauderdale, Florida where he lives today in a beautiful home he designed, built, and decorated himself. Now he is happy with a growing estate planning practice. I am very proud of him and pleased we have each other.

As a young boy, I was fascinated with dancers on television. My first recollection was of the June Taylor Dancers, who first appeared on *The Ed Sullivan Show*, a long running Sunday night variety show on CBS and later on *The Jackie Gleason Show*. Most captivating was the overhead camera shot of the dancers making kaleidoscopic geometric patterns. They were a smaller version of the Rockettes. This also was the era of major movie musicals such as *An American in Paris* with Gene Kelly and the ubiquitous Fred Astaire, both remarkably accomplished dancers. My interest led to me taking tap dance lessons when I was in elementary school. My parents were supportive of this interest, with Mom taking me to the dance studio once a week. I loved it but kept it a secret from my classmates for fear of being labelled a sissy. At the height of this effort, I was part of a three-boy group which performed together at the annual dance review. My entire family came to see me. As I think back on it, my family couldn't have been more supportive, but I feared my classmates would find out about my tap dancing. My brief tap dancing career ended when I entered junior high school; however, later in high school, classmate Donna Stern and I won every dance contest. No one came even close to beating us.

At an early age, I was aware that boys were expected to act a certain way and taking tap dancing lessons was not one of them. While I felt I was different from most other boys, I wanted to fit in. One day in elementary school, the gym class teacher, Mr. Walling, referred to me as "pretty boy" in front of the whole class. I never understood why he called me that, but it was humiliating. He was the same gym teacher who had my older brother climb on gymnastics equipment without mats underneath. Rodger fell and broke his two front teeth, which required extensive dental work. Our mother complained about him but to no avail.

I believe my mother knew I was gay long before I had the conversation with her, and certainly before my father did, mostly because she had a lot more time than my father to get to know me. We were around her a lot more than we were around our father, who was often occupied with work or his beloved golf game. I'm not saying he was an absentee dad; he was firmly in our lives. But it wasn't the split-it-down-the-middle, both-parents-breast-feeding style of modern parenting we have now. In middle American families during the 1950s and 1960s working fathers just weren't around the children as often as the stay-at-home mother. And by stay-at-home, I mean based at home because Mom had a hand in the happiness and well-being of a lot of families in addition to ours. As an example, for more than twenty years she would pick up my grandmother and one of my great aunts and take them on an outing every Friday. They'd go to the grocery store together, then have lunch usually at Frisch's restaurant, then do more shopping somewhere else. She'd deliver them home along with their groceries before heading home herself. She was and is a loving and selfless woman who always had time for her family, especially her children.

Everyone receives two kinds of education. There's the formal education that you get from school, the academic foundation for your future endeavors. And there is the social education, the people and circumstances around you that form the palate of colors with which you paint your life's landscape. It's the look of the houses on your block, the way everyone dresses, the subjects that get brought up at parties. The things I learned at school were always balanced and blended with the things I learned at home.

Like many kids, I got a lot of my social cues from my mom and dad. They were social people. They were not teetotalers, but they also were not heavy drinkers, even though alcoholism ran on my mom's side of the family. They drank socially and hardly ever at home. They would have an occasional beer or maybe a little bourbon on the weekends, but that was about it. Starting when I was about 15, my parents allowed us to have a wine spritzer when they had parties. It was a very unusual mixture: Mogen David wine and 7-Up. While I now gag at the thought of that sweet mix, it bears explanation. The only place in our neighborhood you could get wine was from the Jewish delicatessens, and they had a pretty good selection. You could get Manischewitz AND Mogen David!

I was always in a religious minority growing up. Pleasant Ridge was adjacent to a large and diverse Jewish community, something for which Cincinnati is known. Being a religious minority there was never really an issue for me, just a fact of life. Since my high school class was majority Jewish, I had to figure out how to fit in with people from diverse backgrounds. My brothers and I were raised Presbyterian, yet all but two of the other children in the neighborhood were Catholic and went to the local parochial school.

The garage in our basement was converted into a family room that served as the venue for most of the entertaining we did. It was the classic post-war recreation space, complete with wood paneling and a standing bar, not a wet bar. The couch was a hot orange vinyl type material, and it was the deluxe model with built-in Formica end tables on either side. We also had steel tube chairs with orange plastic seats. My contribution to the décor came from my junior high school art class, which I loved. I made a plaque of ceramic tile that had martini glasses, highballs, olives … the crowning touch in a room oozing '60s chic.

The style sense continued in the kitchen. It was more like a kitchenette. It had an L-shaped breakfast nook booth and a little table. Remarkably, the color scheme here was also orange. The seating was a challenge; the booth sat four and when Greg came along, we were a family of five. The problem was solved with Mom pulling a chair up to the end of the table to make room for five. The point was moot because she almost never got a chance to sit as she was too busy serving us.

Another nugget I picked up at home was a love for gardening. Grandpa Doyle is responsible for my interest in gardening. He started me out at our family's first house with a little patch of potatoes. When we moved to the house I grew up in, there were remnants of a World War II victory garden that had fallen into disrepair in the field behind our house. When I found it, there was only a patch of wild rhubarb and wild strawberries that proved there was fertile ground underneath the tangle of weeds. I started by planting some tomato plants, but by the time I finished high school I had tomatoes, strawberries, green beans, and radishes. I planted corn one year without calculating how the shadows would be cast. That year I got great corn, but the tomato crop was a complete bust. The end came in high school when I planted a melon patch and just as they were about to be harvested, some jerk in the neighborhood decided it would be a good idea to pull them out of the ground. My mother chalked up this vandalism to the same reason she had for anything that went wrong in my world. "People are just jealous of you, Bob, because you can do so many things." Ah, a mother's love. Is there anything else like it?

Growing up, I was a joiner with a capital J. If it held meetings and kept minutes, I was likely part of it. I would also include my mother in the project. With me, you got my mom too, and she loved it and excelled in that role as she did in so many others. A long-standing family joke is my mother saying that she was especially happy when

I graduated high school because I couldn't volunteer her for anything else. A partial list of my club associations included:

Hi–Y: A high school extension of the YMCA which did food drives and fundraisers. I was president and I loved being involved with the organization.

Fraternity: Yes, high school fraternities were permitted, and I was a member. In fact, I was president of that august body.

School Government: A no-brainer. I started at the grassroots level as homeroom representative, but I had my eye on the top slot. I ran for president of the student body… and lost. My high school class of 700 was more than half Jewish, and the Jewish candidate was a solid favorite. He had been president of the Woodward Junior High student council so was better known than I was. I stood a chance of winning until another Christian decided to run, splitting the non-Jewish vote. (Several Jewish classmates referred to the Christian classmates as non-Jews.) This secured the election for Paul Feldman. My first taste of ethnic politics, right there in the heart of the Midwest.

Rising to leadership roles in several organizations throughout my school years and after demonstrated my ability to get along with people and gain their respect. My reputation for being even-tempered and rarely upset was appealing to individuals and organizations looking for leadership. My demeanor was mainstream, and it wasn't an act to cover up a different personality. I was simply being myself. And my sexual orientation wasn't a barrier to gaining leadership roles because, especially at this point, only a few people knew of my attraction to other males, and I kept it that way for years.

I was a solid B student, which was not spectacular until you compared it with my older brother, who had to go to summer school every year just to get out of high school. Rodger and I grew up in the same house, but we could not have been more different in most respects. He was always a handful for our parents, and they struggled to figure out what to do to get him on a better track. In the 1950s and early '60s, there weren't the tools and resources parents have today. Years later, he was diagnosed with paranoid schizophrenia. He wasn't dangerous to himself or others but lived in a world that came to him through voices no one else heard. Looking back on his behavior, there were obvious signs of that illness, even as a boy and young man.

Rodger was a bit different in ways that were not always easy to describe. Once we were both in our teens, we took different paths, most notably in our friends and interest in school generally. Dad told him he could have a car in high school if he could earn the money to buy one, so he worked as a carhop at a local White Castle restaurant. With his earnings, he bought a used car that he drove to high school and drove his friends around on weekends. Incredibly, he charged me a quarter each time I rode to school with him. Given the tension between us, I often walked to school or got a ride from a classmate who would stop by to pick me up. Dad also told him that as long as he owned Wallingford, he would have a job and he did. Rodger started an office coffee division for the company when businesses started providing coffee for their employees in the 1970s. Rodger raised the idea of coffee bars that are ubiquitous today but were unheard of back then. The idea never took hold with Dad.

On the rare occasion when I saw him during adulthood, he spoke so quietly that I couldn't understand him. He was afraid someone was listening through the TV. I recall one particularly bizarre incident with Rodger during a family Christmas visit in the late 1980s. Greg and I were both home visiting for the holidays when Rodger came over for Christmas dinner. As Greg and I were in the kitchen cleaning up, Rodger said, "Bob, you spend time in L.A., right? Then you must see my face on billboards around L.A. I control the gang activity there and can start or stop gang activities." I thought he was kidding but went along with it. The discussion went downhill from there with me asking follow-up questions and beginning to laugh. He correctly sensed we were making fun of him, so he quickly left the house. Once he was gone, Dad said "See what we have to deal with?"

Before this incident, I had no idea the extent to which he fantasized about his own importance and connection to major events. When Dad sold the company to his employees, costs had to be reduced and Rodger was the second highest paid employee in the company next to Dad. With the amount of profit-sharing Rodger had with the company and his share of the proceeds of the sale, he was financially secure for life. He didn't have to work again. With his illness out in the open, we often wondered if he was taking prescription medicines to curtail the disease. He never talked about it and we usually could not tell.

It's a sad part of our lives that Rodger never got to develop close personal relationships once his disease became apparent. I never really had an older brother. I felt so sorry for him as his disease robbed him from the trials and joys of a more normal life. The last time I saw him was when I was in Cincinnati to fly with Mom to Florida to reside full time. She was moving out of the apartment she had rented after selling the house she and Dad had lived in for decades. Rodger came over the day before we were to leave for Florida. I was sitting next to him in the living room and he whispered that he was happy Mom was leaving because she wasn't safe being close to him. There were people out to kill him and they might hurt her if they couldn't get to him. That was the last time I saw him. Sadly, he died at the early age of 71 from pancreatic cancer. When the cancer was diagnosed, he was already in Stage IV and mercifully was spared the pain that so often accompanies pancreatic cancer. We all miss him and know he is in a better place.

Life took an exciting turn when my younger brother Greg (left) came along. This photo is from a Florida family vacation in the early 1960s.

I have fond memories riding in my grandfather's boat on Indian Lake, Ohio. My brother Rodger (left) and I enjoyed many summers with our grandfather Doyle on the lake.

I have always been close with my brother Greg (right). This photo with him and my mother is from the reception that followed his graduation from the University of Chicago Law School.

I took this photo of my brothers Greg (left) and Rodger (far right) and his son, Michael, joining my parents for Christmas dinner.

CHAPTER 5

Awakenings

MY EARLIEST MEMORY OF BEING ATTRACTED TO MEN WAS IN 1958 at age 12 when Mom took me to see *South Pacific*. We both liked musicals and it was something we could do together. In those days, movie studios would sometimes produce hardcover books about a movie to be sold in the theatre lobby. I still have my book from *South Pacific*. I found the actor John Kerr, who played Lieutenant Cable, so attractive and appealing I couldn't take my eyes off him. There is a line in the movie from the Polynesian character, Bloody Mary, that captured his essence when she said, "Lieutenant Cable, you very sexy man!" Perfect. Around that age, I recall going in my grandfather's runabout boat to the location on Indian Lake where a makeshift donut shop had been set up in a trailer. Handsome young college men often worked the counter. I remember asking Grandpa who they were. He said they were probably Ohio State students. We went for donuts as often as I could talk him into it. Also, at Indian Lake, I recall driving or walking around looking at the male construction workers as they worked on cottages, often with their shirts off.

As I was growing up, my sexuality didn't come up with my family in direct conversation for the longest time, but like any other teenager I was discovering new desires and new ways to satisfy them. I had two male friends with whom I had ongoing sexual relationships during high school. The initial idea was not mine but once we started, I felt perfectly comfortable. I knew it was our secret that was never to be shared with anyone. Somehow none of our parents or friends ever figured it out. We had a perfect cover for our escapades; we were friends, and friends spent a lot of time together anyway. So no one questioned what we were doing; everyone just figured we were doing "boy stuff." They didn't know how right they were.

While I was doing a fair bit of same-sex shopping, I also had girlfriends in high school, college, and law school. I even brought my law school girlfriend home to meet my parents. Dad especially liked her because she was exceptionally good looking. My mother liked her but had a change of heart when she learned the young lady had a chronic nervous condition and was even hospitalized once for it, something she had failed to mention to me before. She was Jewish, and contrary to many folks in those days, neither of my parents objected to my dating a Jewish girl. After all, my favorite great-aunt Eva had married a Jew. (My great-uncle Sam Malberg decorated their house with more Christmas decorations than the rest of us Christians combined.) So there was precedent in the family for mixed religious marriages. My parents were considered to have a mixed religious family since in the 1940s Catholics and Protestants rarely married.

The reaction was the opposite when I visited her parents. They knew I wasn't Jewish, but when they saw me, they flashed each other a look that said, "Boy, he's REALLY not Jewish." After meeting them, she told me her father had said to her, "Never marry a gentile because if the marriage doesn't work, they'll blame it on the fact you are Jewish." Oy vey. But I liked her. She was fun and interesting, and she was the first woman with whom I ever had sex. I was twenty-two when we first slept together. It was a big moment for me. My first thought afterward was "interesting … good, but not that satisfying." It was like the sexual equivalent of a Swanson frozen dinner. She wasn't my only bite at the apple, so to speak. Most of my gay encounters had been fireworks; by comparison, the hetero liaisons were more like homework.

My attraction to politics began with an interest in my school's student council. There is an old saying that Washington is full of former student body presidents. I fit perfectly into that category, having run and lost for student body president in high school. Defeat didn't discourage me. My consolation prize or prizes was to be elected president of my high school fraternity and the Woodward HI-Y chapter. I thoroughly enjoyed both roles. The Hi-Y clubs were service-oriented organizations. The Hi-Y clubs did toy drives at Christmas and other community projects throughout the year. Being Christian wasn't a requirement, but Jewish students didn't join. There was a similar organization called Key Club that was predominantly Jewish boys. Looking back, it's remarkable that public schools permitted, even sponsored, fraternities and sororities and religious-based groups. It speaks to how tribal and segregated life was back in those days.

During most of my childhood, Dwight Eisenhower was president of the United States. My parents supported him in both 1952 and 1956. They were small business Republicans. In fact my entire family, grandparents, uncles, and aunts, all were Republicans. As a small businessman, my father was anti-union because he thought unions caused trouble and had the potential to shut down businesses. In the 1960 presidential race that pitted Senator John F. Kennedy against Vice President Richard Nixon, I recall some of the kids in our predominantly Catholic neighborhood going door-to-door with Kennedy literature. When they came to our house, Mom was polite and took their literature, but there was no doubt she and Dad would vote for Nixon. Mom also was active in the League of Women Voters and participated in many of their election-related activities.

Even though my parents were loyal Republicans, they weren't much interested in politics. However, they knew I was, and encouraged me to talk about my views whenever I wanted. Almost no one in my immediate or extended family other than me was enthusiastic about politics. They were busy with their own lives and families. The lone exception was my Uncle Donald, my mother's younger brother. He was very interested in politics. I liked spending time with Uncle Donald and his wife Aunt Vi at their house because he enjoyed talking with me about politics, and our conversations felt like one among peers. No matter the subject, there is no greater feeling for a young man than to be treated like an equal by a full-grown man. Uncle Donald took me to my first political rally, a campaign event for Barry Goldwater at the Cincinnati Gardens in 1964 during his presidential campaign. From that moment on I was completely and irretrievably hooked on politics. The pomp, the band music blaring, the balloons, and bunting, and just the excitement of the people were utterly intoxicating. Those conversations with Uncle Donald and that campaign event were the beginning of my lifetime love of politics, a love that has survived good candidates and bad candidates, excellent policies and wretched ones, private tragedy and public drama

During my junior and senior years in high school, I was one of four students from Woodward to participate in the YMCA's Youth in Government Program that occurred every April in Columbus, the state capital. I served as a state representative the first year and a state senator the second. It was a thrill to participate and compete with other Hi-Y members, first in Hamilton County and then at the state level. These were two of the first trips I made away from home by myself. It was energizing and rewarding.

Having gained the notoriety of being Mr. Republican in my senior class, I was asked to speak on behalf of Barry Goldwater during a school debate in October of 1964. A gifted female student represented President Lyndon Johnson. The debate took place at a school-wide event held in the gymnasium. I was smitten by Goldwater for reasons I can't remember today, but I did my best to represent what I understood was his dedication to libertarian ideas. In a mock poll conducted afterwards, Goldwater got crushed by the Johnson supporters. Just like the outcome of that big Democratic victory in 1964.

In the weeks before the 1964 election, there was another formative event in my life that drove me toward a career in politics. I was thrilled to get selected to represent Woodward High School at Cincinnati's annual Councilman for a Day. The people representing their high schools sat behind the dais in the council chambers. Each student had to address an urban issue of interest to us. I chose prison reform and discussed how rehabilitating some criminals was preferable to incarceration. While it was on a much smaller scale than the Goldwater rally, the City Council Day had similar gravitas and excitement. Important people were there, and they were happy and proud to be there. There was a sense that if you were in that room, you were a part of the city's present and its future. You were somebody. And I felt I was somebody.

The participants in the Councilman for a Day event were invited to a dinner in our honor at a downtown hotel. Dad went with me. As we departed the dinner, Richard Nixon was in the lobby. He was there campaigning for Senator Goldwater. I excitedly shook his hand. I was struck by his height and his overall bearing, but then I was in high school and to meet someone of his national stature was a singular thrill in and of itself. The political hook that had been set was working its way even deeper.

Socially and academically, I was self-motivated; my parents did not push me. They were proud of the things I would accomplish, ordinary and sometimes extraordinary. To my parents and my teachers at school I was different. I was clearly college material. My parents acknowledged both their pride in my success and the fact that although they were willing to pay for college neither of them had a clue as to how to get me in. It was kind of unusual amongst my friends that I had parents who didn't go to college. In most families, we knew at least one parent had attended college. For my Dad, it was probably never an option. Mom spoke now and again of having had a desire to go to college, but she just didn't; none of her siblings did either.

Fortunately, my high school had excellent guidance counselors and I had friends who knew about the college selection process.A high school classmate arranged a trip to Denison University in Granville, Ohio about a two-hour drive from Cincinnati. My classmate's brother had recently graduated, and he offered to take us for a visit. We went for a weekend, spending the night in one of the dorms. It was by far the coolest thing I had ever done. I fell in love with Denison immediately and completely. Granville is a quintessential small-college town, quiet and quaint, with a New England feel. My parents fell in love with it too. So I became a Denison man, as did my younger brother after me. When Greg graduated, our parents were more nostalgic than he was because they wouldn't get to come there anymore for parent weekends.

Kabel Attends Boy's Week Congress; Elected To Office Of City Councilman

Senior Bob Kabel recently attended Boys' Week Congress at City Hall on Wednesday, October 28. In the course of the program of which Juvenile Court Judge Benjamin Schwartz was the chairman, Bob was elected to the office of councilman.

"The purpose of the Congress," Bob stated," was twofold. First, it was to show boys from the Cincinnati area on a small scale how city government is run. Secondly, as Judge Schwartz indicated, it was to give recognition to the youth of the area; something which is very important."

Bob explained that the Congress was attended by approximately 250 boys from Greater Cincinnati high schools, junior high schools, and elementary schools. Fifteen of the boys, one from each of the large public and parochial schools, presented a three minute speech which was accompanied by a prepared, written platform.

Afterward the nine councilmen were elected by the assembly. The mayor, vice-mayor, and president pro-tempore were elected by a voice vote of the council.

"Then," he further explained, "the mayor appointed the remaining six participants to such jobs as city manager and police chief so everyone had some job."

Following the election, the group went to the Sheridan-Gibson Hotel to attend a luncheon given by the Cincinnati Lions Club. "On our way there," Bob commented, "we had the privilege of seeing and meeting Former Vice-president Richard Nixon, who was on his way to address the Cincinnati Womens' Republican Club. This could definitely be called my greatest thrill of the day."

For the final event of the day, the assembly returned to the Council Chambers to attend the regular meeting of City Council. During the meeting Bob sat with Councilman Phil Collins, who was his counterpart on the council.

"This experience, Bob stated, "was very satisfying because we were all judged entirely as individuals presenting our own ideas and feelings regardless of school, race or religion."

Bob Kabel

This newspaper article chronicles my life-changing experience as my high school's representative at City Council Day in 1964. This experience helped spark my passion for politics.

This photo from my 16th birthday is one of my favorites. I was very close to my Uncle Donald (center left) and my grandmother Doyle (back right). Nan Pletz (on far right) lived next door to us growing up and was like a third grandmother.

This 1965 photo is from my high school prom. Thankfully, white dinner jackets were appropriate dress in 1965, unlike the garish formal wear of the mid-'70s when Greg graduated from high school.

CHAPTER 6

Coming of Age

I BEGAN MY FRESHMAN YEAR OF COLLEGE AT DENISON IN September 1965. I had what I assumed were typical freshman jitters, and the drive with my parents and Greg from Cincinnati to Granville didn't help. As we were driving in the station wagon Dad used for his business with all my things in the back, the hood came unhinged, ripped off and flew into the median on I-71 just as we were reaching the suburbs of Columbus, Ohio. I had been in an accident with the car earlier that summer and the hood had not been properly repaired. It could have been a real disaster, but it wasn't. Somehow, we got to a nearby dealership where a mechanic temporarily fixed it. We looked like the Beverly Hillbillies as we drove into Granville and up the hill to my dorm. We were all frazzled, but others must have been too since no one seemed to notice our jerry-rigged car. Once settled into my dorm room, my parents said goodbye and left me to begin adjusting to campus life.

Thus began a journey of learning and growth, both academic and personal. I developed a life-long love of learning during those four years. Liberal arts colleges have proven themselves as places where young men and women can broaden their thinking without being tied to one specific discipline. The liberal arts are, by definition, a broadening experience that helps graduates develop helpful tools they can use the rest of their lives. My freshman class of around 400 was about half the size of my high school class. My Denison education and experience have remained an important part of my life from graduation day forward to today.

I was so happy being in a quality academic atmosphere and, given the intensity of my involvement in extracurricular activities during my high school years, it never occurred to me to run for any campus government office. I was worn out on all that and devoted myself to learning and developing lasting relationships.

In the 1960s, fraternities at Denison held freshman rush before the beginning of classes. I was a very young 18 and didn't know what to make of rush, much less which house to choose. I pledged the Beta house mainly because they invited me, and I was not invited to join the Sigma Chi house where my three male friends from Woodward High School had pledged. I had a rough few months as a Beta pledge and ended up quitting one day in a huff. I wasn't ready for the rough and tumble of pledging and hazing.

The Betas were known as the campus jocks, so I was wondering what I was doing there since I was not much of a jock. I played tennis in high school, but the frat brothers were primarily football and lacrosse players, a more rugged bunch. Even so, I enjoyed the visual treats I experienced as I did my pledge chores around the Beta house. Later in my freshman year, I pledged Kappa Sigma. My freshman roommate Bruce also had pledged it during regular rush. All in all, I was not meant to be a fraternity man but at the time, social life at Denison centered on the Greek system so joining a house was essential.

I lived in the Kappa Sigma house my sophomore year and the first semester of my junior year. My sophomore roommate was also named Bruce. He was a senior no one else wanted to room with because he was diabetic and didn't care for himself, a widely known fact in the house. I soon learned what that meant. He would go into diabetic shock in the middle of the night on a regular basis and it was my job to feed him mints until he came out of it. Once he did, he would go to the kitchen for more food. He never once thanked me for helping him. Despite his lack of gratitude, we developed a decent friendship. In 1967, a group of us even drove in his car to Ft. Lauderdale for spring break. I recall not sleeping at all when Bruce was at the wheel because I feared he would go into another diabetic shock and kill us all. We did enjoy the Elbow Room and similar college spring break spots in Ft. Lauderdale.

Denison in the 1960s was isolated from much of what was occurring in the US particularly in larger cities. The hippie and anti-war movements never reached our small enclave. At the time, Denison was often referred to as a "country club" school given the demographics of most students and the golf course adjacent to campus. The student population was largely Midwestern with many mid-Atlantic and East Coast students as well. Not only was the school geographically isolated, but it felt isolated from the increasingly divided nation. This was long before 24-hour news channels and social media feeds constantly bombarding us with the latest news and opinions. Newspapers were available only in the library and student union building, and dorms typically had only one TV and one phone. I don't recall watching TV or even listening to the radio much during these years. Most of us had stereos in our rooms to play our LP albums.

Since I was closeted on campus, I didn't see evidence of sex, but the talk around the fraternity house indicated otherwise. While I was a Beta pledge, I often came across used condoms during my afternoon room cleaning duties. Add to that a sex scandal on campus involving a female student—a coed in the lingo of that time—and multiple male students during a drunken party. She transferred to another school and at least one of the men was denied a letter of recommendation to medical school for a year.

I had only two gay sexual liaisons during my years at Denison, one during my freshman year. My parents recognized I was having a tough time much of that year and agreed to help me join a group of male classmates on a trip to Bermuda for spring break. It was fun, carefree, and a wonderful break from studying. We had at least six of us staying in one room with two beds. I recall sleeping on a mattress on the floor with one of the other guys next to me. Suddenly one night my mattress companion began initiating sexual contact and, despite my fears that the others would hear us, I gladly joined in the fun. Apparently, we were quiet enough that no one heard us. Curiously, the guy who had initiated the encounter got a girl pregnant and married her before the end of our senior year. I was perplexed by that development, but he turned out to be the first of many bisexual men I would meet over the years.

There was some drug use on campus, but it was not a big problem. Someone caught selling drugs would have been suspended or expelled. Getting caught smoking pot would have resulted in a lesser penalty or counseling. Senior year, one of my roommates and his girlfriend were into marijuana and rumor was he was the campus distributor. My other roommate and I told him we didn't want his "supply" kept in our off-campus apartment. Both of us were applying for graduate or law school and didn't want a drug bust to ruin our chances of admission. As far as we knew, he respected our wishes.

There wasn't much drinking on campus due to the fact Granville was in a dry county. Newark, Ohio, a short drive east, was in a county that permitted liquor, and that's where we would go to party on weekends which sometimes started Thursday evening. For many years, Ohio law allowed 18 years old to drink 3.2% beer, a weaker version of regular beer. On my 21st birthday, I asked a bartender for a "final" 3.2 beer. After hunting around in the cooler, the bartender finally found one. Most Newark establishments didn't care which alcohol level beer they served to Denison students. The situation on campus changed our senior year when beer was made available at special events. Most of the fraternity houses allowed locked refrigerators in rooms stocked with beer.The rule was to be discreet and not allow pledges to partake.

All this means that even though I came of age in the '60s, my young life was far from the stereotypical '60s experience. Not much sex, not much alcohol, and no drugs. Probably as a result, I got good grades.

I quickly got used to the classes and often studied at the library between classes and at night. I especially enjoyed my English and history classes and eventually became a history major. Denison continues to be known for the close relationship students develop with their professors. I especially benefitted from working with my faculty advisor, Professor Wally Chessman, with whom I had several history classes. Larger schools can't offer these close, mentoring relationships that are so beneficial to students. A favorite learning exercise for me was to look up the derivation of words in an unabridged dictionary. I spent hours in the reference room of the library studying the development of words over centuries.This seemingly simple exercise helped broaden my view of history and the intricacies of the English language.

My favorite freshman year class was the art history class I took second semester. I especially loved the Italian Renaissance period and began thinking of how I would see the amazing artworks I was studying. Much like my interest in the derivation of words, the Italian Renaissance had distinct periods that also developed over the centuries. The art history class prompted me to investigate the possibility of spending part of my junior year abroad. I visited the office that had information about junior year abroad programs. Most programs required a level of foreign language proficiency I didn't have and programs in England were almost nonexistent at the time. However, Syracuse University offered a semester abroad program in Florence,

Italy that didn't require any prior knowledge of Italian, I suspect since few American schools offered Italian classes.

With my parents' approval, I took the plunge and entered the program during the second semester of my junior year. Along with a classmate who also was going to Florence on the Syracuse program, I began taking Italian lessons from the wife of one of my history professors. They lived in one of the few truly contemporary houses in Granville, and it was a treat to be invited there. Deciding to study in Italy was the most important decision of my young life. It provided me with incredible experiences that enriched my life in many ways and taught me a new level of independence that a small college town or suburban Cincinnati could not offer.

There were several semester abroad programs in Italy sponsored by American universities, but Syracuse's program was the only one in which students lived with Italian families. I split the semester between two families; my first one was the Bettarinis who lived at 9 Via Guicciardini, a block across the Ponte Vecchio near the center of Florence. A charming older couple, he was a professional artist with summer and winter studios in their large apartment. Signora Bettarini ran an embroidery business with several women working for her. She kept the beautiful linen goods they embroidered in several armoires Signor had hand painted with Florentine scenes. A few weeks after living there, they told me I had learned less Italian than any other student who had stayed with them from the Syracuse program. Seeing the disappointment on my face, they told me it was because I wasn't Jewish as all their other students had been. I still laugh at that, but it was the kick in the pants I needed to focus on learning Italian. Eventually I learned enough Italian to satisfy my host family. I was awakened every morning when the phone rang in the kitchen and Signora Bettarini answered "Pronto!" My bedroom overlooked the Boboli Gardens behind the Pitti Palace which was just up the street from their building. I thought I was in heaven and literally felt like pinching myself daily.

My second host family was a couple with a young son. The husband taught at an industrial design school and the wife was a housewife. There was no joy in the house, and I was happy when the semester ended. Classes were and still are held at the Villa Rossa, a building owned by Syracuse on Piazza Savonarola. Florence is small enough that I walked to and from classes twice a day. We came home for lunch around noon and classes started again in mid-afternoon.

I developed a crush on the woman who was teaching my Italian language class. She was a beautiful woman from Rome who had married a doctor and lived in a villa in Fiesole, a town first established during the Etruscan period, in the hills above Florence. I enjoyed the afternoons we had class in her villa. She once told us that the Roman were "evil" people since they viewed their version or dialect of Italian to be the pure one.

Groups of young Italian men hung around the Villa Rossa every day and whistled and called out endlessly to the American girls in my class. They often tried to befriend the guys in the class, hoping we might introduce them to the girls. We were all appalled by the behavior. Similarly, the Ponte Vecchio was a hang out at night for gay men. Conveniently for me, crossing the Ponte Vecchio was the most direct route back to the Bettarini's apartment so I walked across it daily. I was stared at often as I crossed the bridge. I was young and didn't understand that most of them probably were harmless, but I was on guard. I recall talking with an older Italian man one evening who invited me to join him in his car in a nearby parking lot. I politely declined.

Another evening as I was walking across the bridge, I noticed a handsome younger man on the Ponte Vecchio. He was clearly not Italian; he turned out to be an Australian who was working in Florence. We had an immediate attraction, so he invited me to his hotel. After arriving, he told me to be quiet because his visiting parents were asleep in the adjoining room. We saw each other a few times, including for a day trip to a beach on the coast. For my first affair as a young adult, it was fun but too brief.

There was another time in Florence when I had a brief moment of intimate same-sex contact. I was in the courtyard of the Accademia where Michelangelo's statue of David is displayed, when a fellow male classmate saw me, grabbed me in a bear hug, said something like "What would you think if I did this" and kissed me on the lips before I knew what happened. To say the least, I was surprised. I wondered at the time if there was something about me that led him to believe I would like his kiss. Maybe I did and wasn't aware of the vibes I was sending. It didn't happen again.

1968 was a momentous year for so many Americans but it didn't impact me much, at least until I arrived back in Cincinnati that August. I vividly remember the early April day Martin Luther King Jr. was assassinated while I was still in Florence. I had returned to the Bettarinis' apartment for lunch when they told me the terrible news. I was stunned. They often had guests for lunch; that day they had a married couple visiting and as I recall one or both worked for the United Nations. I remember being speechless and embarrassed by this tragedy. I don't recall getting any news about the riots that followed King's killing in major cities across the U.S. Some of the worst rioting was in Washington D.C. where the damage was still visible until just a few years ago before a wave of gentrification changed the face of the city. While in Italy, it was difficult getting news in English, and the Italian papers didn't cover these momentous events in the same way as U.S. papers.

I was in Paris in early June of that year when Robert Kennedy was assassinated. The French capital was an armed camp with military service members at every street corner. The uprisings were largely over the Vietnam War, but the students were also rioting over a range of other issues. It was difficult getting around the city as I tried to live on what little money I had left. I contacted my parents to ask for money for the rest of the trip and to get home. American Express offices were centers of communication between family and friends when traveling overseas in those days; both for cash (that had been wired) and mail. I recall visiting several American Express offices that summer. Credit cards were just beginning to be issued in the US, but college students like me didn't have them, so the Amex offices provided our lifeline.

I initially traveled that summer with two young women from my program. We hitchhiked through Italy heading south with the specific objective of visiting the town of Siracusa on Sicily. It was an advantage for a male to hitchhike with one or more females. Sometimes I hid behind a tree or a bush while they secured rides. I popped out only when the car door opened. For good reason, the women would not hitch by themselves.

We hitched rides in cars, buses, and once in Southern Italy, on a donkey-powered hay wagon. We made it to Siracusa and stayed most nights in youth hostels. Sicily was breathtakingly beautiful. One of the girls departed, and the other one and I hitchhiked to Brindisi on the Adriatic Sea before taking the ferry across to Greece. One night we slept on a beach and were awakened at dawn by a herd of passing goats. We eventually made it to Athens.

Once she departed, somehow, I hitched a ride on an American tourist bus going north through Yugoslavia. It was an era where hitchhiking was commonplace in Europe and the US. People took pity on us and were so kind. The bus ride through communist Yugoslavia was a life saver. I have no idea how I would have made it to Austria without their kindness.

One evening in Munich I met a guy about my age while returning from a beer hall. We were waiting for a ride to return to the youth hostel where we both were staying. He was from Holland and he offered for me to stay with him in Amsterdam if I found my way there. After visiting Paris on my own, I took him up on his offer and stayed with him in his small apartment. His offer was much appreciated as I was quickly running out of money and a free room was a blessing. He took me to a pub that was frequented only by men. I was so naive I didn't realize he had taken me to my first gay bar. He was a good companion during my stay. I suppose he was as cautious as I was as far as intimacy was concerned, but it remains a favorite memory.

I flew back to the U.S. on Icelandic Air and, much to my parents' consternation, I stopped to see a college friend in Wilmington, Delaware. Daniel was an artist and gay. So was his older brother, I later learned. I wasn't sure what to expect when I arrived, but apparently he told his family he was interested in me and that was the purpose of the visit. His mother left their house while I was there. We slept on a bed in the basement for a couple nights. During the visit, he told me he loved me. I was stunned and didn't know what to say except that I had similar sexual desires, but apparently I gave off a vibe that I wasn't much interested in him. It was awkward. I flew to Cincinnati a few days later and was told to take a bus to downtown where my mother would pick me up for the drive home. Since the airport was only a few miles from downtown, they were clearly punishing me for not coming directly home to Ohio after being in Europe for almost six months. My stubbornness and independence were clearly showing.

When I returned to Cincinnati, the Governor had called out the National Guard, and there were armored personnel carriers patrolling the streets in the suburban area where we lived. No specific riots broke out, but there was considerable tension throughout that long summer. Race was an issue in Cincinnati and not just by skin color. Growing up, my schools were predominantly white, with a mix of Christians and Jews. When my parents decided to join a country club, I suggested they consider the one closest to us, Losantiville Country Club. Mom said we couldn't because they only admitted Jewish families. Losantiville was founded as a Jewish club because they were not welcome in most other country clubs in Cincinnati at the time. The one my parents joined had a few Jewish members but was primarily white Christians. There were only a few black students at my high school and no Latinos or Asians that I recall. We all got along, but we were clearly divided by race and religion. Cincinnati has always had a significant Roman Catholic population with some excellent schools such as St. Xavier High School and Xavier University. As noted, my immediate neighborhood was predominantly Catholic, and the children attended the local parish grade school and a variety of high schools. During the tumultuous year of 1968, Cincinnati did not experience the violence other American cities experienced but the tension was there.

I got home from Europe in time for the Republican National Convention in Miami where Richard Nixon was nominated in early August and for the Democratic National Convention in Chicago later that month where Hubert Humphrey was nominated. The 1968 Democratic National Convention pitted ultra-liberal Eugene McCarthy, a strident anti-Vietnam War Minnesota Senator, against former Senator and sitting Vice President Hubert Humphrey. The convention was one of the most divisive in American history as the Democratic Party was divided by President Johnson's Vietnam War policy. Fights broke out on the convention floor, with delegates and reporters being hurt. Tens of thousands of anti-war protesters flooded into Chicago to make their voices heard. Chicago's hard-nosed Mayor Richard Daley was determined to crack down on the protesters. Hundreds of protesters, reporters, and doctors who had arrived to treat the injured were roughed up and beaten by Chicago policemen. It all happened on live TV. Like most Americans, I was watching as all three television networks covered the convention and the protests around the clock. The nation seemed to be coming apart. The Democratic Party couldn't come back together after the divisive convention, helping propel Richard Nixon to a narrow victory over Vice President Humphrey that November.

By the time I returned to the U.S. in late July, it was too late to work for Dad's business for the rest of the summer, so I got a job at the local McDonald's for a few weeks before beginning my senior year at Denison. It was fun making milkshakes by hand and learning how to flip hamburgers and make French fries.

I lived in an apartment off campus down the hill in Granville during my senior year. I shared it with two friends, Bruce who had been my freshman year roommate and Jim, another friend. It was a lot of fun and after living in Europe for more than six months, it seemed a better option than living in a dorm or the fraternity house. By then I had my first car, a pale yellow four-door Corvair. It got me around the Granville area and back and forth from Cincinnati. Jim borrowed it one evening and totaled it in an ice storm. Fortunately, neither he nor the others in the car were injured. That was remarkable since the Corvair was the subject of Ralph Nader's book, *Unsafe at Any Speed.* Nader targeted the car because serious injuries were happening in Corvair accidents since the engine was in the rear of the car and an empty trunk was in the front.

The Vietnam War was raging when I returned from Europe. While Denison's campus was not the hot bed of anti-war protests that other larger campuses were, we had intense on campus debates during my senior year. Both Senator J. William Fulbright (D-AK), a long-time chairman of the Senate Foreign Relations Committee and a strong anti-Vietnam voice, and Secretary of State Dean Rusk, a strong supporter of the Vietnam war, spoke on campus as part of an ongoing lecture series. I recall attending both speeches.

I knew I was likely to be classified 1A in the Selective Service system the summer after graduation and, therefore, a prime candidate to be drafted. President Nixon eventually granted all graduate school and law students a one-year academic deferral if they began their studies in the fall of 1969. The first Selective Service lottery was scheduled for the end of that year, so a deferral made sense. As a result, I began my law studies in the fall of 1969.

Despite the turmoil, senior year flew by and suddenly graduation day had come and gone. My father was particularly proud of my attending Denison and the things I achieved there. While my father wasn't one for dishing out the L-word (love) very often, I knew he loved me. I took more daily comfort in the assurance that he was proud of me, something I was secure in because he told me so quite often. Twenty-five years after I graduated, I was chosen to receive an Alumni Citation given to accomplished alumni of the school. For Denison, and for me and my parents, it was an important occasion. My parents drove from Cincinnati to Granville to attend the awards ceremony, no doubt filled with excitement about having a chance to visit the campus that they had enjoyed so much when Greg and I were enrolled there. Dad was in his late seventies then and not in the best health, but he did not hesitate to make the trip. He told me again and again how proud he was of me and all that I had accomplished; it felt sublime to hear those words from him.

I had great experiences in college at Denison University. One of my college friends, Bruce Brett (far left), celebrated my birthday with my brothers Greg (second from left) and Rodger (right).

I studied in Florence, Italy during the second semester of my junior year in college, spring of 1968. This photo is with a friend during a weekend trip to Venice.

Basilica di San Marco in Venice is one of the most iconic and beautiful churches in the world. My semester in Italy was a life-changing experience.

It's graduation day from Denison University in the spring of 1969. This is with my mother (left), brother Greg, and Nan.

CHAPTER 7

Approaching the Bench

AS A TEENAGER, I EXPLORED A FEW POTENTIAL CAREER PATHS. MY mother occasionally urged me to become a dentist. I dismissed this idea quickly because as someone who didn't enjoy going to the dentist it was unbearable to think of having my fingers in someone's mouth for the rest of my life. Due to my interest in art and architecture, as a young teenager I talked to a neighbor who was an architect. I may have caught him on a bad day because he tried to talk me out of it. I wasn't ready to give up on the idea, so a classmate took me to his dad's architecture firm one day after school. The man looked so overworked that when his son asked to see some of his drawings, he threw a roll of drawings at us. That was further discouragement. A few of my friends' fathers were practicing attorneys. In fact, the fathers of two classmates, John Kimpel and Jim Allen, were law partners. I was around John's dad a few times and was impressed with his demeanor and presence. He was Perry Mason-like in my eyes. I loved the idea of using facts and analysis to build arguments that could win a case or just a point.

Speaking of Perry Mason, he also impacted my decision to become a lawyer. He was the most widely known and popular attorney in the country in the late 1950s and early 1960s. Well, he wasn't technically an attorney, but he played one on TV. *Perry Mason* was the wildly popular TV series about a tenacious defense attorney who always won his cases. Growing up, this TV show was at the height of its popularity and I never missed an episode. I was fascinated with actor Raymond Burr's portrayal of the character written by Erle Stanley Gardner. Aside from the fact that Mason always won, I was drawn to the air of wisdom and reliability he projected. He was the go-to guy for those who had no place else to turn. No matter how bleak the outlook, Mason always kept his calm. In the courtroom, he not only would get his client off the hook; he also would correctly identify the actual guilty party, an amazing twofer. All I knew was that when I grew up, I wanted to be just like Perry Mason. I wanted to be a lawyer. I was in law school before I realized that rarely were cases resolved like they were on Perry Mason. Mason typically wrapped up the case in a preliminary hearing, the purpose of which was to determine whether there was sufficient evidence to charge the alleged perpetrator with a crime! That was the only way to tell a really good story and resolve the "case" in an hour. It was literary license at its best and, for me, most entertaining and persuasive. It turns out that Raymond Burr was gay in real life. He had to be in the closet because his Hollywood career would've been destroyed had his truth been revealed. It's quite a coincidence that the actor who played the character I admired and wanted to emulate in real life was in fact a gay man.

My senior year at Denison was filled with angst over preparing for and taking the LSATs that were required for applying to law schools. Denison had an advisor who focused on law schools, and he provided invaluable guidance as the process unfolded. Eventually, I was accepted at Vanderbilt University Law School along with three Denison classmates. I was accepted to other schools but decided on Vanderbilt partly after visiting the campus and talking with a few professors, including Professor Bob Covington, one of the most sophisticated individuals I had met then or since. My first semester, Covington taught a course called Legal Methods, sort of an introduction to legal thinking and writing. Ironically, or perhaps not, Professor Covington called on me the first day of class to state whether portions of a court case were holding or dictum, both of which were new concepts for me and most of my classmates. I got them all correct and was momentarily the smartest person in my section. I soon learned not to let it go to my head as studying law got tougher from there.

My roommate for those three years was a Denison classmate, Francis "Sandy" Cherry, so I didn't have to worry about finding a roommate as I arrived in Nashville to begin classes in the fall of 1969. To my pleasant surprise, I quickly realized Nashville was a pretty gay city. I was 22 and anxious to explore my sexuality after four largely closeted years at Denison. I don't recall how I discovered gay life in Nashville, but it seemed to be everywhere, partly I am sure because I came across to other gay men as open to exploring that side of me. That being said, I had no sexual liaisons with anyone in the law school. I was careful to keep this part of my life separate from my law school life, including from my roommate.

In the spring of my first year, I met an undergraduate student at Peabody Teachers College, which was adjacent to Vanderbilt's campus. He was a stunning young guy who was a state gymnastics champion and had the sculpted body to prove it. It was fun for a while to spend time with him on a regular basis. I would call his room from the lobby phone in the law school library to see if I could stop by his dorm on my way home. The following year, I met an interesting and attractive Vanderbilt undergrad whom I saw for several months until he graduated. Over the five and a half years I lived in Nashville, I had several liaisons with men and even a few I could call boyfriends, but I didn't want to be seen in public with them for fear of having to explain where we met and why we were out together. Perhaps I just wasn't clever enough to come up with answers to such questions. Also, I was dating a few women from time to time and it seemed wise to keep the two activities separate. After graduation, I was invited to become a member of the local Bachelors, an informal group of young professional men who were invited to attend occasional dinner dances and escort younger single women. Once I moved to Washington, I ran into a fellow Nashville Bachelor at a gay bar. I imagine we weren't the only closeted gay men in the group.

Aside from going to classes and dating, I also had a job during most of law school; my first year I worked in the main library shelving books a few evenings a week. During my second year, I landed my first job in politics. I worked part-time in the administration of Tennessee GOP Governor Winfield Dunn. I was introduced to the Dunn staff by a Vanderbilt classmate who had been involved in his 1970 campaign. I applied for a job after learning the governor's legal counsel was looking to hire law students part time. I was thrilled to get hired. Initially, I worked to fill vacant seats on the many state boards and commissions. It was essential for the state's three Grand Divisions to be appropriately represented. The Grand Divisions were the geographic parts of the state: West, Middle, and East Tennessee.

Another early task was being part of interview teams that met with prisoners who had requested a clemency hearing. During the 1970 campaign, Dunn made an issue of how Democrats had mishandled clemency. It was common knowledge that clemency could be purchased, so Dunn had promised to end this illegal and immoral practice. He told voters that if he were elected, any prisoner in the Tennessee system could receive an interview by a member of the governor's staff. My classmates and I were the governor's team to do the interviews along with a member of the state Board of Pardons and Paroles.

It was an eye-opening experience. We reviewed the official profile and medical records of each prisoner we interviewed. We all were shocked at the high percentage of those who had been subject to sexual abuse during their childhood, often by a family member.

Governor Dunn commuted the sentences of several primarily older African American men who had been convicted of murdering a wife or girlfriend. After years of imprisonment, they were no longer considered a threat to society, and he commuted their sentences to time served. A full pardon was rare, but I respected Governor Dunn for permitting several inmates in this population to return to their families and communities.

Most of our interviews were at the state penitentiary in Nashville. During one visit, the warden was escorting us into the main courtyard when a handsome young blonde inmate walked by us. The warden said, "We lock him up at night in solitary, so he doesn't get raped." We quickly learned prisons have their own hierarchy. It was not unusual to see an inmate wearing eye makeup and acting effeminate. From what we could tell, none of the other prisoners thought anything of it.

During law school in the late '60s and early '70s, the Vietnam War was raging. Every day brought news from the war zone, including dramatic images of the fighting, both photos and film. The three TV networks and every major newspaper covered the war with correspondents in the field. With such close media coverage, Vietnam was brought into the living rooms of every American house in a way no previous war had been.

Almost three million Americans served in the Vietnam War, including almost 650,000 who were drafted. I was conflicted about the war. I have always been a strong supporter of our national defense and believed in the domino theory of why it was important to keep Vietnam out of the hands of the communists. Hindsight is always 20/20, but we were at the height of the Cold War with the Soviets and communism was spreading around the globe. But as the war dragged on and it became clear that our military leaders were not given the tools or authority to win, it was increasingly difficult to support. The Pentagon Papers made that clear when they were released in 1971.

Attending college resulted in an automatic deferment until the early '70s, so the war was largely fought by young men who didn't go to college. I often said I would have considered taking a year or two off after graduating college, but I most almost certainly would have been drafted so I decided to immediately begin law school.

At the height of the war in 1969, my senior year in college, there were 549,000 American service members in Vietnam; by 1972, that number had fallen to 69,000 because of President Nixon's decision to have South Vietnamese regulars do most of the fighting. In 1968, Nixon ran for president on a platform of restoring law and order and ending the Vietnam War. In March of 1968, as the death toll rose and the prospects for total victory diminished, President Johnson announced he wouldn't seek re-election so that he could devote his full attention to the war effort.

The war was tearing the country apart, and as I witnessed in Europe in the summer of 1968, protests and riots over the war were commonplace there as well. More than 58,000 Americans were killed during the Vietnam War with many more wounded and many listed as MIA. It was a dark period in our history. During my 50th high school reunion, those of us who had served in the military were recognized. I was astonished to learn that from our class of more than 700 students, only one classmate had died in Vietnam. He was killed the first day he arrived there. He had not attended college and was immediately drafted into the army. The Vietnam War remains a lasting tragedy for our nation, especially for the families of all those who never came home and for those who returned with serious injuries, medical issues brought on by Agent Orange and other reminders of how ugly war can be for those who actually fight.

I entered law school in the fall of 1969 at the height of the war. Several of my classmates were returning Vietnam vets and many of the rest of us were subject to being drafted. The first Vietnam era lottery was held on December 1, 1969 and determined my fate and that of many others. I recall sitting in the study room of our apartment with my roommate as the numbers were called out for the lottery. My roommate was ineligible to be drafted due to an old high school football injury. If my birthdate didn't receive a high number, I knew I would be eligible unless I was willing to declare myself homosexual which never crossed my mind. If it had, I would have rejected the thought outright knowing how society felt about gays. I believed it would have ruined my life in the early 1970s, so it remained a closely guarded secret.

There were 366 balls in the bin, one for each day of the year (including February 29th). Dates would be selected at random and my birthday, November 30th, was picked early on, so I had a low number. That meant I was certain to be drafted in the summer of 1970. President Nixon had granted all law and graduate students a one-year draft deferral, but that would end in the spring of 1970. Panic quickly set in. I wanted to finish law school without interruption. I wasn't anxious to join the military, but the priority was to delay induction until graduation in June 1972. That left two choices to keep me in law school: join either the Navy ROTC program or the Army ROTC program on campus. I first tried the Navy program at Vanderbilt only to learn it was at capacity with undergraduate students. Apparently, the Navy was a favored branch of the military in the south. The Army ROTC program on campus was nowhere near capacity. It needed law and graduate students to maintain sufficient numbers to remain on campus, so I joined along with a few classmates who also had low lottery numbers. As a result, while most of my classmates were getting summer clerkships at law firms and other legal related summer positions, I spent the summer after my first and second years at Army ROTC boot camp, first at Ft. Knox, Kentucky and the second summer at Ft. Bragg, North Carolina. I recall at least a few nights of anxiety when I suspected some of the guys in my unit were onto my sexual orientation. I was discreet to a fault, but I feared what would happen if

I was exposed. I had a migraine headache one night in the barracks at Ft. Bragg. My head hurt so much I could barely put it on the pillow. It was a tough night, but I made it through all in one piece.

During my second and third year of law school, we had ROTC classes weekly and Thursday afternoon drill on the field next to the law school. Plus, we had occasional weekend drills. I remember one of my boyfriends during law school would sometimes come by my ROTC unit drills to watch us march. I enjoyed having him there and knowing our relationship was our secret. Joining the ROTC allowed me to finish law school with the rest of my class and provided a welcome monthly stipend. By the time of my graduation in 1972, the Vietnam War was rapidly winding down, and I could not have begged my way into the full-time Army. We received our commissions on graduation day, and I have a wonderful picture of my mother pinning my Second Lieutenant bars on my uniform. I waited more than six months to start the required active duty for training at Ft. Eustice, Virginia. As a result, my law career was put on hold for almost a year after graduation, but I continued to work for the governor's office. That job was a godsend because it kept me active in politics and public policy.

During and after my time in law school, I continued discovering gay life in Nashville. Besides the campus area, there were other places to meet gay men, including a couple of bars downtown near the bus station, a typical location for gay bars in inner cities during that era. One evening, I got up the nerve to go into one and immediately regretted it. It was dark, smelled of stale beer, and was populated by older men, all of whom looked lecherous. All eyes were on me as I ordered a beer and took a few gulps before quickly leaving. There were two primary cruising spots. There was one downtown called "the block" where gay men would drive around looking for hookups. The other was in Centennial Park close to the Vanderbilt campus where gay men would drive around or park and wait in their cars. It was a seedy way to meet other gay men, but during most of my time in Nashville, there weren't bars where I felt comfortable. Of course this was decades before the internet and dating apps would make finding other gay men much easier.

A couple of years before I moved from Nashville, a gay nightclub opened in the warehouse district. Warehouse areas were a common location for gay bars in urban areas, in part because of cheap rent and in part because of the privacy they offered patrons who didn't want to be seen entering a gay establishment. The bar, The Other Side, was fun and the crowd was closer to my age. I began meeting guys I felt more comfortable with and wanted to get to know. The beginning of the gay bar scene in the late 1960s and early 1970s was a healthy development for gays as it gave us an alternative, safer venue in which to meet others.

I began living on my own as soon as I graduated from law school, my roommate having moved to begin his legal career in Richmond, Virginia. I made a point of being careful who I invited back to my apartment and usually preferred meeting elsewhere. Being gay in Nashville, as in many cities at that time and even now, could be dangerous. Gay men could be preyed upon by unsavory characters looking for money or someone to gay bash. I learned this lesson the hard way, in what might be the understatement of my life. One evening as I was studying for the bar exam in June of 1972, I decided to take a break and went downtown by myself to see a movie. On my way home, I picked up what I thought was a clean-cut young guy who was hitchhiking my direction home just outside of downtown.

Even though I had hitchhiked my way through Italy and much of Europe just a few years earlier, I rarely picked up hitchhikers in the U.S. This young man was good looking and friendly. As soon as he was in the car, he began asking questions. At first, I thought he was just curious and perhaps trying to make what should have been a short trip more enjoyable. I told him I had just graduated law school and was studying for the bar exam which I suspect in hindsight indicated to him that I had money. I didn't, but he didn't know that. After hearing I was soon to be a lawyer, he pulled a gun on me and told me to drive to my apartment. That was the first and only time I have had someone pull a gun on me. I was terrified. My mind raced in search of a way out, but with a gun pointed at me, my choices were limited. I drove him to my apartment, which was in a small house in a quiet neighborhood. The entire time, I kept thinking about how I could get out of this situation.

He ordered me to go into the apartment, I suppose so he could see what he could take. All I had to my name were some clothes, law books, an old TV, and a few pots and pans. As we left my apartment, he pointed the gun at my head and told me to get in the trunk of my car. In hindsight, I should have tried to get the gun away from him at that moment, but I didn't try. He proceeded to drive my car around Nashville with me in the trunk in what appeared to be an effort to recruit an accomplice. He stopped at least twice and got out of the car to talk with people, but I could not hear what they were saying. I listened for anything that might sound familiar or if I could hear anyone just outside the car when he stopped at a traffic light. If I heard someone, I planned to loudly yell for help. He must have found an accomplice because what happened next required one.

He drove somewhere outside the city and suddenly I could hear the car was in a field with tall grass. He stopped in the field and got out and yelled at me through the trunk, demanding where he could find money in my apartment. I didn't have cash sitting around or even much in my bank account but to get rid of him I told him I had some cash in a dresser drawer. With that information, he left me in the trunk and ran off, apparently with the accomplice, to search my apartment. Even now all these years later, it's difficult recalling this situation. I prayed for help but knew that was unlikely because I was in a rural area and probably hidden from view. I thought I might die in that trunk before anyone found me. I tried repeatedly to find a latch to open the trunk or figure out a way to get into the back seat of the car. Years later, perhaps because people got locked in trunks, car makers began making ways to open trunks from inside but not in time to save me from this situation.

After what seemed like an eternity, I heard footsteps in the grass. He opened the trunk, yelled at me for lying to him because he didn't find any money and shot at me twice and ran away leaving the trunk open. The bullets hit the left side of my chest. My left arm went numb. I got out of the trunk and somehow managed to drive myself to the closest house with signs of someone still awake since it was early morning by this time. I woke up a couple who called the police. After what seemed like endless questioning, they took me to an emergency room in Nashville. Fortunately, the bullets were from a small caliber pistol and didn't pierce my ribs. My doctor later told me I was lucky the bullets hit my ribs otherwise they would have pierced my heart and killed me on the spot. One bullet was removed before I was discharged from the emergency room, but doctors could not locate the other one. The second bullet remained in my chest for years and would show up on chest X-rays until it dissolved on its own. The probing to find the bullets left my chest sore and bruised for weeks.

I stayed for a few nights with a married couple I knew from law school who also were remaining in Nashville for the bar exam. The next day, my classmate accompanied me to my apartment to make sure the perpetrator was not inside. He brought a handgun with him just to be safe. I soon moved to an apartment in a large complex that would provide more safety, especially since the perpetrator knew where I lived.

The next Monday I went to work with my arm in a sling and the left side of my chest bandaged from the exploration the doctor had made trying to remove the bullets. I attended the bar review course that evening and never missed a class. I continued to study diligently while trying to put this incident behind me as quickly as possible. My life easily could have ended that night. I had learned a traumatic lesson about the importance of recognizing and avoiding reckless situations. For years, I would wake up at night in a panic thinking of being in that trunk. Fortunately, like so many things, time pretty much healed even that. For years, only my closest friends and family knew of this incident, and it's difficult but important to include it here. With my shirt off, the bullet holes are clearly visible and sometimes a topic of inquiry. I thought of not telling my family but decided they should be told. It's a good thing I did since a suburban newspaper in their area of Cincinnati had a short article saying I had been stabbed in Nashville. Some of my parents' friends saw it and called to express concern and find out more about what had happened. The paper got the story wrong, but not by much. My Uncle Donald and his wife came to visit me in Nashville. He didn't say so, but I think he brought one of his guns with him and may have thought he could help locate the shooter. He had been an Ohio Highway Patrol officer some years earlier and had a bit of a John Wayne personality. They stayed just a couple of days, but it was nice of them to visit. I tried to put the shooting out of my mind and return to studying for the bar exam in July.

I certainly never picked up a hitchhiker again and nor did anyone who knew of this frightful evening. In the days after the shooting, I scheduled a follow up meeting with the Nashville police. I wanted to know what they were doing to find the guy who shot me. Their answer was "nothing" as they didn't follow up on crimes perpetrated against people who picked up hitchhikers. The message was clear: I was a gay man and deserved what I got.

Many years later, the matter was raised again at two separate school reunions. In 2015, at my 50th high school reunion, a classmate tapped me on the shoulder and said he had heard "something about my being stabbed somewhere and left on the side of a road." I corrected him on what happened and fortunately that ended the inquiry. Then in 2017, at a law school reunion, we were at dinner at a classmate's home in Nashville, when another classmate saw me and said to the gathering, "Hey, Bob has a story to tell about a car trunk.." I didn't let him finish his sentence when I quietly said, "I don't talk about that." He apologized later in the evening. Even so, I wondered how anyone could think I would want to talk about that nightmare incident again. This classmate was one of the nicest guys in our class but apparently lacked emotional intelligence. I became more cautious and aware of my surroundings, something that served me well as I moved to Washington in 1975 where crime was a more significant issue than in relatively quiet Nashville. The fact I was closeted at Denison and at Vanderbilt Law School stayed with me for many years. The more difficult moments I have had as a gay man involved these two schools. Even when I served on the Board of Trustees at Denison, while it was known I was a gay man, I never spoke about it.

At my 40th Denison reunion, I took the man I was dating at the time. He offered to go with me as I seemed ambivalent about going, and he said he had heard so much about Denison that he wanted to see it for himself. Everyone on staff at the school knew he was coming and were wonderful to him. He was considerably younger, so we stood out. During the opening reception, a classmate asked how long we had been together. During the class picture, one classmate asked him to join the picture saying, "You could be one of our sons." I was nervous the entire time. More recently at a large dinner on campus to announce a new capital campaign, a contemporary alumnus said he could not understand why I never married. I hesitated and responded that marriage was not for everyone and left it at that. Indeed, it is not. Several of my straight friends in Washington never married. Most were married to their jobs and who knows why they didn't marry. As with so many situations, I tend not to ask personal questions as I am still reluctant to respond to personal questions about myself.

In preparation for our 50th reunion from Denison, we were asked to send in a piece about what we have done since graduating and talk about anything we wanted. It was liberating for me to say two of the highlights of my life have been chairing the Log Cabin Republicans board and being part of filing the organization's lawsuit that led to the repeal of "Don't Ask Don't Tell." The statements of those of us on the 50th reunion organizing committee were sent to the rest of our class as examples of what they might send. I was pleased when a male classmate sent me a message saying he was glad to have found the "other" gay member of the class. This classmate moved to New York City after graduation and became a successful male model over many years. More recently, he was the head of publicity for a major design house. I encouraged him to attend the reunion and to send in a statement about this interesting career. I also gladly told him we were not the only gays in our class. At Vanderbilt, I talk openly with the dean and others at the law school. I have offered to speak to the LGBT group at the law school and undergraduate school. I feel I have finally resolved the baggage I have held for decades at both schools.

I enjoyed living in Nashville while in law school at Vanderbilt University. This photo with my parents is from graduation day in the spring of 1972.

This is another photo from graduation day. My mother pins my Army Second Lieutenant bars on me. I joined the Army ROTC unit at Vanderbilt after getting a low number in the first Vietnam War draft lottery. Doing so allowed me to complete my legal education without interruption.

After graduating from law school, I continued serving in the Tennessee Army National Guard until I left the state in 1975.

This 1970 photo is from my apartment in Nashville. I enjoyed exploring the city's gay life, but it was a dangerous time to be out. I was lucky to survive a kidnapping and shooting that happened in the summer after law school graduation.

CHAPTER 8

Mr. Kabel Goes to Washington

FOR MOST OF ITS HISTORY, THE OFFICE OF GOVERNOR OF Tennessee was limited to a single four-year term with the possibility of running again in the future. (After a change in state law, in 1982, Lamar Alexander became the first two-term governor in modern state history). Before Governor Dunn was elected, two Democrats tag-teamed the governorship back and forth between them, with one serving a four-year term then giving way to the other one to serve a four-year term. It was very much a Southern Democratic state at the time, and the tag team strategy was meant to keep one individual from building a dynasty.

In 1970, Winfield Dunn became the first Republican governor in Tennessee in fifty years, winning a challenging primary and then defeating Democrat John Jay Hooker, a candidate so dubious that the incumbent Democratic governor endorsed the Republican Dunn in the November general election. Dunn was a dentist in Memphis before being elected governor. He had been serving as Chairman of the Shelby County Republican Party when he caught the attention of U.S. Senator Howard Baker and other senior Tennessee Republicans. Dunn and his wife, Betty, were right out of central casting. They were an attractive couple with a young, growing family. Both had outgoing personalities and were extraordinarily likeable. Senator Baker offered some of his key staff, including Lamar Alexander and Lee Smith, to help run the Dunn campaign. Smith became his counsel and later chief of staff.

When I started working full-time for the governor's office after graduating law school, I continued focusing on clemency matters. Eventually, I became the governor's liaison to the Tennessee congressional delegation. The role required me to go to Washington on a regular basis to meet with members of the Tennessee Senate and House delegation to advance the governor's agenda. I quickly got hooked on D.C. and realized I wanted to move there after Dunn's term would end in 1975.

In time, I got a new job in Dunn's administration, working side-by-side with the governor as his scheduler. I was thrilled to be offered the job by Dunn's chief of staff. Soon after beginning my new role, I decided to join the Tennessee National Guard. After completing my Active Duty for Training commitment in early 1973, I approached the State Adjutant General, the head of the Tennessee National Guard, for his suggestions on how to proceed. Shortly after, I was assigned to the state headquarters in Nashville. The commitment involved serving one weekend a month at state headquarters and occasionally going out in the field with some units. One weekend, I was flown by helicopter to a remote area where a unit was conducting training maneuvers. As I got off the helicopter, the officer in charge shouted out: "Which one of you is from the governor's office?" I replied I was, and he looked a bit stunned. After all, I was 27 years old and looked even younger. I decided not to join the National Guard when I moved to Washington in January of 1975.

During the last eighteen months of the Dunn administration, I spent much of the day with the governor when he was in his office in

Nashville. My office was one of two directly connected to his office, so I could pop in on a frequent basis. My role was to work with his administrative staff to develop his schedule and then make sure the day went smoothly. It was a heady job for a 27-year-old. I got to know his cabinet members, some of whom called on me to relay messages to the governor on developments in their departments. Given my experience working with the Board of Pardons and Parole during law school, I served as the liaison to the Board on all clemency matters, including reviewing all files before they went to Governor Dunn for his decision.

Even though Democrats controlled the state legislature, Dunn passed nearly all his priority legislation. He brought a new level of professionalism to the governor's office and its dealings with the legislature. In his last year in office, Dunn was elected chairman of the Republican Governor's Association. Dunn left office in 1975, after serving the one term allowed by law, as the state's most popular political figure. After leaving office, he worked primarily for Hospital Corporation of America, which was headquartered in Nashville and founded by the Frist family. (Republican Bill Frist later won election to the U.S. Senate from Tennessee in 1994.) For his part, Dunn tried to make a comeback in 1986. Then Gov. Lamar Alexander was term limited. Dunn ran again for governor and lost to Democrat Ned Ray McWherter, the speaker of the Tennessee House, by a margin of 54% to 46%.

With the end of Dunn's term in 1975, I had some decisions to make. I could have stayed in Nashville, but that wasn't a terribly appealing option. While my career was going well, I wasn't happy on a personal level. Nashville was a beautiful place, full of all the antebellum charm that makes the South so attractive to many people. And the fact that Nashville was one of the music capitals of the world added an entirely different appeal. And it wasn't just the country and western stars. All the greats from rock, rhythm and blues and even jazz came to the world-famous studios in Nashville. From its sun-dappled summers to its barely-there winters, the Nashville I knew was modern and exciting while exhibiting just the right touch of seersucker suits and lace doilies. The parties, the hospitality, just the general pace and quality of life were appealing on many levels. And I was in a good position professionally, after making a name for myself by doing good work. I probably would have been a sought-after young professional in the legal and political worlds.

I was still a gay man in what remained the old South, and although I was seeing a few people, it was furtive and secretive. If I stayed in Nashville, eventually I would have to literally play it straight: get married, have kids, join a country club, join a law firm, and live a lie. I instinctively knew I could not pull it off for long and would hurt the woman I married, not to mention our children. I resolved that at the end of Dunn's term I would depart Nashville for more favorable personal environs. I fashioned my escape using the contacts I had made through my duties as the governor's liaison to the Tennessee congressional delegation in Washington. As a part of my responsibilities, I had been regularly going back and forth to D.C. and I had loved it.

There were two Republican Senators representing Tennessee at that time. One was Howard Baker, who was well on his way to becoming a national political figure. Serving with him in the Senate from Tennessee was Bill Brock, who had defeated country western singing star Tex Ritter in the Republican primary and Al Gore Sr. in the 1970 general election. These men were young, powerful, and on top of their game. It was a thrill to be around them, and I soaked up as much as I could about the issues and the way Senate staffers conducted their business. I worked with the House members, too, but the Senate suited me more for a couple reasons. Senators had a six-year term, so you had time to drill down on important issues and really accomplish something. By contrast, the U.S. House of Representatives is the home of what are quite possibly the worst political jobs in the nation. With only two-year terms, House members never stop campaigning, which means staffers never really stop. It's year after year of non-stop, hyperventilating activity. And the potential of losing an election meant the prospect of unemployment was never far off. I was also drawn to the Senate because of the thrill and prestige of working in the world's most powerful legislative body. Henry Kissinger once said power is the greatest aphrodisiac; all I know is for me, the U.S. Senate had me at "Hello."

Working in the Dunn Administration was an important factor in solidifying my identity as a Republican. Tennessee Republicans were growing in number; most tended to be younger individuals with forward-looking ideas. In my travels to Washington, I spent considerable time with Senator Howard Baker and his staff. He was smart, articulate, and had a wonderful dry sense of humor. I spent less time with Senator Brock's staff due to the perceived political rivalry between Dunn and Brock. Baker and his staff were great role models for me. Both Baker and Brock were pro-business and supported a strong national defense. I identified with the policies they espoused which were in stark contrast to what I saw many Democrats in Washington advocating. Social issues had not yet become divisive political issues. That didn't occur until after I moved to Washington in the mid-1970s.

I told Governor Dunn about my intentions. He had many Washington connections through his position as head of the Republican Governors Association and kindly set up appointments with several GOP senators. After interviewing with all of them, I got precisely zero job offers. It was humbling, but I was determined to move to Washington and get a job bartending or waiting tables if I had to, as long as I was closer to my ultimate goal of a job as a Senate staffer.

There's an old saying that says, "Follow your dreams and the universe will accommodate you." Back in Nashville, my humble apartment building had a fair number of Vanderbilt students and recent grads like myself. One of my neighbors, a Vanderbilt medical student, told me his sister was planning to visit from Washington where she had just finished a tour on the staff of Senator Paul Fannin, a Republican from Arizona who was widely rumored to be retiring in a couple of years at the end of his second six-year term. My neighbor's sister had moved to a new job at the Department of the Interior, but she was aware that Fannin's staffer who worked for him on the Senate Finance Committee was taking a newly created position with the Finance Committee itself. This meant Fannin was looking for a new Finance Committee staffer, and she suggested I apply. My heart leapt as she discussed the opportunity; the job sounded perfect for me. Tax and trade work were my absolute bailiwick when it came to the law, and to be able to pursue my specialty in service of a U.S. Senator was a potential dream come true. I packed a suitcase with clean shirts, a toothbrush, and a bushel of positive thoughts. I interviewed a couple of times before they hired me. My hiring was helped by the reality that no one from Arizona wanted to come to D.C. to be a part of a term that only had two years left. I had no such prejudices; I had a job with a senator. And not just any senator. While largely unknown outside of Arizona, Fannin was the second-ranking Republican on the Senate Finance Committee. This meant that for any major legislation, he would be named to the all-important Conference Committee, the bipartisan committee of legislators who negotiate the final wording of any bills that are passed by the House and Senate. It promised to be an incredible experience for me, being able to witness the crafting of some of the most significant legislation of the era. Senator Fannin was heavily involved in the hearings, the markup, and the debate of key legislation on the Senate floor and, just like with Governor Dunn, I was going to be there with him every step of the way.

Moving to Washington, D.C. was a life-changing event for me, both professionally and as a gay man. Even the physical act of moving itself was memorable. I rented a U-Haul truck large enough to haul my few worldly possessions including the car I had bought after passing the Tennessee Bar Exam, my beloved blue Fiat Spider convertible. Somehow, I got the car inside the truck and loaded my furniture, books, and clothing around it. I was off for my new adventure. Driving a truck that size was new to me. I had driven a small delivery truck when I worked for Dad's coffee business in the summers, but this was much bigger and was filled with items that could shift. I stopped about midway between Nashville and D.C. to find a motel for the night. I almost didn't make it. Exiting the freeway to look for a motel, I took a turn too fast and almost overturned the truck. I felt it leaning hard and almost lost control but somehow, I didn't. It was quite a scare, but I got up the next day and drove into D.C. where I stayed with a law school friend for a few days before moving into my own apartment on the 100 block of E St. S.E., a 10-minute walk to the Dirksen Senate Office Building where I would work for the next seven years.

I quickly made friends with a group of gay men about my age, all professionals getting started in their careers, some with a few more years under their belts. Meeting these individuals was the best thing to happen to me in many ways. Having friends with whom I felt comfortable and not having to hide our interaction as I would have been compelled to do in Nashville gave me a sense of security and a growing sense of family. These friends introduced me to the gay bar and entertainment scene that was lively and growing in 1975. I was young and single for the first few years in D.C. and enjoyed an active social life both bar hopping on the weekends and having dinners and parties at friends' homes.

From the outside, Washington gives the impression of being a straight-laced city and, for the most part, that is true. It didn't have the glamour of New York or San Francisco. Most of the people who make their living in D.C. are traditional types, policy wonks who feel more at home with a policy brief than a dancer in a bikini brief. But there were plenty of people in Washington of all sexual bents who wanted to let their hair down, and there were plenty of places ready to serve them, including my friends and me. A typical Friday and Saturday night started with meeting a small group of friends at one bar and then heading to two or three others before the night was over: places like Pier 9, Grand Central, or Cinema Follies. Typically, we started at one of the bars or clubs in the former warehouse district in Southeast D.C. Most of those places were demolished to build the new Nationals baseball stadium in the early 2000s. Before the stadium was built, that area hosted some of Washington's most famous and most infamous nightlife, such as Cinema Follies and Club Baths Washington. There were porn theaters, bathhouses, strip clubs, bars, and hookup joints to satisfy every desire and every budget. It wasn't a surprise to see a cab driver and the mayor sipping champagne from the same woman's slipper. Southeast was the home of several very popular gay bars that catered to the gay community.

Although the Capitol dome was visible from the area, it seemed far away from official Washington and consisted mostly of warehouses and industrial parks. The seclusion gave gay men a sense of comfort, with the feeling that anyone who saw you there was probably doing the same things you were. That seclusion worked both ways. There were more than a few cases of young gay men being attacked and beaten, sometimes by servicemembers from the nearby Marine barracks. To protect against this harassment, one gay ex-Marine formed a little group called GEM (for Gay Ex-Marines) who took it upon themselves to help patrol the area and prevent violence against gays and lesbians.

A favorite Southeast hangout of our group was the Lost & Found (often referred to as Lucy and Fred's.) The Lost & Found had a large dance floor and several big bars. It was always packed on the weekends with familiar faces and more than a few newbies. I met a lot of wonderful people there including, one Sunday afternoon, a man named Joe, who would soon become my partner and move in with me. After the L & F, we would drive downtown where there were several gay bars and other gay establishments on 9th Street Northwest. This was a totally different atmosphere from Southeast. The bars on 9th Street were sharing city space with federal government buildings and prestigious law firms.

Prominent among these bars was the original Eagle, a leather bar. (For the truly naive reader, I will specify that "leather bar" refers to the preferred attire, not the furnishings). But even though I have never been into the leather scene, I somehow managed to fit in enough in jeans and a flannel shirt to pass muster with the bouncers at the front door. During this era, all bars had to serve at least some food to keep their liquor license. Most of the gay bars had grills where they would cook burgers and fries. The Eagle met its requirement at least in part by serving home-cooked dinners on weekends early in the evening and then moving the tables and chairs to make room for the bar scene that started around 9 p.m. The food was better than one would have expected in a leather bar.

Down the street was a fun dance bar called the Eagle in Exile and close to that was the Chesapeake House, another bar with male strippers. The Chesapeake was on the corner of 9th and Massachusetts Ave. N.W., a busy corner for traffic. I never went there for fear of being seen by someone driving by. But there were others in the Washington establishment who operated with less caution. The Chesapeake House was the place where then Republican Congressman Bob Bauman of Maryland would hang out. Bauman was elected to Congress in 1973 in a special election to replace the previous member who had committed suicide. A devout Catholic with a wife and four children, Bauman established a reputation as a faithful conservative, often bemoaning the decline of morality in the United States. By the late 1970s, after founding several conservative activist groups, Bauman was considered a rising star in the conservative movement and Republican Party. But Bauman had a secret, and he had as rough a coming out as anyone I can remember. On October 3, 1980 at the height of his election campaign, he was charged with soliciting sex from a sixteen-year-old who had lied about his age to get a job as a dancer at the Chesapeake House. Bauman blamed the incident on a bout with alcoholism. After a public apology and completing a rehab program, the charges were dropped. Nevertheless, Bauman lost the November election just a few weeks later to an opponent who wouldn't have had a chance prior to the scandal. Bauman ran again in the next election cycle but bowed out prior to the primary election. He left public life and fashioned a very successful career as a specialist in offshore tax havens. I have always admired Bob Bauman for his allegiance to conservative principles and for the way he handled the scandal that destroyed his political career. He eventually came out of the closet and wrote a compelling memoir in 1986.

There was another restaurant and bar just a block from the J. Edgar Hoover FBI building in downtown D.C. It served lunch and dinner and had strippers who would dance on the bars and tables during meals to entertain the guests. During the day, the strippers were female but during evenings they were male. All the 9th Street bars were closed around 1980 to make way for the new D.C. Convention Center which was demolished in the early 2000s when the new but cavernous convention center was built a few blocks away.

Even though gay men and women lived throughout the city, Dupont Circle in Northwest was considered the heart of gay D.C. at the time. As the 9th Street bars were being closed for demolition, 17th Street was quickly becoming the gay "strip" with bars and restaurants that catered almost exclusively to the gay community. The original Annie's Steakhouse was a wonderful place because it had a sense of family that emanated from its genial, charismatic owner. Annie's eventually moved from its original location to a to a larger space up 17th Street. JR's, a successful gay bar from Dallas, opened in Annie's original place. Others opened over a few years, many of which are still going strong. Nearby was Rascals, a townhouse with several floors of entertainment, including a female impersonator show, and on the top floor a male strip club called Shooters. Close by was Mr. P's on P Street and the Fraternity House in an old brick stable in an alley behind P Street. Finally, there was Friends, a fun piano bar on P Street.

Whether in Southeast, 9th Street, or Dupont Circle, there were places to go to cruise and look for sexual encounters. Little did anyone know that the AIDS virus was being spread by anyone having unprotected sex. In those days, that was pretty much every gay man having sex. No one knew about what was later called "safe" sex. I got out of the club scene soon after I met Joe in 1979. We met one Sunday afternoon at the "tea dance" at the Lost & Found. We soon started dating and became a couple, settling into a different life that didn't involve going to bars every weekend. Instead, we discovered how wonderful D.C. could be during the day on Saturdays and Sundays. We biked most weekends, had friends over for dinner, renovated our house, and had an active social life. We also started collecting dogs, a small herd, and they became an important focus of our relationship. Despite the ups and downs all relationships have, it was a good and fun time in my life. My friends and partner became my extended family and that gave me great comfort. Being content in my relationship and not having to worry about what I was doing the next weekend allowed me to focus on my career more intensely. But for a while, I had a case of Saturday Night Fever, and I loved almost every minute of it.

My relationship with Joe lasted fifteen years. As with any relationship, it had its ups and downs; I had to learn how to argue, something that was avoided in our house growing up. My career was moving along nicely but Joe struggled with his, finally becoming a real estate agent and doing reasonably well. When I sold the Capitol Hill house, together we bought a new townhouse in Georgetown for us and the dogs to live in and an older town house on the Hill for Joe to renovate. It seemed like a great idea at the time, but our relationship was already strained. The renovation project proved too much for us to handle.

There were constant arguments about money and how stressful this project was for both of us, but especially me because he had quit his real estate job to devote full time effort to renovating the house. I was paying two mortgages with the high interest rates of the '80s and '90s and trying to find the money to continue the renovation. While Joe was tremendously talented at design and had great taste, his main shortcoming at that stage of his life was his inability to finish anything. I should have known that from the history of how long it took to finish renovation projects on the small house we had sold. Eventually, we had to rent our Georgetown house and moved into the still unfinished Hill house. Tensions got worse.

Our relationship was pretty much over when we moved into the Hill house. He lived in the rental apartment we had built out below and I lived upstairs with the dogs. Eventually I had to sell the house as the burden was too great and creditors were chasing me. I wasn't used to this level of financial strain and it troubled me greatly. The stress was having an impact on my law and lobbying practice. Once we sold the house, I moved into another Georgetown townhouse I had bought since the one we both owned was still under lease. Despite his assurances that he had located somewhere to live, on my scheduled moving day he had nowhere to go. Given all that had happened, remarkably, I agreed to let him move in with me and stay in the guest bedroom. He came down with hepatitis and couldn't move out, but weeks turned into months and, finally, I told him I would change the locks and put all his belongings outside if he didn't move out in a few weeks. He moved out and for a while we stayed in touch. That was a difficult ending to a difficult relationship. It took a long while to emotionally recover from it.

During my early years in Washington, the modern gay civil rights movement had taken shape. More people were coming out and pushing for equal rights. The Stonewall rebellion of 1969 had been an important turning point. In 1973, the year after I graduated from law school, the American Psychiatric Association removed homosexuality from its manual of mental disorders and called for the enactment of antidiscrimination laws. That was a key turning point because as long as homosexuality was classified as a mental illness, business and government weren't going to treat gay and lesbian people any better. Also, pop culture and the news media began including gay and lesbian people and sometimes even in a positive light such as the famous episode of *All in the Family* when Archie Bunker's bar buddy, a masculine retired NFL player, came out.

Some cities around the country started enacting gay non-discrimination laws. This incremental political and social progress on gay rights inevitably led to a backlash. It came in the form of Anita Bryant, a former beauty queen and rather unpleasant woman. In 1977, she led the effort in Miami-Dade County to overturn a non-discrimination measure passed by the local government. Bryant succeeded with the campaign and took it to other places around the country such as Minneapolis and Eugene, Oregon. Like so many things in politics, it's two steps forward and one step back. During this period, I made my one and only trip to Atlantic City. A gay friend of mine and I were walking on the beach when a lifeguard saw us and shouted out "F— Anita Bryant." I guess we were the only two men walking together on the beach that day, and he correctly assumed we were gay. Her crusade continued for several years with some ordinances being overturned by the voters and elected legislative bodies and then reinstated years later. Her crusade against gays symbolized some of the turmoil of the 1970s.

I began visiting New York City during my first years in Washington when I met an interesting guy my age named Jim at a bar in D.C. and he invited me to visit him in New York. Little did I know when I accepted his invitation that for someone so young, he was a successful art dealer. Jim graduated from the Georgetown School of Foreign Service and worked for a wealthy art collector for a while and then went out on his own. He lived in a beautiful, large apartment at 75th and Park Avenue. I had never seen anything like it. It came with its own elevator and a series of large, gracious rooms. He told me he paid $75,000 for the apartment during the New York City financial crisis in the mid-1970s. Today, it would sell for several million dollars.

As comfortable as we were with one another, it was a sign of the times that he could not take me to the parties and receptions where he met his clients. Two single young men together at such events was not acceptable in the mid-'70s, even in New York. Instead, he went to his parties, and I entertained myself by going to plays and roaming the clubs of New York. We met later in the evening back at his place. The time together during the day was special. Jim was sophisticated in a New York sort of way. His interest in art and wide-ranging knowledge on a variety of subjects was so appealing. I can't explain why we stopped seeing each other, but I have always been thankful we met.

A favorite memory took place in Central Park one afternoon. We had picked up sandwiches at a deli and were sitting on a park bench when a man dressed head to toe in pink came by us riding a pink bicycle. I turned away, being slightly embarrassed by the biker's flamboyance when Jim said, "Look at him. You don't think he dressed up like that to be ignored!" Of course, he was right.

I have enjoyed going to New York ever since. Joe and I went several times a year and we always had a good time. We usually stayed with friends in their apartments and sometimes in hotels with weekend rates that included parking, so we could drive and save on travel. We enjoyed roaming around town, shopping, and eating without any agenda except perhaps a play in the evening. When the AIDS crisis hit, some of the friends we had stayed with were among the first to die. That included our wonderful friend Axle. New York, San Francisco, and Los Angeles were among the first cities to be hard hit. D.C. was not far behind.

This photo is from a camping trip to the Great Smoky Mountains in the mid-'70s. I knew I had to leave Nashville if I was going to be openly gay and have a successful legal career.

I got my start in politics working for Tennessee Republican Governor Winfield Dunn. I worked part-time for the Dunn administration during law school and had several jobs with him after graduation, including a stint as his scheduler.

CHAPTER 9

The Price of Admission

AFTER I HAD MOVED TO WASHINGTON FOR THE FIRST YEAR OR so, my father would sometimes say, "I'm surprised you aren't shacked up with somebody by now." Of course, he had the expectation that the "somebody" would be a woman. For most of my life, he really didn't have any idea about my sexual orientation, but I think my mother always knew. I can pinpoint the time when they both got the unmistakable message their son was gay. In the middle of 1975, my parents came to visit me, and they brought the daughter of one of their best friends with them. They told her they were coming to D.C. to visit me, and when they extended an invitation to her, she eagerly accepted. My reaction to the news was decidedly less sunny. I liked her; she was a fun person to be around in the time we had spent together. But my parents were clearly looking at her as daughter-in-law material. She had two of the most important qualifications. First, she got along very well with my mother. Second, her family was reasonably wealthy. (They owned a chain of restaurants in the Midwest.) So she comes to town with them, and while everyone had a pleasant time, a pack of wet matches could have produced more sparks than she and I did. I needed someone to talk to, so I turned to my psychiatrist. I had started seeing him about six months after I got to Washington. I was kind of a wreck at the time. Not only was I suffering from culture shock, a frequent hangover from exploring the bars, and a touch of homesickness, I somehow had started an affair with a woman who worked in the Senate. Correction, a married woman who worked in the Senate.

What was I thinking? Good question. I knew I was attracted to men and didn't think there was anything wrong with that. But, like a lot of young gay men of my generation, I also had a faint notion that my attraction to men was a "phase" and that I would one day find a wife, kids, pet, and a house in the suburbs ... you know, the typical middle American family life from whence I came. And now, I had not only become involved in a serious relationship with a woman, but that relationship was immoral and potentially damaging to both of us. It quite thoroughly shuffled my mental deck. My paramour had located the doctor for me. She found another doctor for herself. I went to him with a simple request: I want to be straighter. His response was encouraging.

"You can do that if you want," the doctor told me. After a few months of individual sessions, he recommended I join one of his therapy groups, the entire composition of which was straight. Everyone was in the group for different reasons. It took me months to come out to these strangers. To their credit and my relief, they were very accepting, so the scars left from the group therapy experience were minimal. But I remained fundamentally confused and conflicted about who I was and what I was doing with my life.

It was into this highly emotional stage of my life that my parents had come to D.C. with their marriage candidate in tow. It proved to be the straw that broke the camel's back. The next time I was in Cincinnati, I broke down and begged my parents to stop putting pressure on me about women. I was as upset as I had ever been, only getting my words out between sobs. After a half-hour of this, my mother said it was good for my father to hear this from me and to see me like that. "He thinks you are made of steel," she said, "but you have feelings, just like everyone else." My father just sat there not saying a word. But it made him realize that whoever I was and whatever I was going to be, I needed space to be my own person.

Although my father didn't ask me if I was gay that day, he probably came to that conclusion. Ironically, within a year, my father asked my younger brother Greg if HE was gay. It was pretty much a rhetorical question; unlike me, Greg was more open about his sexuality. Greg confirmed he was gay, to which Dad responded, "I think your brother Bob is, too." Greg replied, "You will have to ask him that yourself." But the answer was clear.

My sexuality was more of a mystery to my parents than Greg's, but when I was so emotional with them about not trying to fix me up with women, a switch clicked for them. My speech was more than a typical "stop meddling in my life" screed. It was more like a, "if you love me at all, please don't make me feel more confused and upset about myself than I already do and please don't ask me what the real issue is because I'm not sure I want to tell you but I'm damn sure I don't want to lie to you" kind of screed. Looking back at these events from more than 40 years ago, I can now see I was a victim of my own deep-seated internalized homophobia; I felt that being attracted to men was okay but being gay might not be. Young people today might have a hard time understanding my difficulty. I never felt badly about my orientation toward other men, but I was aware it could create trouble for my career and other aspects of my life. Consequently, I was always very discreet and, candidly, that was a big reason why I was always a very private person, especially in the workplace. I didn't talk too much about myself and my life while I was at work. In fact, I recall several instances when acquaintances would ask why I didn't talk more about myself. I know I was a mystery to some of my law school classmates, but I didn't want to let them in on my big secret.

Coming to grips with my sexual orientation was a struggle. It's not hard to imagine how difficult it was to "come out" and trust that my loved ones would be any better at understanding me than I was at understanding myself. By the way, even if I had let my parents do their *Fiddler on the Roof* thing and fix me up with a female partner, chances are it wouldn't have turned out well. Remember the girl my parents had brought to Washington? Turns out she was a lesbian and has been in a committed relationship for many years. I finally found self-acceptance only after meeting Joe. I grew comfortable accepting myself as an openly gay man. I found comfort in being close to Joe and our gay friends. There was an emotional and physical bonding there I had not found elsewhere.

There always has been a part of me that looks at the authority figures in my life as potential role models. Some have had qualities I found admirable and sought to emulate, but most did not. Paul Fannin, the first senator for whom I worked, didn't fit the "mentor/role model" bill for several reasons. One, he was on his way to retirement when I worked for him, so he wasn't interested in taking on protégés. He also had a large family and they took up most of the spare bandwidth that potentially could have gone into bringing a guy like me along. And the final stumbling block was the not so insignificant fact that he wanted to fire me.

It happened during my first year on Senator Fannin's staff. Over the August recess, I had gone to California for vacation. When I came back for my first day of work after vacation, I didn't even get to my desk before the chief of staff called out to me from his office. When I poked my head in the door to see what he wanted, I was told to come in and close the door. The chief of staff, Joe Jenckes, was a former professional actor who had been on popular TV series such as *Gunsmoke* and *Daniel Boone*. At some point, he stopped acting, finished law school, and eventually was asked by Senator Fannin to serve as his chief of staff. His title was Administrative Assistant, a title that was much more common in those days than Chief of Staff. Later, I became good friends with Joe and his wife. But that was in no way apparent as I sat in a chair across from him. He looked like the Western character actor he had once been, and on this occasion, he was playing the role of the local hangman. "Look," he said in very direct tones, "the senator is not happy with you. You're not doing what he wants."

Everything moved in slow motion. I had just come back from a great vacation, and now I was about to get fired from my dream job. No one had instructed me on my exact role and responsibilities. Truth was that everyone in the office except me knew I was skating on thin ice, although I still don't know why someone didn't give me a heads-up. I had only myself to blame. Being a typical male, I never asked for directions.

"Really?" I said, genuinely shocked to be hearing this.

"Yes," he replied. After I fought off a wave of combined panic, fear, and shock, I was able to speak to my defense.

"You know," I said, "I accept that the senator is not happy with what I'm doing. But no one has ever told me exactly what it is that I am SUPPOSED to be doing around here. No one has ever given me any direction on anything. I just had to learn by doing." He listened to my argument and thought it over for what seemed like an hour but was probably only a few seconds. Eventually, he spoke. "Well, if that's the case, then that's our fault." I tried my best to maintain a calm exterior, but inside I was rejoicing at having at least earned a stay of execution. The next step was to achieve a full pardon.

After the come-to-Jesus meeting with the chief of staff, other staffers came to me and told me I had been put in an impossible position. Fannin was a senior member of the Senate Finance Committee and Interior Committee, and he was a senior member of the Joint Economic Committee (which, for the record, issued endless reports but didn't have any legislative authority.) Fannin liked to participate in these committees and have smart things to say at them, but nobody told me it was my job to produce those nuggets of wisdom for him. You would have thought Fannin's legislative director might have been tasked with that, but his sole responsibility was Indian Affairs. To be honest, I also wasn't giving full effort at work. Like I said before, I was enjoying life as a young man in a city where I could finally experience a robust social life. I was in D.C. and loving every minute of it, but I was slacking off and it was costing me professionally.

I asked Jenckes what he thought I should do. He said I should schedule a meeting with the senator and ask him what he wanted. I did exactly that, and in the meeting the senator told me what he wanted in clear and explicit terms. The most significant thing was his desire to introduce a bill that reduced taxes across the board. So, I went through the proper channels and processes, and I produced a bill that met his expectations. He introduced the bill and got lots of attention for his work trying to promote it. Miraculously, within a month of what was almost my last day on his staff, I was the senator's favorite legislative staffer. And while the bill I had drafted did not pass the Senate Finance Committee, it came to the attention of a young conservative House Member, Jack Kemp from Upstate New York. He partnered with Republican Senator Bill Roth of Delaware who was adept at finance issues, and together they used the bill I had drafted as a template for their vision of tax reform. When Representative Kemp spoke about the origins of the Kemp-Roth tax bill, one of the most significant pieces of tax legislation of the twentieth century, he made it clear that he had seen Paul Fannin's bill and quickly realized it was something he could champion after Fannin's imminent retirement. And Paul Fannin's bill was my bill, mine and the Senate Legislative Counsel's. It's important to remember the centrality of this tax bill in the legislative agenda of President Reagan. The bipartisan 1981 law enacted historic across-the-board tax cuts and formed the foundation of President Reagan's success during his first term, helping create morning in America.

My role in crafting this historic legislation has always given me a sense of accomplishment and pride; there are so many hours spent on policy and legislation that never see the light of day. This was one instance when something that was equally good and important came at least in part from my efforts. As a participant in the craziness that is our federal legislative process, it really doesn't get any better.

Despite how well I was doing in Senator Fannin's office, occasionally I was reminded how essential it was to remain closeted at the office. One Monday morning, as I was walking past Joe's office, he yelled out, "Hey, Bob, how was your weekend?" I responded it was a good one including meeting some friends one evening at a particular bar in Georgetown, to which Joe asked, "Is that the bar where the queers hang out?" I quickly responded it was not and left it at that. At the time, there was a bar in Georgetown, Mr. Henry's, which gays frequented, including myself but not that night. That exchange in front of coworkers, sent a chill up my spine and served as a reminder how homophobic D.C. was in those years.

Homophobia was common almost everywhere with gay jokes and snide comments. On Capitol Hill, homophobia was common in both Democratic and Republican offices. Senator Sam Nunn (D-GA) fired a friend of mine for being gay, saying he was a security risk. The AIDS crisis that began in the early 1980s vividly demonstrated the level of homophobia in politics, the news media, and other areas.

Abortion became the first prominent social issue, starting in the mid and late '70s. The AIDS crisis brought out the homophobic feelings of many members of Congress initially on both sides. Senator Jesse Helms (R-NC) was the lead homophobe in opposing all AIDS funding. Clearly, it was uncomfortable being in the same party as Helms, but there were other Republicans who quickly became compassionate about AIDS victims, most of whom were gay men at the beginning of the crisis. Members such as Senator Specter (R-PA) and

Congressman John Porter (R-IL) were leaders in appropriating funds for AIDS research and treatment. I decided to shun Senator Helms and those who agreed with him and work with groups such as AIDS Action Council to encourage Republican members to support various HIV/ AIDS initiatives.

I was fortunate to work for two United States senators between 1975 and 1982. Being at the center of power was exhilarating and stressful.

I spent two years working for Arizona Republican Senator Paul Fannin. Early in my tenure, I nearly got fired. I eventually found my sea legs and helped write a tax reform bill that would become the basis for the historic tax cuts signed into law by President Reagan in 1981. Photo courtesy of the U.S. Senate Historical Office.

CHAPTER 10

The Guy Behind the Guy

IN EARLY 1977, PAUL FANNIN RETIRED AND WENT HOME TO Arizona at the end of his term. That same year the former mayor of Indianapolis, Richard Lugar, came to Washington as the newly elected junior senator from Indiana. The political scene in Washington that year was a mad scramble, especially for Republicans. Jimmy Carter narrowly defeated Gerald Ford in the presidential election, and everyone who worked in the Ford administration was hunting for new jobs. Many of them focused their search on Capitol Hill. Despite Carter's win, a wave of GOP newcomers began their initial six-year term in the Senate. In addition to Lugar, S.I. Hayakawa from California, John Danforth from Missouri, John Chaffee from Rhode Island, David Durenberger from Minnesota, Orrin Hatch from Utah, John Heinz from Pennsylvania, Harrison Schmitt from New Mexico, and Malcolm Wallop from Wyoming became freshmen GOP senators. This was one of the most talented freshman Senate Republican classes ever. They came from backgrounds ranging from ketchup king (Heinz was the heir to the condiment company fortune) to urban cowboy (a native New Yorker, Wallop had returned to the state of his ancestors' birth to be a rancher) to former astronaut Harrison Schmidt. Most of them had beaten incumbents to take their seats. They were smart, savvy, and ready to take their place in the nation's capital. To be effective policy makers, they would need quality staff to help navigate the waters. This sequence of events would lead to a wonderful relationship on a professional and personal level between me and Senator Lugar.

Typically, when a freshman senator comes to Washington, 90% of the staff comes from the campaign. These people know their home state down to the last fire hydrant but know very little about the ways of Washington. Almost invariably each new senator would look for people who could literally direct them to the Senate floor. That's where I came in; I did in fact know the way there, in addition to a few other things I had to recommend me. I was fortunate to have received two job offers, one from Hayakawa and one from Lugar. I accepted the offer from Lugar. Given the political situation, competition was fierce. I have always believed one key factor in getting the job with Lugar was that we both were Denison University alumni. He had become a member of the Board of Trustees at Denison during his tenure as mayor of Indianapolis, and I was a Denison undergraduate at that time. In later years, I was very proud to be selected to serve alongside Lugar as a member of the Denison Board of Trustees.

In Lugar's first year in the Senate, I handled his finance and banking work along with some other domestic issues. When his legislative director departed to return to private law practice, I was chosen to be his successor. It wasn't Senator Lugar who hired me. That was the responsibility of Lugar's chief of staff, Mitch Daniels, who would eventually become governor of Indiana and subsequently president of Purdue University. Richard Lugar and Mitch Daniels made quite a formidable team and adding me to the mix to anchor the legislative team made it even better. Working with Lugar and Daniels was fascinating. They were so much on the same wavelength politically that they could sit together and discuss an issue without talking very much, especially on issues concerning Indiana politics, about which I had almost no clue. A raised eyebrow here and a nod there would bring consensus between them.

Richard Lugar is the single smartest person I have ever known. But he didn't rely on pure intellect. He was incredibly well studied; his idea of a fun weekend was to read through a stack of technical reports and scholarly papers. Often on a Monday, I would find one of the reports he had read in my inbox, with a cryptic note attached that said, "Interesting report, Bob." I didn't know what I was supposed to do with the paper or the comment, but I always read the paper to find out what had caught his attention. He told me some years later that while at Denison he would rise early to study before anyone else in the fraternity house was up. He graduated first in his class but didn't want anyone to know how hard he worked for that honor.

Lugar rarely wanted speeches written. I learned that first-hand during his first Senate speech. The event is an auspicious one for a new senator, and many choose to use prepared notes or full texts. Even seasoned veterans like my ex-boss Paul Fannin wouldn't take the dais without notes. I asked Lugar if he wanted me to prepare something for him; the way he reacted, you would have thought I had asked him if he wanted me to tie his shoes or comb his hair. He paused, gave me a quizzical look and said, "Well, no, Bob. No."

All Lugar needed to prepare for a speech was background material, the preparation of which was often my responsibility. It didn't even have to be typed. These were the days before computers and printers. All we had were typewriters, and there were times I didn't even have access to one of them. But Lugar would say, "Just send me a handwritten outline and some backup materials." He would take those threads and fashion an hour-long speech that was both substantive and entertaining. With his Rhodes Scholar education and his speaking prowess, Lugar was kind of like Bill Clinton without the good ole boy twang or the penchant for getting into trouble.

Lugar was smart, but he was also incredibly savvy and almost immediately well regarded. In 1978, Senator Bill Proxmire, a Democrat from Wisconsin, chaired the Senate Banking Committee. Proxmire opposed most legislation before his committee, but his modus operandi was to let the committee work its will and go with whatever a majority of members supported, even though when it came time to vote he was often in the minority. At the time, New York City was virtually bankrupt. The Carter administration and Democratic Congress responded by trying to bail out the city. Earlier, when Gerald Ford was still president, the *New York Daily News* ran a picture of Ford under a headline that read "Ford to City: Drop Dead." In reality, Ford never said those words, but he was vehemently opposed to a bailout and promised to veto any legislation that provided for it. By contrast, President Carter had just wanted to give New York and later Chrysler, a blank check. The negotiations had started ugly and went downhill from there.

As a former mayor with practical experience in municipal matters, Lugar was brought in as a negotiator between the many factions, especially the unions that needed to be appeased to reach a deal. A bailout was eventually approved, and New York paid it back with interest. Lugar played a similar role in the rescue of Chrysler during the late 1970s. Lugar and fellow freshman Democratic Senator Paul Tsongas of Massachusetts brokered the deal, eventually reaching an agreement that saved thousands of jobs. From his time as a mayor, Lugar understood that when you have unions, private enterprise, and government sitting around a table, the key to reaching a deal is to make sure the final product involves everyone having some skin in the game.

In addition to being tapped early on as a skilled crafter of domestic policy and negotiator, Lugar was also soon acknowledged for his expertise in foreign affairs. He was named to the Foreign Relations Committee only four years into his first term. Lugar had the makings of an ideal public servant. He was only 44 when he was elected to the Senate. He was a runner, and because he encouraged his staff to run, I became one too. He also started the annual Lugar Fitness Festival, a program he initiated to address health and fitness issues in his home state. He felt that in addition to promoting a healthy lifestyle, it was a way to reach out to people, namely fitness-conscious liberals, who would normally not connect with him. It was enormously popular, and so was he.

His signature accomplishment, and the work that he would want to be remembered for, was in nuclear missile non-proliferation. I attended a lunch where Lugar, in what would turn out to be his final term in the Senate, was the special guest. He recalled how he alone was asked to take a trip to Eastern Europe to continue his work in nuclear non-proliferation. It was a great honor to be given such individual responsibility, and a testament to his knowledge and wisdom on the subject. At the end of his talk, he mentioned that The Hague had created a new peace prize; it was named for Sam Nunn and Richard Lugar. They were also the first recipients.

As a physical presence, Dick Lugar wasn't particularly imposing. He was a committed runner and therefore quite fit. But he wasn't tall like former professional basketball player Senator Bill Bradley from New Jersey, a man who made a ripple in the room just by showing up. What he lacked in physical stature he more than made up for in gravitas. When he left the room, everyone knew he had been there. Lugar was gracious but not garrulous. He was friendly, but not necessarily as approachable as some politicians. He didn't have dizzying highs or lows in his moods. He was a family man who married his college sweetheart. He had four successful sons, with an extended family that could comprise a congressional district. There is a lot more praise I could heap upon Richard Lugar. Above all, he was a gentleman and a scholar, someone who embodied the true spirit of the Senate. I am better for having known him and immensely privileged to have worked for him. Washington and the world are diminished by his absence.

I didn't have what could be really called a "father/son" relationship with Richard Lugar. Our age difference wasn't big enough for such a connection.Add to that Lugar was a stark contrast to my father. As I mentioned, my father had a tremendous amount of street smarts, the kind that made him successful as a salesman and businessman. But my Dad was not an educated man by any means. He was not what you would call sophisticated or erudite. He often spoke English poorly; something I found embarrassing when I was a kid. I couldn't understand why he didn't work on improving it. All my life, I had watched and listened to others I admired learn the "right and proper" way to do things. It wasn't that I wanted to mimic them; I just wanted to learn from them. I wanted, whenever and wherever possible, to be and do better. I often wanted to ask my dad why he wouldn't or couldn't do the same.

Despite any shortcomings, I respected and cherished my father, but Richard Luger was a person I could more easily recognize as a mentor. He was polished without pretense, educated, savvy, and sophisticated. I could model myself after him on a day-to-day basis. I was fascinated by his intellect and his political skills. He gave practical advice that has stayed with me and proven useful on a variety of occasions. For instance, he understood it's better to listen rather than always speaking up to prove you are the smartest one in the room.As an example, the senator and I were attending a policy meeting where an issue came up on which I wanted to be heard. However, it was difficult to get a word in. Finally, I got my chance and I laid out my thoughts on the issue, which to my dismay left those around the table utterly unimpressed. Sensing my disappointment, Lugar took me aside after the meeting and said in his matter of fact way, "Bob, some things are better left unsaid."

Lord knows there are plenty of people like that in Washington, Type A personalities who must have the first and last word. I was like that before working with Lugar, and to be honest it is a tendency I still have and try to keep in check. I don't feel like I am the smartest in the room; that delusion was dispelled years ago. It is just habit. As the saying goes, the longer you live, the less you know. What that means to me is that if I keep quiet and listen, I'll probably learn something from what others are saying. And I do enjoy hearing a new fact or a new perspective and saying to myself, "Wow, I really didn't know that."

After serving six full terms in the Senate, Lugar was defeated in 2012. Ironically, he lost in a Republican primary to Richard Mourdock, the State Treasurer of Indiana. While Mourdock had been twice elected statewide as treasurer, he was not initially thought to be a serious challenger to Lugar. But he was recruited by the Tea Party because Lugar had the audacity to vote, from time-to-time, in a fashion that did not match the ideology of the GOP's ultra-conservative wing. For example, he didn't vote against the Supreme Court nominations of Sonia Sotomayor and Elena Kagan, two extremely competent jurists who were confirmed by overwhelming margins. Lugar believed in the Senate's mandate to advise and consent on the choices of the president. Only rarely did he withhold support from a presidential nomination, and in the cases of Sotomayor and Kagan, he felt it was not warranted. He also voted for a few other things that were probably reasonable and rational to most people but were tantamount to treason for the Tea Party activists.

When Lugar and Orrin Hatch came to the Senate together in 1977, they were considered by far the most conservative members of the Senate. It's another sign of our nation's current and rather strange political climate that a lifelong conservative such as Lugar was defeated because he was considered too moderate. Lugar was also defeated by a lot of money; as many as eleven super-PACs came into Indiana to defeat him, a staggering number for a primary election. I was part of a Super PAC that raised about $1.5 million for him, enough to buy some TV time and possibly survive the challenge. But the prevailing winds against him were too strong, and voter turnout was extremely low, a recipe for defeat for many moderate, thoughtful Republicans.

That election was a good example of why American politics is broken. The only real challenge Richard Lugar ever had was from the right wing of his own party. He never had a serious challenge from the Democrats, but there was always someone willing to take him on for not being "conservative enough." He was so well-respected in the state that people just didn't buy into it. But this time an energized group of activist conservatives ganged up on him; they found a candidate in Mourdock who had won twice in statewide elections and who lots of people thought was a fairly reasonable guy. In his campaign, he shied away from personal attacks on Lugar. He was very respectful, taking a position that Lugar had served well but that he was 80 years old and it was time for him to move on. Lugar himself acknowledged that on occasion he would be approached by long-time supporters who felt he should have retired fifteen years ago, not so much because he was no longer effective or vigorous (he was still putting in 14 to 15 hour days on a regular basis during his last term) but because he was just "older than a senator ought to be."

As he did with most things, Lugar took the primary defeat with dignity. It's not that he didn't have deep regrets and disappointments; he did. But he was not one to let his disappointments show outwardly. He was disappointed to have lost in the primary, but I have seen him more upset at other times. The most upset I've ever seen him was in 1988, when George H.W. Bush chose Dan Quayle, the junior senator from Indiana, to be his running mate in that year's presidential election. That was very difficult for two reasons. First, Lugar had himself been on the shortlist for the VP slot on the ticket. Second, I don't believe Lugar and many of his staff ever had much respect for Quayle. They thought Quayle wasn't very smart, and that he was a glad-handing kind of guy with a good head of hair but not much else. For all the abuse Dan Quayle took, some of it deserved, Quayle was considered by his peers in the Senate to be a very well-studied and serious member of the Armed Services Committee. A former congressman from Fort Wayne who had won his Senate seat by defeating three-term incumbent Democrat Birch Bayh in 1980 as part of the Reagan landslide, Quayle started slowly but turned out to be a politically astute senator. He knew defense matters well, and those who tried to slip something past him in hearings found out just how well. And Washington insiders knew Quayle's biggest asset was his wife Marilyn; she was smart, tough, and extremely ambitious, really a force to be reckoned with. If he had wanted to, he could have been reelected to his Senate seat ad infinitum. But when the White House calls, it's a very difficult to say, "No, thank you." Quayle was in, and Lugar was out. The deal was done in the privacy of the White House, but it now had to play out in public, complete with the inevitable awkward social moments.

Quayle was elected on the ticket with Bush 41 in the 1988 Presidential election. In 1989, the Quayles came to the Indiana State Society inaugural dinner. Lugar of course also was there. We were seated at our table watching Quayle take his victory lap. It was a moment that had been coming since Bush had called Lugar and instead of offering him a spot on the ticket said, "Dick, I have decided to reach down to the next generation on this choice. I'm going with Dan." As Quayle worked the room, I caught a look at Lugar and saw him like I had never seen him before. He was pale and drawn, but I knew that his outward appearance only reflected a fraction of the humiliation he felt. For Lugar, a man who had prepared all his life for The Call to come, it was a cruel mixture of insult and betrayal. When The Call finally did come, it was far from what he had waited to hear all those years.

The late summer day in 1988 when Bush officially announced Quayle as his running mate, I was at the Republican Convention in New Orleans. It was being held in the Superdome, and I was roaming around the arena floor soaking up the atmosphere. I ran into C. Boyden Gray, a respected man, and almost a unique Washington figure.

Gray is fabulously accomplished; he clerked for Earl Warren, was White House counsel for Bush 41, and served as U.S. Ambassador to the European Union. Gray is a wealthy, patrician kind of guy; his was one of the founding families of R.J. Reynolds Tobacco in his native North Carolina. Standing six feet eight inches tall with a shock of salt and pepper hair, a prominent beak of a nose and the hunched shoulders of a man who has spent a lifetime having conversations with people a foot shorter than him, Gray looks like Ichabod Crane but has smarts and savvy few can match.

Gray saw me (at his height he saw everybody) and shouted over the crowd, "Hey Kabel! You know Quayle, right?"

"Yeah," I said.

Gray shot back, "Can you give me one good reason why Bush picked him?"

Bear in mind, this was Bush's current vice presidential counsel who was loudly and publicly questioning his boss's pick to be his running mate. While there were many potential answers to Gray's loaded question, I chose the high road. I answered truthfully.

"Nope. I can't think of one."

Personally, I liked Quayle. When you got to know him, you find he's a decent and studied man. I often thought that after he became Vice President, he had the best political instincts in the Bush 41 White House. That wasn't hard because the rest of the senior staff was tone deaf, at best. One who stood out, in particular, for tone deafness was Dick Darman, the Director of the Office of Management and Budget. Darman convinced the President to reverse his "Read My Lips" position on taxes, a decision that heavily contributed to his 1992 defeat against Bill Clinton and Ross Perot. Quayle, as always, has landed on his feet. He lives in Arizona, making a lot of money in the private equity business, which he can add to the money from his family's newspaper fortune. It's worth mentioning that Quayle's son Ben was elected to

Congress in 2010; he was defeated in 2012 in a primary election by a challenger who accused him of not being conservative enough.

Eventually, Senator Lugar came to know I was gay when I was working for him. We never had a direct conversation about it because I never felt it was necessary, nor did I get the feeling that he did either. But I never went out of my way to hide anything from him. I met my first partner Joe in 1979 while I was working for Lugar, and we became a couple shortly thereafter. On occasion, Joe would accompany me to office parties and other functions. I can safely say that in my office everyone knew I was gay, and nobody cared.

This was not the case in every Senate office, not by a long shot. There were several offices where being exposed as a homosexual was grounds for immediate dismissal. Democratic Senator Sam Nunn of Georgia fired a friend of mine because he was gay. Today, such an action would not be politically or morally acceptable, but in the early 1980s there was nothing to prevent such blatant discrimination. There were no statutes, no commissions or boards to which one could appeal. As a staff, we were "at will" employees, meaning that our employer could fire us at will without cause or justification beyond the fact that you were no longer wanted. Now there are some protections afforded to LGBT congressional employees. For the LGBT community, the employment practices and conditions on the Hill mirrored the situation across most of America. In some parts of the country, sexual orientation is a protected class, but in many parts of the county, it is not. In fact, more than half the states don't have employment non-discrimination protections for LGBT people.

For the most part, I never faced workplace discrimination for being gay, except on one occasion, during the 1980s when I was working at the Manatt firm. One of my favorite clients was the California League of Savings Institutions, the trade association representing savings and loans or thrift institutions in the Golden State. In 1987, the league's new president hired our firm to represent their interests in Washington. After landing the business, I knew we had our work cut out for us because the thrift industry had been damaged by the 1986 Tax Reform Act's repeal of key provisions affecting real estate taxes.

I enjoyed working with the president and his staff. Unbeknownst to me, the president had leukemia some years before, and it returned. After he died, the association began looking for his replacement. The association's staff wanted the league's board to hire me. They had gotten to know me, felt I was doing a good job for them, and we effectively worked together. The position would have required me to be bicoastal, which at the time appealed to me.

During the interview process, I first met with the Washington counsel for the largest member of the association whose CEO served as chairman of the league. I had known and worked with this attorney for several years. I was surprised during our interview when he asked, "Bob, you have never been married, correct?" I replied that was correct. The next step was to meet the chairman of the league who asked the same question. It was clear the league, or at least the CEO, did not want to hire me because I was gay. I was dumbstruck by this blatantly discriminatory treatment. I could understand that in the late 1980s industries such as tobacco and perhaps oil and gas would not hire an openly gay man, but the financial services industry was among the first to have a nondiscrimination policy for LGBT employees. Additionally, this financial services trade association was in one of the country's most liberal states. Add to this the general counsel for the thrift was a flamboyant guy who wore pink ties and matching pocket squares. When I mentioned this situation to a former Capitol Hill colleague who was working for another California thrift, she laughed and indicated there probably was another reason why they decided not to hire me.

As with so many things in life, not getting this job was a blessing. A few years later, the thrift industry on the West Coast collapsed, and the California League of Savings Institutions was merged into the stronger California Bankers Association. I would have been without a job. Instead I remained a partner in my law firm where I continued for many more years.

On its face, almost all forms of discrimination are absurd and counterproductive. Growing businesses need qualified, talented employees to succeed; they could not afford to discriminate based on anything other than pure talent. That standard should hold true everywhere, and perhaps it will, if Congress ever passes federal employment protections for LGBT people. Legislation, which for a long time was known as the Employment Non-Discrimination Act, has been bouncing around Congress for decades. At different points, versions passed the House and Senate with bipartisan support, but not in the same Congress.

Historically, this legislation has been sponsored by Democrats with some Republicans joining as co-sponsors. A stumbling block to enactment is the decision by Democrats to add provisions, particularly regarding religious freedom, that many Republicans find unacceptable. Democrats blame Republicans for blocking passage and keeping this wedge issue alive to use with the LGBT community, a key part of their coalition. In 2019, Congressman Chris Stewart, (R-UT) introduced the Fairness For All Act, a compromise bill that would ban discrimination against LGBT people in employment, housing, education, and public accommodations but carves out broad exemption for churches and religious organizations. His was the first Republican sponsored bill introduced on this important issue. This issue won't be resolved anytime soon. This wedge issue remains.

The progressive attitude in Senator Lugar's office towards Joe and me is another reason I loved working there. The time I spent in his office was the most rewarding and fun five years of my professional career. Senator Lugar lived a long and meaningful life. He died at age 87 in 2019. He was a good man who had a great life. Working for him early in my career was a blessing. The first term staff, what we refer to as the "original Lugar crew," became family. Years later, we remain close and know we can rely on each other in times of need.

After Senator Fannin retired, I joined the staff of freshman Senator Richard Lugar (right) from Indiana. He quickly made a positive impression with his colleagues, including Sen. Howard Baker (R-TN). Baker (left) became Senate majority leader after the Reagan landslide in 1980. Lugar had been chair of Baker's short-lived 1980 presidential campaign. Photo courtesy of the U.S. Senate Historical Office.

It may seem like a foreign concept today, but Senator Lugar (left) wasn't afraid to work closely with Democratic colleagues. He had an especially strong working relationship with Indiana Democratic Senator Birch Bayh (right). Lugar was one of the smartest and most capable senators of the last 50 years. I learned so much from him about life and public service. Photo courtesy of the U.S. Senate Historical Office.

Future Indiana Governor Mitch Daniels (left) was Lugar's top advisor and my boss. As Senator Lugar's legislative director, I worked closely with Daniels. This photo is from my farewell party in early 1982.

This is a 2003 photo with Senator Lugar. I'm second from the right. Lugar served six terms before losing a 2012 Republican primary. His values and philosophy remained consistent, but GOP primary voters turned on him as the Tea Party wave crested.

CHAPTER 11

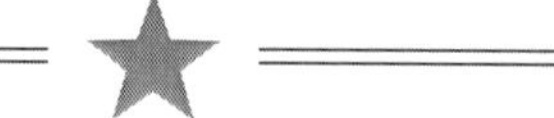

Life On the Hill

RONALD REAGAN'S 1980 VICTORY INCLUDED SOME LONG COATtails as a wave of Republican Senators came to Washington. The class included some colorful personalities who would put their stamp on Washington for a generation. The best of the bunch included Don Nickles of Oklahoma, Alphonse D'Amato from New York, Frank Murkowski of Alaska, Warren Rudman of New Hampshire, Chuck Grassley of Iowa, and Arlen Specter of Pennsylvania. D'Amato was smart, savvy, funny, and nasty, all at the same time. Don Nickles was one of the truly nice guys in the Senate, a smart but humble man who, unlike many in Washington, didn't have to dump on other people to make himself look good.

Some of the other freshman senators who came in on Reagan's coattails were way out of their league; they knew it and their colleagues knew it. You wondered if they had come in on the 4 o'clock Greyhound bus. I wasn't alone in that assessment. Once when I was working out of the vice president's legislative office close to the Senate chamber, I overheard Pete Domenici, Republican Senator from New Mexico, commiserating with a couple of his Republican colleagues. "You know," he lamented, "if we'd known we were going to take over the Senate we would have run better candidates."

One example of that sentiment was Paula Hawkins from Florida. She was an energetic campaigner, but she was politically tone deaf. One time she held a luncheon for the media to talk about the evils of overspending on the food stamp program and the need for immediate entitlement reform. Her intellectual argument was overshadowed by the lunch menu; she served steak. How does a senator offer up suggestions on cutting food stamps while sitting down to a ribeye with reporters?

Senator Jeremiah Denton of Alabama was in a league of his own. And not in a good way. The retired Navy admiral was a hero during the Vietnam War and spent nearly eight years as a prisoner of war. Not long into his Senate career, the *Washington Post* tagged Denton as the "Dumbest Person in the Senate." It's best to ignore "publicity" like that, even if it comes from the *Post*. But Denton chose to deny the "allegation" in an official news release, thereby confirming the *Post's* original hypothesis. Further proof: After proposing federal funding for teenage chastity centers, Senator Denton was asked what he meant by his use of the term "juvenile promiscuity." "I'm not talking about scratching where it tickles," he bellowed. "I'm talking about screwing." The senator also proposed legislation to provide criminal immunity for raping a spouse. His reasoning for such a law? "Dammit, when you get married you kind of expect you're going to get a little sex." This heroic military man was not cut out for politics. It was not surprising when Alabama voters reached the same conclusion by voting him out of office in the 1986 election.

As the title of this book suggests, while I have been discreet, I also have been open and honest about my sexual orientation for the vast majority of my adult life. There are others who have chosen, for one reason or another, not to live that way. While I didn't choose it for myself, I try not judge anyone else for living a more closeted life, especially someone in public life. In Washington, I know of many people who chose to lead what can only be called a double life. Their proclivities and preferences may be a secret outside the Beltway, but inside it the political community is too small to keep it a secret. A prime example is Larry Craig, the former three-term GOP senator from Idaho who dominated the news in the summer of 2007, for all the wrong reasons. He was arrested for suspicious behavior in a Minneapolis-St. Paul airport bathroom which was notorious as a rendezvous point for gay sexual encounters. Craig vehemently denied the charges, even making a speech with his poor wife standing next to him to (allegedly) lend credibility to the spectacle. Ironically, Craig started his statement to the assembled reporters by saying, "Thanks for coming out today." Like a lot of Washingtonians, I knew Craig was attracted to men, especially after having been cruised by him more than once at a reception.

On one hand, I felt sorry for Craig and the way his situation played out in such a public, sensational, and humiliating way. On the other hand, I thought to myself, "C'mon, Larry. Picking up guys in bathrooms?" It's just embarrassing. He is a grown man who serves as a United States senator, has a wife and several adopted kids. He had a nice life, but he chose time and again to risk that life with his sketchy behavior. Maybe the danger was an inseparable part of the thrill. Maybe he got off on the risk; he wouldn't be the first one. Men like comedian Paul Reubens and singer George Michael ruined their careers by indulging in public liaisons. What they all have in common is they don't have to; they can afford the privacy of a secluded hotel and meeting men online or even professional escorts. But they chose to satisfy their sexual desires in public places rather than protect their futures and often their families.

Craig wasn't the only elected official who had me in the crosshairs at some point or another. Before he came out, former Democratic Congressman Barney Frank of Massachusetts hit on me. It was a standard ploy; he followed me into the supermarket close to the gym where I had been working out and started talking to me. I must admit, it was a little flattering. But for me, both physically and politically, Barney Frank personifies the words Not My Type!

When Senator Lugar came into office in 1977, it was fun being a Republican; there was a real sense of mission trying to turn back the continued expansion of the federal government that had started during the Johnson administration and continued unabated through the Nixon and Ford administrations. There were 38 Republican Senators and 62 Democrats on the other side of the aisle, either of the big labor or conservative southern variety. This was the era of Hubert Humphrey, Ted Kennedy, Gary Hart, and other progressives. For years, whatever big labor wanted, the Democrats in the Senate would make sure to deliver it, on time and nicely packaged. While politics was not nearly as contentious as it is today, there was a sense Republicans were a minority party on a mission to shake things up.

In 1977, the Democrats were pushing legislation for major labor law reform to make it easier for unions to organize. Senate Republicans and the business community went to Lugar and Orrin Hatch to lead a filibuster against the bill. In today's Senate, the term filibuster usually refers to the threat of a filibuster. In those days, it meant the real thing. A senator or a group of senators had to take the floor and keep it with continual debate, sometimes for days at a time. The Lugar-Hatch filibuster was staged out of our office, where we set up a kind of war room to provide the senators with talking points and other necessary support. We lost a few Northeastern Republican votes, but eventually, with the help of our reliable partners, Southern Democrats, we defeated the bill. It was the Democrats' big push to cement big labor's influence, and our band of resistance stopped them. We didn't know it then, but this political fight marked an important turning point in the slow but steady decline in big labor's outsized and harmful influence.

It was a joy to be part of something significant, something I felt strongly about and to have the opportunity to do it alongside some incredibly talented people. One of those people was Nancy Maloley. Like me, she joined Lugar's staff on the first day of his term. Before that, she had worked for the Ford administration at the Environmental Protection Agency. She was a beautiful, vivacious, energetic woman. We were about the same age, and had I been straight, I would have been interested in her. But I wasn't and we both knew that, which was another reason it was easy for us to be close friends. Of Lebanese descent, she was one of those women who could be cute as a button and drop dead gorgeous at the same time. Her family was just as warm and friendly as she was. Her father owned a chain of grocery stores in Fort Wayne, Indiana. She was also as feisty as they come. During our time on the Lugar staff, her father sold the grocery store chain and there was an item about it in the *Wall Street Journal*. I was with her in the Lugar office when she was reading the story and suddenly shrieked, " I can't believe he said that!" Startled, I asked her what the problem was. "My father said he sold the stores because he had daughters and not sons! How could he insult me like this?" Insulting Nancy or making her angry in any way was not something one wanted to do. She called her father and reamed him out; she probably made up a few curse words along the way. It was classic Nancy. I'm sure it was unpleasant for her, but I must admit it was great fun watching Nancy lose her temper. It was so over the top sometimes, it was comical. But that was just a part of the package that made Nancy so wonderful. When I think about Nancy, it is a reminder that Washington isn't just marble buildings and policy papers. Ultimately it is about people, many of them quit extraordinary. Sadly, Nancy died of breast cancer twenty years ago at the way too young age of 52.

Unlike some Hill staff, I wasn't in it for the social contacts. I loved the work and I liked my colleagues well enough. But most of them had forged strong bonds from their home state and from working on the campaign trail. After work, they would go to bars and swap war stories, which was fine, but I made a point not to do it very much.

Not that I was anti-social. I would occasionally join the happy hour crowd, and in my first year in the office, I was on the softball team. But mostly when I was asked, "Why don't you come out with us?" my answer would be, "I've spent all day with you, and I actually have a life outside the office." It sounded brusque, but I opted out of things partially out of consideration for them. I had my gay friends and I had my partner Joe. I had several dogs. I wanted to enjoy my private life, and I also didn't want to rub that life into the faces of my colleagues. Better to keep the two worlds contentedly separate.

There were a lot of people who got into the whole hookup scene on the Hill, but that pastime never really attracted me, especially after the disastrous dalliance with my female colleague early in my Senate staff tenure. I was never one to mix business and pleasure, or to make my profession my pastime. I did have several gay friends on the Hill, but I didn't hook up with them. Matthew Scocozza was one good friend. I got to know him socially at first before realizing he worked for the Senate Commerce Committee. He was a talented guy and a very entertaining person. Eventually Matthew became HIV positive and, like too many of my friends, he died way too young. He was a lawyer who worked on aviation issues for the Commerce Committee. He moved from the Senate to the State Department where he worked on international aviation agreements. When Elizabeth Dole left the White House Office of Public Liaison to become Secretary of Transportation during the Reagan administration, she brought Matthew in to be her Assistant Secretary for International Affairs. I was at the White House at the time, and Matthew told me his FBI report came back noting that he was living in a homosexual relationship with another man. The White House approached Secretary Dole and said, "This is something we think you should know." To her everlasting credit, Dole responded, "I know and don't care; I need him." And she got him. He sailed through his Senate confirmation hearing, which was held by a group of senators most of whom knew that he was brilliant, competent, and gay.

His death was not an easy one. When I first met him, he was already battling brain cancer. Eventually he developed other cancers that spread throughout his body. He was literally an NIH case study for the treatment of aggressive cancer. Later he contracted HIV, a certain fatal diagnosis in those days. And yet he remained funny, charming, and engaging right to the end. Even when he was very sick, he and his partner liked to host big dinner parties. They had a wonderful small house on A Street SE, and all of us would enjoy ourselves tremendously, especially Matthew. Matthew became more than a friend; he became a part of my extended family. I mourned his death then and I still miss him now.

Suffice it to say that when I was active on the Hill, there were some great senators and some not so great senators. There were scholars and there were shysters. There were visionaries and there were hardened realists. There were senators who had happy hour at 10 a.m., and there were others who were so pious you could practically see the halos over their heads. It was the characters who gave the Senate its character. And despite the full spectrum of talents and personalities and ideologies present in the upper chamber, it functioned well, especially when compared with today's dysfunctional Senate.

Nancy Maloley was my closest friend in Sen. Lugar's office. She was charming, funny, and brilliant. It was tragic she died from cancer at the young age of 52.

CHAPTER 12

Honorable Bob

MANY YOUNG MEN AND WOMEN COME TO WASHINGTON WITH dreams of participating in government at the highest levels. But of all the seats of power in the city, one address stands alone: 1600 Pennsylvania Avenue. The White House. It's so iconic you can just say "1600" and everyone knows what you are talking about. It is the most powerful place in the most powerful city in the world, and people would just about kill to have the opportunity to wear that coveted White House pass with their picture on it and walk through those gates.

So it's funny to recall that when I got the call from Senator Howard Baker's counsel in late 1981 to tell me Baker wanted to recommend me to the White House for the open Senate Legislative Affairs position, I was ambivalent at best. First, Senator Lugar's office was so junior in the Senate roster that we never got attention from the White House, so I didn't know what the job involved. Mitch Daniels, Senator Lugar's administrative assistant at the time, had a call from Baker's chief of staff at the same time his counsel was calling me. Mitch tried to talk me out of it, saying there surely would be more high-profile positions offered in the future. Then, I spoke with David Gogol who had joined Lugar's staff shortly after I did to handle housing and urban issues (which I hated, by the way.) David is the type who cuts to the chase immediately with few niceties. When I told him of the offer and my ambivalence, he looked at me with disbelief and said, "Bob, the White House only calls once. If you turn this down, they won't ask again. You have to do this regardless of what Mitch and the senator think." He was right. I made the decision at that moment. I went home that evening to tell Joe that Senator Baker wanted to recommend me to the White House for the open Legislative Affairs position. Joe loved Ronald Reagan and was more excited than I was. But in my own gradual, Midwestern way, I was in the process of becoming attached to the idea of working in the White House.

The official offer from Ken Duberstein, Assistant to President Reagan for Legislative Affairs, came a few days later, and I went to meet with him in his West Wing office. I was mesmerized by the fact I was in the office of an assistant to the president in the West Wing and was being offered a chance to work there. He explained that it took time to get me cleared through Presidential Personnel and the Political Office since I had not been an early Reagan supporter during the campaign. Having worked for Lugar who was Howard Baker's presidential campaign chairman initially was a problem, but they worked through it. I was offered the job and I accepted on the spot.

Candidly, I didn't think too highly of Reagan in the years before he became president, thanks in part to an experience during my tenure working for the governor of Tennessee. In the spring of 1974, I accompanied Governor Dunn to a Republican Governors Association retreat at a tennis resort outside of Austin. I had never been to Texas before, and political retreats were new to me, so I was delighted to be included on the trip. The program featured panel discussions on issues facing states and the federal government. This meeting was the first time I saw Ronald Reagan in person. At the time, he was wrapping up his second term as California governor and was focused like a laser on his upcoming 1976 GOP primary challenge of President Ford. At least twice, Governor Reagan made an entrance with his entourage to a panel discussion already underway, made a prepared statement and then left the room. I remember him discussing welfare reform which had been a key issue during his gubernatorial years and one on the mind of many conservatives. At the time, it seemed like grandstanding, and he appeared stiff and very formal. Most governors were casually dressed; Reagan was dressed in a dark suit, white shirt, and tie. At the time, I was a bit put off by him and his staff, but in hindsight I recognize I was witnessing a higher level of professionalism and focus from Reagan and his staff than any other governor in attendance. Years later I saw a similar, disciplined atmosphere in the White House. Anyone who had the privilege of working there benefitted from the atmosphere that had been created by him and his staff throughout his earlier political career. He was a man on a mission.

For three years, the White House was my life. Working in Congress I could look forward to week-long recess periods and the typical extended August recess to rest up and rejuvenate. Not at the White House. If we were traveling, we had to tell the White House telephone operator where we could be reached at all times. This was long before cell phones, so we had to have a landline phone number to give the operators. They prided themselves in being able to connect with anyone in the world that the president or White House staff needed to reach.

One Fourth of July, Joe and I were staying at a guest house in Provincetown, Massachusetts, an LGBT vacation community on Cape Cod. It was an annual trip that became a tradition Joe and I both loved. One morning, I was awakened by a furious knock at our door as someone yelled, "It's the White House calling for Bob Kabel." I was momentarily famous as the guy who had received a call from the White House. Despite the gay community's growing demonization of Republicans, a call from the White House was still a remarkable event, even in a rainbow enclave like Provincetown.

When Congress was in session, we wrapped up on the Hill and spent whatever time it took to draft memos to the president, the vice president, and relevant cabinet officers. The memos often listed follow-up phone calls that needed to be made to senators on the day's hot issues. Typically, these calls were in advance of important committee or Senate floor votes, and the White House was in full swing to secure enough votes to win. This was before computers with spell check and cut and paste among other advantages now taken for granted. Each memo was done on an IBM Selectric typewriter and had to be letter perfect. That meant we didn't leave for home until after 8 p.m. I would arrive home with the "clack-clack-clack" of the typewriter still in my ears, have a quick dinner, and go to bed. I'd get up early the next morning and get to the White House in time to meet our four-person Senate team at 8 a.m. to prepare for our 8:30 meeting with Ken Duberstein. Rinse, repeat. Rinse, repeat. By the time Friday night came, I was so drained that all I wanted was peace and quiet. Joe and I had a weekly routine. We would walk three blocks to Machiavelli's, an inexpensive Italian restaurant on Pennsylvania Avenue, to have one of their specials and split a carafe of their Italian red wine. Then we went home, and I quickly went to bed. It was a simple but effective way to decompress.

Despite the long hours, no one ever complained. We understood the importance of our job; working for the president of the United States. Ronald Reagan ran and won with an agenda to make several significant changes that we all believed in: strengthening our national defense and stature in the world and getting our economy rolling again after a decade of high inflation and high interest rates. My colleagues and I recognized how fortunate we were to work at the White House and be a part of our nation's history, if only for a short while.

As the only lawyer on the Senate Legislative Affairs team, I was the lead for the Senate Finance, Banking, Judiciary, Commerce, and Labor Committees. When issues of interest to the White House came before these committees, I was the lead for the White House team.

We often worked with departmental and agency legislative affairs offices. These offices were responsible for all legislation impacting their departments or agencies. The White House Legislative Affairs staff focused on top Reagan administration priorities.

One part of the job I especially enjoyed was attending cabinet council meetings for the Legislative Affairs office. The cabinet councils (Commerce and Trade, Economic Affairs, Food and Agriculture, Human Resources, Legal Policy, Management and Administration, and Natural Resources and Environment) discussed important domestic policy matters. Most cabinet councils had a secretariat, chaired by the executive secretary, who announced meetings, compiled agendas, and supplied other support. Working groups were formed to study specific issues and make recommendations to a particular cabinet council which would then present decision memos to President Reagan. Since I primarily covered domestic issues, I often attended the Economic Policy Council meetings chaired by Treasury Secretary Donald Regan. I recall one meeting which was billed as a briefing on the accounting system then used by the savings and loan industry. This briefing was scheduled because from early in Reagan's first term, it was becoming clear there was a financial crisis brewing in the S&L industry. Secretary Regan, a former Marine and CEO of Merrill Lynch, was an imposing figure and commanded the attention of everyone in the room. After the briefing, Regan's face was white as a sheet. "This," he declared, "is a house of cards." As the former head of Merrill Lynch, Regan recognized that the thrift industry's accounting system was based on smoke and mirrors. He also understood that after the 1982 Garn-St. Germain banking law expanded the lending powers of thrifts to commercial lending, many thrifts institutions were engaging in highly risky investments about which they knew nothing. Add to that the Reagan White House's budgets reduced funding for financial regulation, and you had a recipe for disaster. Regan's comments were borne out a few years later when much of the thrift industry collapsed in what would become the most expensive financial industry bailout in U.S. history until the 2008 financial crisis.

Early in his presidency, Reagan had nominated his long-time associate Ed Gray to be chairman of the Federal Home Loan Bank Board, the agency which regulated the federally chartered thrift industry. Gray, who had a public relations background, including with Reagan when he was Governor, was thought by some as not the brightest bulb in the chandelier, but he quickly figured out what was occurring in the thrift industry and worked diligently to address the issues. As noted, Congress had recently passed legislation, the Garn-St. Germain Act that deregulated the thrift industry, giving these institutions the authority to make a wider range of investments. Additionally, the Reagan budgets cut deeply into the financial regulatory agency budgets, including the FHLBB. Ed Gray, to his credit, argued against these cuts, but the forces behind deregulation were too powerful.

My own story here goes further. I got a call one day from a friend in the Office of Presidential Personnel asking if I knew of anyone who would be interested in being considered for an opening at the FHLBB for General Counsel. I said, "I'd be interested." "That's what I thought," he said. "That's why I called you." He knew I had experience and expertise in the area and that I knew my way around Washington, both prerequisites for the position. Sometimes it's not who you know; it's who you know who knows what you know. Got that?

I scheduled an interview with Ed Gray in his office across the street from what was then called the Old Executive Office Building. I knew Ed casually from staff table discussions in the White House Mess before he became chairman of the FHLBB. Since I handled some nominations, I was surprised by his nomination given what I understood was a PR background. Nonetheless, the Republican Senate confirmed most of Reagan's early nominations. During the interview, Ed was friendly, but I found out shortly thereafter that he had his sights on someone else for the position, a Democrat no less, not a popular position to hold in the Reagan White House. I was the White House's candidate, but Ed eventually got his way.

But back to my interview. I am still troubled by the fact Gray had a long-time friend sit in the meeting. This man was well known in D.C. as one of the most prominent California thrift lawyers who represented many of the state's large thrifts. On one level, I could understand that Ed, not a lawyer himself, would want a lawyer to advise him on who to hire for this key position, but having this particular lawyer in the room was clearly a conflict of interest. The entire thrift industry and its trade association in Washington were already suspect. This occurrence confirmed my suspicions. The S&L collapse was on our doorstep. It was one of those events that was both frightening and exciting to be a part of. Like so many disasters, it was caused by a perfect storm of bad decisions and policies. Even though Gray and Regan understood the risk, the disaster was nearly impossible to avoid by the time its symptoms were discovered.

Daily life on the White House staff was guided by certain principles. Primary among them was to keep your head down and never, ever be quoted in the news media or accused of leaking information to journalists, unless you were one of the anointed ones authorized to do so. Soon after joining the Reagan administration, my mother sent me a Cincinnati newspaper profile of a nurse from the city serving on the White House medical staff. Being still new to the staff and a bit naive about the way the White House Communications Office tightly controlled messaging, I mentioned the article to a friend in that office to ask if a similar local story could be written about my service in the White House. The answer was a quick: "No. She's a nurse; you deal with policy and politics. Just keep your head down." I probably should have known better than to ask, but it seemed worth a shot to make my parents even prouder than they already were.

The reaction was not surprising. As in most White Houses, there are only a few people allowed to talk to the news media. Anyone who decided to be an "unnamed source" might soon be a "former staffer." In the Reagan White House, people who thought leaking information would get them places were sadly mistaken. In the first place, the White House staff is remarkably small, and there is limited possibility for advancement. Basically, everyone is hired for a specific role, and they are expected to work at peak performance all the time. I might have advanced if my boss, Pam Turner, had left and I had been selected to run the Senate side in her place, but that was pretty much it. The staff is small and relatively stable. The opportunities for advancement through the ranks are better at the large departments or agencies such as State, Defense, or Justice that have huge staffs for legislative affairs, but it was rare for someone to move from the White House to an agency.

Unlike recent Presidencies, leaking was kept to a minimum during the Reagan administration. Except for a few senior staff whose job it was to talk off the record, on background, or without attribution to certain reporters, unauthorized leaking was rare. In Legislative Affairs, we had strict orders not to talk with any members of the news media. Ken Duberstein and later M.B. Oglesby sometimes spoke with reporters on the down low, but it was part of their job and, more importantly, authorized by more senior staff. The Reagan administration's approach to reporters was one part of a tightly run operation.

More recent administrations have had quite different policies. The Trump White House is one big leaking operation, though it's better now than the early months of the administration. The factions around Trump battled each other by leaking juicy tidbits to their favorite reporter. This undermines staff cohesion, undercuts the president's agenda, and causes so much distrust that it makes effective governing nearly impossible. Of course, this problem is nothing new. President Nixon's downfall, after all, started with a White House effort to stop leaks. A small group of operatives, which became known as The Plumbers, launched a secret effort to identify leakers in the administration. Their efforts eventually led to the Watergate break-in and the downfall of the president. Maybe it was the lessons learned from watching Nixon fall that made so many of Reagan's White House staff reluctant to leak without authorization.

I am asked from time to time who my best friend was in the White House. My "best friends" were not a part of my work, but my best White House friend was my boss Pam Turner. We had a lot in common; she had been legislative director for Texas Senator John Tower, the same position I had held with Lugar. Tower was a major player at the time; when the GOP took over the Senate in 1981, he became chairman of the powerful Armed Services Committee. He was a short man in height but had a personality and drive the size of the state of Texas.

As I look back on my White House career, I was fortunate to have worked with some extraordinary people who would go on to accomplish remarkable things in government and the private sector. When I was in the heat of it working with them, for the most part, I couldn't really envision the careers they would have. I had a difficult enough time envisioning my own career, much less anyone else's. Although I had some ability and some ambition, I didn't have a detailed roadmap for how my professional life should play out. I tried to work hard, keep my reputation for being honest and trustworthy and take new opportunities as they presented themselves.

There are a few people who stood out. One of them was future Supreme Court Chief Justice John Roberts. He was initially at the Justice Department when I met him, and he was working on some of the legal issues I was involved with as Senate liaison. Since I was the only lawyer on the Senate Legislative Affairs staff, the legal issues and some of the nominations that had a legal component usually ended up on my desk, and it was in that capacity that we first crossed paths. Later, Roberts was brought on as a member of the White House counsel's staff. People often ask me, "So what was Roberts like?" When we had occasion to be at the same meeting, I noticed that Roberts didn't say much, but you always knew he was the smartest guy in the room. Although he was very young at the time, he was a person to whom everyone paid attention. He had gravitas without being pompous. An Indiana native, he was the nicest guy in the world. He had a dry sense of humor and a kind of polite gentility that was rare in politics then and is all but extinct now. He was one guy I thought was really special; obviously, a lot of people agreed with me.

Another staffer who impressed me was Rob Portman, now a senator from Ohio. A native of Cincinnati like myself, Portman, who was elected to the House of Representatives from Cincinnati, had served in the Legislative Affairs office for Bush 41 and was director of the Office of Management and Budget for Bush 43. One can't have a much better résumé than that. As further proof that it really is a small world, while he was a member of the House Ways and Means Committee, Portman visited the coffee roasting plant after Dad had sold the company to his employees using an ESOP. Portman was sponsoring some ESOP-related legislation and used the visit to publicize his interest in this issue of importance to the small business community. The visit was punctuated by Portman's committing a bit of a party foul. Most of us who had been associated with Wallingford thought our plant was a pretty big operation. At some point Portman exclaimed, "It's hard to believe you can process so much coffee in a facility that's so small!" The silence he heard in response let him know he had put his foot in his mouth.

Another colleague, Bill Barr, eventually became U.S. attorney general under George H.W. Bush and again under President Trump. When we met, he was a special assistant on the White House Domestic Policy Council. One of the issues I led on was tuition tax credits. I was asked to handle it because the issue had become a political football that

Treasury Secretary Don Regan was reluctant to carry. It was a key issue for President Reagan and his bid for re-election because it appealed to many Catholic and Jewish voters who sent their children to private religious schools and therefore might benefit from the credit. Amazingly, Regan said he wouldn't do it (although I don't know how you say NO to your president), so Ken Duberstein came to me and said, "You do Finance Committee; this is your issue."

So that began a seemingly endless round of meetings with legislators, constituent groups, and other stakeholders. We finally got it passed out of the Senate Finance Committee, which was followed by a vote on the Senate floor. As expected, the bill did not pass the full Senate. By passing it out of the Senate Finance Committee, which was quite difficult to accomplish, we had met our objective of demonstrating dedication to an issue that meant a lot to President Reagan personally, to his reelection effort, and to certain constituencies. Among the senators most active in the effort were Democratic Senator Bill Bradley, a co-sponsor and staunch supporter, and John Chaffee, one of my all-time favorite senators, a Rhode Island Republican, who was vociferously opposed to it.

At one point during the long build up to congressional action on the bill, I attended a meeting in the Secretary of Education's conference room strategizing with several constituent groups that were interested in seeing tuition tax credits enacted. Bill Barr and I were the two White House special assistants in attendance. During the meeting, a representative from the Moral Majority leaned back in his chair and said, "Well, Mr. Kabel, we trust President Reagan on this, but we DON'T trust you and Mr. Duberstein." That was just how the Moral Majority operated; they thought of everyone as the opposition, which meant they were some of the nastiest people in Washington at the time. They were always looking for enemies under rocks. They had just found one. I was livid, about as angry as I have ever been about something work-related because he had made it personal. As we left the meeting,

I turned to Barr and said, "If this guy is ever at a meeting again, then I won't be." Barr was embarrassed. They both understood I had my limits and they had just been crossed. It was another lesson learned, but on this occasion instead of being the student, I was the teacher.

The Moral Majority was founded in 1979 by Jerry Falwell Sr. It played an important role in mobilizing conservative Christians as a political force in the Republican Party. The Moral Majority was a key factor in the rise of social conservatives in the GOP. While the Moral Majority disbanded in 1989, the influence of Christian social conservatives continues.

It was exciting to have a front row seat for the Reagan Revolution. I joined the White House staff in 1982 as Special Assistant to the President for Legislative Affairs (Senate).

President Reagan autographed for me this photo of a 1984 meeting on tuition tax credits in the Cabinet Room. You need a magnifying glass to see me, but I'm there, against the window just behind Senator Bob Dole.

White House colleague Ken Duberstein hands me my Presidential Commission in 1982. Being a special assistant to the president was equivalent to being a one-star general in the military.

CHAPTER 13

Hollywood On the Potomac

THE LASTING IMPRESSION OF NANCY REAGAN IS THAT OF A woman who loved and protected her husband. That, in fact, was her self-declared role; to be the staunch protector of the office and even more so of her beloved husband. I wasn't around her much and don't ever recall speaking with her directly. There was an understanding among most of the staff that if you didn't need to have direct contact with the First Lady, it was better to avoid it. She could shoot daggers with her eyes and damage careers in a single breath if she saw something she didn't like. And she was always on the lookout for something that didn't seem right, particularly self-promoting staff. There was no good reason to be on her radar screen unless you had to deal with her or her staff. She trusted Jim Baker (Chief of Staff), Mike Deaver (Deputy Chief of Staff), Ed Meese (White House Counsel), and Fred Ryan (Scheduler) but that was about it. For President Reagan, his team of rivals, other than the vice president, was the senior staff surrounding him. Jim Baker was instrumental in the Bush presidential campaign as was a key deputy, Dick Darman; Ed Meese was an early Reagan staffer from California as was Mike Deaver, who was by far Mrs. Reagan's favorite as they went back many years to the gubernatorial days. Deaver understood that staging and showmanship were critical to the success of the Reagan presidency. Deaver was the stage manager; it was his job to make the president look good at every turn and he had the gratitude of the first lady because he performed his job flawlessly. Fred Ryan was another California transplant who served faithfully under Reagan and has had a spectacular career after the White House, including being one of the founders of *Politico* and more recently as publisher of the *Washington Post* by its new owner, Amazon founder Jeff Bezos. Reagan's team made sure nothing was left to chance in the planning of events - from the look of the room, the audience, the music, and every other more minor detail. Everything had to be perfect.

Mrs. Reagan elicited strong opinions; most people either loved her or hated her. She got a bum rap from the news media as being an elitist. A lot of that came from the sense of style the Reagans had cultivated during their years in Hollywood. She also took some heat for things like overseeing a huge renovation of the White House and for ordering a new set of china for the White House at a cost of over $200,000 even though all the renovations, including the new china, were privately funded. Because it was happening against the backdrop of an economic recession, journalists portrayed the Reagans as out of touch elitists. The contrast was especially harsh since their direct predecessors, the Carters, went to great lengths to take any semblance of glamour out of the White House and even out of the office itself. The truth is the Reagans were glamorous people who brought a lot of class to the White House. That's who they were, naturally and without pretense. Mrs. Reagan took a lot of the steam out of the negative press when she appeared at a White House Correspondents' Dinner and did her version of "Secondhand Rose," rag costume and all.

One of the obscure facts about a special assistant position in the White House is that in addition to being chosen to serve the president, you are a commissioned officer with the rank of a one-star general. In most situations, it doesn't really mean anything, but the fact is that special assistants and above serve the Commander in Chief of the United States and, as such, are officers on his staff. I didn't get a uniform or a weapon, but I did get an impressive commission certificate signed by President Reagan and Secretary of State Al Haig, one of the last certificates he would sign as Secretary before resigning. That certificate still hangs proudly in my office. Although I don't use the title, I occasionally receive mail to The Honorable Robert Kabel. With the title of Special Assistant to the President of the United States comes the life-long title of "The Honorable." I find it too pretentious to use, but it makes for a clever title for a book chapter.

I was still working for Senator Lugar when President Reagan was shot. It was March 30, 1981, and it was a typical day for me. I was busy at my desk in Senator Lugar's office listening to the Senate proceedings on the "squawk box" on my desk. Senate proceedings had not yet begun to be televised, so every office was allocated a couple of "squawk boxes," which were small receivers that broadcast live from the Senate floor. Around 3 p.m. that day, Senate Leader Majority Howard Baker came onto the floor and announced, "It is my duty to inform the Senate that the President of the United States has been shot." Of course, the news itself was stunning, but the lack of additional information was almost as bad. Baker mentioned the president had been taken to a local hospital, but that was it; no word on his condition. My first thought was, "Oh no…not again." I remembered the wrenching tragedy of John F. Kennedy's assassination and how it tore the country apart. I was in high school when Kennedy was assassinated. Our principal came on the PA system to announce Kennedy had been shot in Dallas. They were very difficult times and the shooting of another popular president brought those memories flooding back to me. Reagan had been in office a bit more than two months. He was at the Washington Hilton on Connecticut Avenue speaking to the AFL-CIO's Building Trades Union. (Yes, Republican Presidents used to do that, and, after all, he had been president of the Screen Actors Guild years earlier.) After his speech as he left the hotel, Reagan was shot by John Hinckley Jr., a mentally deranged man in his mid-20s. Everyone was stunned and basically silent for what seemed forever, until word came that the president was alive and being treated at George Washington University Hospital. Only much later did we learn how close Reagan came to death.

One direct impact on my daily life was that when I joined the White House staff several months later, security for the president had been tightened significantly, including inside the White House. When we walked from our offices in the East Wing to the West Wing, we went through the ground floor corridor known as the First Lady's Hallway where their official portraits were displayed, we were required to display our staff photo IDs at all times. There are two types of ID. After passing a full field FBI background check, staff gets a color photo. While the background check was in process, staff got a black and white photo. When I had my black and white photo, I got a little extra scrutiny. Nothing too bad, but enough to let you know they were being vigilant.

A full field FBI investigation is exactly what it sounds like. Someone required to have one first fills out an extensive form listing every place he or she has ever lived or worked. Addresses were a challenge, but my parents helped me with addresses I couldn't remember or didn't have. FBI agents interview numerous people with whom I had worked, including at Dad's company, Governor Dunn, key members of his administration, both Senate offices, D.C. neighbors and individuals listed as close friends. It's an intrusive but necessary process. The key objective is to understand whether the individual is loyal to the U.S, is subject to being blackmailed for any reason, or has drinking or drug problems. Historically, there has never been an example of a homosexual who has been blackmailed into giving up state secrets. Even so, U.S. government officials often used the blackmail myth to deny security clearances to gays and lesbians, especially during the 1940s through the mid-'70s.

Years later, I did a Freedom of Information Act request to receive a copy of my reports. Since I had been nominated by President Reagan to be a member of the Foreign Claims Settlement Commission after I departed the White House, I received two reports. In the first report, an agent interviewed Joe as my roommate, and it came through as just that. In the second report, the agent noted that Joe and I were involved in a lawsuit over a house we were trying to purchase. The message was subtle but clear that we were more than roommates. The same agent asked for names of neighbors who could verify I lived at my home address. I gave him the name of a neighbor across the street in a group house who worked for another senator. I called him to make sure he would agree to be interviewed which he did. He called me after the interview and said something along the lines of "I talked with the agent. Good luck if you know what I mean." My second FBI report inferred that I was in a same-sex relationship in such a subtle way that readers could have missed it. I was hired for the White House position and confirmed by the Senate to the part-time commission seat.

White House security was tight, as it should be, but sometimes it could be too tight and not very clever or efficient. Senate Majority Leader Howard Baker was often at the White House to meet with President Reagan or senior staff. Too often, he was stopped at the gate because the Secret Service did not recognize him. One day, after Baker had been stopped again and asked for his ID, I was waiting in the West Wing reception room for his arrival. With a look I had never previously seen from him, he told me with an angry low voice, "Look, Bob, if I come here one more time and they don't recognize me, it'll be the last time I ever come!" From that day forward, pictures of the congressional leadership were posted at every station, to prevent the injury of Washington egos and the career demise of well-meaning public servants like me. The White House got Baker's message.

The Reagan White House was still a much more open and accessible place than it has been since terrorism became a bigger threat. Pennsylvania Avenue was still open to vehicle traffic and there was even parking on the grounds. I parked on East Executive Drive that separated the East Wing of the White House where our offices were located from the Treasury Department. Since 1995, in the wake of the Oklahoma City terrorist bombing, Pennsylvania Avenue and East Executive Drive have been closed to traffic.

A key function of those of us in the legislative affairs office was to educate White House staff on how the Senate and House actually operated. Even some senior staff had little understanding of the legislative process, so our years of experience became invaluable. One example was when Ed Meese used to ask me questions like, "Bob, I thought we controlled the Senate. Why can't we get more done?" In response, I offered a tutorial on how the Senate actually worked. In those days, several Northeast Republicans often voted against Reagan's initiatives, while many Southern Democrats voted with him.

A number of senators were not particularly impressed with Reagan early in the administration. On one occasion during his first year, Senator Lugar came back from the White House after meeting with Reagan and said, "I don't know if the President is really in touch." This was from a man who rarely had a negative thing to say about anyone. After I got to the White House, I discovered it wasn't that Reagan wasn't in touch, it was just that he was going to talk about what he wanted to talk about when he wanted to talk about it. There could be a meeting in the Cabinet Room or Roosevelt Room talking in great detail about the stated topic of the meeting. Reagan would listen to everyone and then often begin talking about something else completely different that was important to him at that moment, usually from his omnipresent three-by-five cards. This often led to a room full of people looking at their notes, then at each other, while silently mouthing, "What the?" I soon figured out there were two agendas for meetings the president attended, the meeting agenda and his agenda. His approach may have confused some, but he was president. They were at the White House and he was going to talk about whatever was on his mind.

One of our jobs in the Legislative Affairs office was to help prepare the president for meetings with congressional leadership and for meetings focused on policy or political issues.These meetings regularly happened. Some were bipartisan, but most included only Republicans because they focused on discreet legislative issues and political strategy. My colleagues and I somewhat humorously described our job at these meetings as "white towel duty." We met the leadership in the West Wing reception, chatted with them as we waited to be summoned to the Cabinet Room or Roosevelt Room and then escorted them into the meeting. At that point, we entered listening mode for the remainder of the meeting and then tried to debrief with the lawmakers afterwards.

President Reagan would enter the room after attendees were seated. Often these meetings were in the morning, so the leadership could return to the Hill in time for the beginning of the day's legislative session. Reagan typically would have just come from his daily national security briefing, so there was no telling what was on his mind. In virtually every meeting, he pulled from his pocket a set of three-by-five cards with talking points for the topic of the day, or sometimes talking points on whatever was on his mind. He invariably used them which struck many attendees as a sign he was not engaged in a meaningful way.After a few such meetings, I realized that the notes were helpful to make certain he covered everything he intended. Reagan was a good listener and always made his points in a firm, usually gentlemanly way.

Reagan was known for being a genial Irishman, but he had a temper. There were occasions where he clearly was annoyed and everyone in the room knew it. Early in my White House service, there was a lot of grumbling from some freshman Republican senators who were elected in 1980 and 1982, and they insisted on a meeting with POTUS to air their grievances. Reagan listened to their complaints and wish lists until he couldn't take it anymore and then he exploded. "Where were you on my budget!? Where were you when I needed YOU!?" he bellowed. We were working with a very slim majority in the Senate and a strongly Democratic House, and the President knew that to get anything done, there needed to be a two-way street of cooperation between Republicans in Congress and the White House. When he needed to bring the full force of his office and of his personality to bear to get results, he didn't hesitate to do so.

Legislative matters originating from the White House were carefully managed, especially in the Senate, where Republicans had at least nominal control. The administration never wanted to lose a vote on the Senate floor, and if they weren't going to win, they would either pull the bill or cut the best compromise possible. The concern was obvious; if the White House began to lose votes on important administration priorities, then the Democrats would smell blood and use these failures to try to pick off vulnerable Republican seats in the next election.

At the time, we often could count on votes from the Southern Democrats, but we had to be sure. As an example, when working on a highly controversial Department of Labor nomination that was before the Senate Labor Committee, it didn't look like the nomination was going to make it out of committee unless we got some help from the other side of the aisle. Some northeastern Republicans were siding with the unions to oppose the nominee. The Senate Labor Committee was part of my beat so in our nightly memo of recommended calls for President Reagan, I recommended the president telephone Senator Jennings Randolph, the senior Democratic senator from West Virginia, to seek his support for the nomination. My memo recommended that the president not go so far as to ask Senator Randolph to vote for the nominee because that was unlikely, but to ask him to vote to send the nomination to the full floor without recommendation. We felt we had the votes on the Senate floor to confirm this difficult nominee. The call came during the Labor Committee's consideration of the nomination. I saw Senator Randolph get up from his seat on the dais and go into the conference room that adjoined the Committee hearing room. He came out a few minutes later and announced he would vote to send the nomination to the Senate floor without recommendation. The call he took was from the president, and when I went up to Senator Randolph to thank him afterwards, his response was "I'm old-fashioned. If the President of the United States asks me to do something, I try my best to help." I was proud of that moment and outcome. It was the kind of respect for the office of the president and for the institution of the Senate that rarely exists today. It's the kind of thing that had to happen every day then, and really needs to happen every day now.

Ronald Reagan was elected promising an ambitious agenda and much of it required legislation. The agenda was extraordinarily bold and aggressive on domestic policy, national defense issues, and foreign affairs. He had a different vision of the U.S. at home and abroad than his immediate predecessor, President Jimmy Carter. President Carter was known as a micromanager and had a difficult time delegating authority. He and most of his staff were in way over their heads. Inflation took hold in the country and he did little to try to stop it. He made some progress in foreign affairs with the Camp David Accords, the historic peace agreement between Egypt and Israel. However, the oil embargo and resulting energy crisis and the national embarrassment of Americans being held hostage in Iran, among other crises, led some seasoned commentators to wonder aloud if the presidency was too big for any one person. Ronald Reagan ran on an optimistic and hopeful platform focused on curtailing the size and scope of government, cutting taxes, and eliminating many regulations and rebuilding the U.S. military after a post-Vietnam collapse. The Reagan administration started positively, moments after the inauguration, when news broke that the 52 American hostages held by Iran were freed.

President Reagan set the policy and delegated to his senior staff the job of turning it into a legislative agenda that Congress, especially Senate Majority Leader Howard Baker, could advance. The architects of the administration's legislative policy were Ken Duberstein and White House Chief of Staff Jim Baker. Both of them did their job extraordinarily well. They had a very fine understanding of what the administration wanted to do in terms of legislation and were excellent at setting priorities and sticking to them. They always had a willing partner in Reagan and in Vice President George H.W. Bush in scheduling as many congressional meetings at the White House as necessary and in making personal calls to senators and congressmen to get things done. There were many times when I, in my most persuasive tone, would contact senators about a specific bill or issue and get a response like, "Well, Bob, if it means that much to the president, have him call me." That meant another memo to the president, another call from the president, and eventually, another vote won or accommodation reached, but not always. At the daily morning meetings with Ken Duberstein, he would show us the memos back from the president. All calls had been made or at least tried and Reagan's handwritten notes were on them. Not every call was a success, but he never relented and always followed through on the recommended calls. His call memoranda with his handwritten notes are at the Reagan Library in Simi Valley, California. These memoranda debunk the myth that Reagan was above the fray and ran the government like a CEO. He was always hands-on and surrounded himself with staff who understood the power of the Presidency and carefully managed it for maximum effect.

The best example of the working relationships Reagan was able to create across the aisle was with the Democratic Speaker of the House. Thomas "Tip" O'Neill would say horrible things all day about Reagan in the news media and on the Hill, and then go to the White

House at night to have a drink with the president and often hammer out an agreement on the issues of the day. It went the other way, too. More than once, Reagan's position on legislation that O'Neill and the Democrats sent to the White House to be signed was "I oppose it, I oppose it, I oppose it...I'm signing it." He could do that because he had gotten just enough concessions from O'Neill to make the bill palatable to him.

This represented the waning golden days of a legislative process in Washington that actually achieved results. People wanted to accomplish something in those days. Invoking cloture was a heavy burden so members found ways to compromise to pass controversial legislation. Before 1975, Senate rules required a 2/3 majority of the Senate present and voting to invoke cloture, thereby cutting off Senate floor debate. Eventually the rules were changed when Democrats had strengthened their numbers. The revised cloture rule required a "constitutional" three-fifths, or 60 votes, which made achieving cloture somewhat easier. That is until recent years when the Senate became hyper-partisan and members rarely broke party rank. It's no wonder Washington is suffering from gridlock.

Besides Tip O'Neill, Reagan developed other productive relationships in the legislative branch. He had an excellent relationship with Senate Majority Leader Howard Baker and with the various old bulls, who in those days ran certain committees on the Hill. Reagan was no stranger to Washington when he was elected president; he had logged many hours in D.C. as the head of the Screen Actors Guild and he even set up what turned out to be a kind of "Mini White House" within the governor's office in Sacramento. After all, California was the largest state by population, and its economy dwarfed most countries. He had a reputation as a governor who was highly principled but would compromise, if necessary, to get things done.

Reagan painstakingly developed his positions on important issues while he had his syndicated radio show in the years after he left the California governorship and before he started running for president. He took meticulous notes for his radio addresses and seeing the actual hand-written script, one could see the ideas and positions evolving in his mind. Contrary to the belief of some critics who think Reagan was an unsophisticated thinker, he was a considered and capable man with a firm grasp on what he thought were the right policies on many national issues. Martin and Annalise Anderson, the husband and wife team who worked in the White House Policy Office during much of the Reagan presidency, are credited with finding the handwritten radio show scripts in the enormous Reagan Library and published many of them in a book called *Reagan, in His Own Hand, The Writings of Ronald Reagan that Reveal His Revolutionary Vision for America*.

His intense interest in important issues was made clear to me in reviewing decision memoranda that went from Cabinet councils to Reagan for his final decisions on specific issues. The issues and alternative approaches were laid out clearly for his review and, what struck me, was how consistent his decisions were on a variety of topics.

Being part of the White House staff involved long hours and work that seldom let up, so a few little privileges were appreciated. From a day-to-day perspective, the most important perk in being a special assistant was admission to the White House Mess. We had breakfast there every day Congress was in session before heading up to Ken Duberstein's office for our morning meeting. It also came in handy for entertaining friends and family when time permitted or grabbing a quick lunch between meetings in the White House complex. Each of us received a bill for our White House Mess charges at the end of each month. It was money well spent.

When the president was out of town, staff sometimes brought their pets to the office. I had two miniature dachshunds, Fred and Ethel. (Lucy and Mickey would come along later, one from each of Fred and Ethel's two litters). They were my little family in addition to Joe. Sometimes during those periods, I would bring them to the White House and let them run around the office and would take them out on the White House lawn to do their unofficial business. They were quite popular but, as I said, they were not the only pets brought to the White House when the president was out of town. Fred and Ethel managed to turn themselves into a national security issue one afternoon. During one outing, the Secret Service agent at the East Gate came up to me and informed me that there was a system of motion detectors in the basement of the White House and that Fred and Ethel had activated virtually all of them.

I apologized profusely, hoping to avoid the worst. But it was not to be; the next day, the dreaded memo came down from on high. No more personal pets would be permitted to visit the White House. Fred and Ethel were barred from their fun trips to the White House. But shortly after the no-pet policy came down, Ethel was pregnant with several puppies. When it was clear she was about to deliver; I had to go to work, but I didn't want to leave her alone. Months before, I had arrived home one evening to discover she had miscarried a sole pup and we didn't even know she was pregnant, so I didn't want a repeat to that scenario. After much consideration, I decided that my duties as a dog owner far outweighed an internal memo regarding canine visitation at the White House. I settled Ethel, who weighed about 10 pounds, into my canvas beach bag and covered her with towels and headed to the White House. As I approached the security gate, I was confident we could pull off the caper; little did I know Ethel had tunneled her way through the towels and was making her way to the surface. The guard looked at me, looked at the bag, and then looked at me again. I looked down at the bag and saw Ethel's brown muzzle in plain sight, sniffing away. The guard raised an eyebrow, and then raised the gate. I had a long sofa in my office, and I made Ethel as comfortable as possible. I carried her out to the East Side gate area to do her business, careful not to get anywhere near the grassy areas. My efforts paid off that Saturday when Ethel birthed her puppies in comfort and with family at home.

I worked at the Republican National Convention in 1984 as part of the Official Proceedings staff. My daytime assignment for the week was to be in the trailer set aside as rehearsal space for speakers. The campaign had hired a professional speech coach to work with any scheduled speaker, and virtually all the speakers took advantage of that resource. My role was to be the eyes and ears of the White House to make sure no one was going to say something that would embarrass the president. Discreetly, I was introduced as the timer. The only two speakers who did not appear in the rehearsal trailer were Ronald Reagan and Barry Goldwater. Reagan obviously needed no handholding when it came to captivating a crowd, especially one as friendly as he would face at his own party convention. Goldwater took the position of "I'm Barry Goldwater, this is my final convention speech and I'm going to say whatever the hell I want." No one was going to try to stop him.

There were two speech rehearsals I still remember. One was by Jeane Kirkpatrick. As fiery as she was, she preserved her energy; when she practiced her speech, her voice was barely a whisper. I was also struck by the fact that she was so very feminine. Because of her position as Reagan's Ambassador to the United Nations, she was surrounded by security agents. Her interactions with them were thoroughly ladylike and genteel, the antithesis of the iron-willed, almost butch conservative that was her public persona.

The speech that she was practicing in those hushed tones turned out to be one of the more famous in in the history of the party conventions. It was her Blame America First keynote speech. She praised Reagan's foreign policy while excoriating the leadership of what she called the "San Francisco Democrats" for the party's shift away from the hawkish policies of former Democratic presidents such as Harry S. Truman and John F. Kennedy to a more strident anti-war position that the left wing of the Democratic Party had pushed since Vietnam. (The Democrats had just held their convention in San Francisco.) It was the first time since Douglas MacArthur's 1952 speech that a non-party member had delivered the Republican convention keynote address.

The other rehearsal that stood out in my mind was former President Jerry Ford's. One afternoon, I was in the trailer minding my own business and with full White House credentials on display, when former President Ford came in with his Secret Service detail literally elbowing me aside and anyone else in the way. But he was iconic at the time, so everyone pretty much shrugged it off.

The only wild card was Goldwater, and there wasn't much anyone could do about him. He was just going to be Barry Goldwater. By that point, he was an irascible old man, a far different person than the one I represented at my high school assembly in 1964. To his credit, after he retired from the Senate in 1987, he became an advocate for allowing gays and lesbians to serve in the military. He famously said, "You don't have to be straight to shoot straight."

Of course, when I saw Clint Eastwood's performance at the 2012 Republican National Convention, I was reminded of my role in 1984, and I asked myself if the Reagan staff would have allowed that to happen. The answer was a resounding "No." The whole thing seemed like it could have been a clever idea if it was perfectly executed, but Eastwood came off as bizarre. The best thing I can say for the whole performance is that it gave the Republicans a bit of Hollywood star power, something that is difficult to come by in the town dominated by liberal Democrats. In a similar way that Goldwater was an icon, so is Clint Eastwood. You must respect and/or love Clint Eastwood, but if you are running a national political convention, you must have a little better idea of what he's planning to say and how he's planning to say it. It seemed to me that the party gave Eastwood carte blanche, and he maxed out the account. It's a sign of how desperate Republicans can be for Hollywood-style star power.

Given Reagan's own history in Hollywood, it has been widely reported that he and Nancy knew and were friends with many gay people, including during their time in the White House. Before being elected president, Ronald Reagan had taken a huge political risk on behalf of the gay community. He spoke out publicly against the Briggs Initiative, which would have prohibited gays and lesbians from teaching in California public schools. His opposition to the 1978 ballot initiative helped lead to its defeat. Even though Reagan, who had finished his second term as California governor less than four years earlier, was a national conservative political leader, he ignored the advice of his political advisors to oppose the initiative. Doing so spoke volumes about his common decency and commitment to making sure all Americans were treated fairly. Not long before election day, Reagan wrote an op-ed in the *Los Angeles Herald-Examiner*, later reprinted in the *San Francisco Chronicle*, in which he stated, "Whatever else it is, homosexuality is not a contagious disease like the measles. Prevailing scientific opinion is that an individual's sexuality is determined at a very early age and that a child's teachers do not really influence this." Polls showed the Briggs Initiative headed towards passage until Reagan came out against it. Voters rejected the measure by a margin of nearly 60%.

My Senate Legislative affairs colleagues eventually became aware of my sexual orientation. My secretary was known to loudly state, "Hey, Bob, Joe is on the line and wants to know when you will be home for dinner." No one thought anything of it. Working at the White House was a pressure cooker that left little time to think about people's personal lives.

The Republican Party has always had gays and lesbians working at all levels of the party. In the early 1980s, privacy was still largely respected, including whether one was gay or straight. When the Christian Right became involved in GOP politics in the 1980s, being gay became a liability in some circumstances. The Reagan White House had staff assigned to working with the Moral Majority and similar Conservative groups. My run in with the Moral Majority at the Department of Education was the only time I recall being in a meeting with them.

I was part of the White House team that accompanied President Reagan to Orlando, Florida for what became known as his Evil Empire speech he gave to the National Association of Evangelicals. This speech was made during the heated debate over a nuclear freeze. There was no mention of social conservative causes. The AIDS crisis was just beginning in the early 1980s. Gay men were targeted as the source of spreading what soon would be known as HIV. A lot of people made a lot of nasty comments about gay men, including some in the Reagan White House, politicians from both parties, and the news media. Republicans didn't have a monopoly on disparaging remarks and actions during this dark period for LGBT people.

As part of my job, I often shepherded members of Congress and other politicians into the White House. I'm on the left as President Reagan speaks with Minnesota GOP Senator Rudy Boschwitz and Baltimore Mayor Donald Schaefer.

This photo is from a White House luncheon for freshman Republican senators. There were a lot of them after the 1980 Reagan landslide. I'm in the center of the photo at the second table.

I have always been a dog person. I've owned six dogs over the years. During my White House tenure, two of my dogs, Fred and Ethel, caused a security alert after they set off sensors on the White House lawn when I took them out to do their business.

CHAPTER 14

AIDS in America

DURING MY TENURE IN THE WHITE HOUSE, THE AIDS EPIDEMIC was beginning to devastate the gay community. Thousands of men were dying, first in the larger cities and then all over the country, as the virus moved into other communities and populations, including straight people, IV drug users, and hemophiliacs. By early 1982 when I joined the White House staff, reports indicate 250 victims of AIDS had died, often dying a painful death from a virus about which we knew very little. I attended a few funerals and memorial services during my time at the White House and many more after departing.

I first learned about the strange disease in a newspaper article. It was scary to learn that gay men were dying of a mysterious illness in San Francisco, Los Angeles, and New York. In those early days, I remember a discussion with a New York friend during a weekend visit he made to Washington. He told me how he and his friends were frightened about this unknown disease. The first friend to fall ill and die was a Senate staffer who worked for another member of the Senate Banking Committee when I served on Lugar's staff. Joe and I went to a few parties at his house. He and his partner bragged about the number of sex partners they were having. We always left their house before the sex parties started. When he got sick, he became increasingly weaker.

Eventually, his partner couldn't care for him, so he sent him back to his hometown where he died soon after.

As more of our friends started getting sick in 1983 and '84, Joe and I became increasingly concerned. Often when we didn't see someone for a while, it was a shock when we did since their appearance had changed. They would lose a lot of weight and maybe get Kaposi Sarcoma (KS) spots. KS is a rare form of cancer that people with AIDS can get because of their weakened immune system.

In those early years, we lived in constant fear we would get the disease. Since no one yet knew what caused the disease or how people contracted it, there were all sorts of theories floating around. One of the strangest targeted amyl nitrites, popularly called poppers, as the source of the disease. This theory caused a lot of panic because so many people used poppers on dance floors and during sex to achieve a temporary high. It was such a prevalent theory that some states outlawed the sale of poppers. As the epidemic intensified, like many in the gay community, Joe and I spent less time in bars. There was more entertaining in homes. We hosted dinner parties and cookouts for our friends. After the development of a reliable HIV test, those who tested negative were relieved. However, the lack of treatment led many to skip testing.

Gay activists strongly criticized President Reagan for not responding to the AIDS epidemic forcefully enough in either his words or government action, including research and treatment initiatives. President Reagan was blasted from the beginning of the crisis, but the vitriol toward him grew as more and more people died in the 1990s after he left office. Reagan was an easy target when so many had ignored AIDS and there is much blame to go around. It's true the Reagan administration should have done more, but the same could be said of Democrats in Congress, the news media, and the gay community.

First, let's look at Reagan's record. It's not as if nothing was being done in the early years of the epidemic. The Reagan administration increased AIDS funding from $8 million in 1982 to $26.5 million in 1983, which Congress increased to $44 million. The amount spent on research doubled every year for the remainder of his presidency. To ACT UP members and other AIDS advocacy groups, there never would have been enough funding or attention given to this deadly disease. And that's understandable given how it was cutting down people in their prime and in such excruciating ways. For those who critique the level of government funding, it's important to remember that Democrats controlled the U.S. House and then the Senate during Reagan's last two years in office. Democratic leaders had the power to extract more funding from Reagan had they asked for it. It's not as if Democratic House Speaker Tip O'Neill was a strong advocate for gay rights.

Aside from funding increases, various parts of Reagan's administration were working tirelessly to respond to the AIDS epidemic. Secretary of Health and Human Services Margaret Heckler, whose nomination I handled for the White House, visited an AIDS patient in 1983 at a hospital in New York and held his hand to demonstrate to Americans that AIDS was not spread by casual contact. In early 1986, the president visited the Department of Health and Human Services where he stated that one of his administration's highest public health priorities was a continuing search on treatments for AIDS.

Reagan was criticized for not speaking about AIDS until several years into the crisis. He should have, but where was the news media? There wasn't a question about the epidemic at a presidential news conference until 1985. Why weren't journalists asking the president about this issue in 1982, '83 or '84? Did they not want to "waste" precious time in a news conference with a question affecting only homosexuals?

Politicians didn't do enough to respond to the crisis, but neither did journalists. That can be seen in an incredible and infuriating White House briefing from October of 1982. Several years ago, *Slate* highlighted the incident in which conservative radio talk show host Les Kinsolving asked Deputy Press Secretary Larry Speakes about the horrifying new disease.[1] "What's AIDS?" Speakes asked.

"It's known as the 'gay plague,'" Kinsolving replied.

Everyone laughed. "I don't have it," Speakes replied. "Do you?" The room erupted in laughter again. Speakes continued responding to Kinsolving's questions with jokes, including a statement that Kinsolving himself might be gay simply because he knew about the disease. Speakes eventually acknowledged that nobody in the White House, including Reagan, knew much about the epidemic. "There has been no personal experience here," Speakes said.

Instead of follow-up questions from the assembled journalists, the room was filled with laughter. What Speakes said was outrageous. However, why weren't his comments on every evening newscast and on the front page of every paper in America? Because the journalists were laughing along with Speakes. They were part of the problem.

Meanwhile, *The New York Times*, America's so-called newspaper of record, was essentially AWOL on the AIDS epidemic throughout the 1980s. Abe Rosenthal, Executive Editor at the *Times* from 1977-88, was notoriously anti-gay, according to reporting from Michelangelo Signorile.[2] Reporters and editors had to be in the closet or risk being fired. Rosenthal prohibited use of the word "gay" in its newspaper, instead requiring the more clinical term "homosexuality." He reportedly discouraged positive articles about gay people and encouraged stories

---

1 Stern, Mark Joseph, "Listen to Reagan's Press Secretary Laugh About Gay People Dying of AIDS," *Slate*, December 1, 2015, http://slate.me/1ImCYwE (accessed March 1, 2018).

2 Signorile, Michelangelo, "Out At The New York Times: Gays, Lesbians, AIDS And Homophobia Inside America's Paper Of Record," *HuffPost*, February 2, 2016, http://bit.ly/2Fb4vVQ (accessed March 1, 2018).

that demonized homosexuality. Given his record, it's not surprising the paper had little reporting about the AIDS epidemic throughout the 1980s. According to Signorile, AIDS activist and playwright Larry Kramer blasted the *Times* for its lack of coverage. It was a similar story at other news outlets across the country.

The government and journalists can share blame regarding AIDS, but the same is true for the gay community. Too many gay men were in denial about how the disease was spread. Some fought efforts to close gay bathhouses where the disease was being spread the fastest. How would gay activists have responded if President Reagan sent in the national guard to shut down every bathhouse in America? Then mayor of San Francisco, Dianne Feinstein, waged a two-year battle to close bathhouses in her city. Her efforts were delayed by courts and gay activists. In a 1986 speech to the U. S. Conference of Mayors, she criticized gay groups "who have turned this into a civil rights issue rather than a public health issue."

I have sympathy for every person who contracted HIV, but the cold hard fact is that too many in our community refused to change their sexual behavior, even when it became clear how the epidemic was being spread. That isn't Ronald Reagan's fault. It's our fault. Of course, many gay men changed their sex lives, especially when it became known that it was caused by a virus spread sexually. Condom sales skyrocketed, and AIDS and other community organizations regularly handed out condoms at gay bars and bathhouses. I had some friends who quit having sex at all; others became more careful in their sex lives or, so they said. However, too many gay activists found it easier to blame President Reagan for failing to lead on the issue. I still hear that from time to time, but recent articles clearly point out what he and his administration did to respond to the AIDS epidemic. Nothing was enough at that time but soon the virus would be identified, and early treatments developed that started to extend lives and make AIDS victims more comfortable.

As much as I didn't like the tactics of groups such as ACT UP, I think they made a difference. They were particularly active and effective during the Clinton administration. Outside pressure helped speed up and improve the government's response. Log Cabin and other mainstream LGBT groups took an entirely different approach. As has often been the case during the gay civil rights movement, it took a combination of approaches: angry outsiders protesting along with people trying to push change from the inside. I've always been more comfortable and effective on the inside, working within the political process.

Looking back on those dark days, it's important to remember the level of homophobia that permeated all levels of society. While I led an "open" life in Washington, I was very much aware of the level of homophobia in many areas of the city. I and others often were cautious where we went and what we said for fear of a homophobic reaction. Anti-gay jokes were commonplace in daily life, including on television. One of the silver linings of the AIDS pandemic was the realization by many heterosexuals that they knew gay people and that fact alone began changing attitudes, albeit slowly. However, this sea change was a crucial factor in the level of acceptance many LGBT people experience today. Critics of Reagan's response to AIDS accused him of being anti-gay. That's simply not true, either in his rhetoric or actions.

I lost many friends to AIDS in the 1980s and '90s. One of them was Tim Furlong who was instrumental in guiding me through the interview process at the Manatt firm after the 1984 election. He died in 1988.

CHAPTER 15

Inside and Out

THE TIME I WAS MOST PROUD TO HAVE BEEN A PART OF THE FIRST Reagan administration was when he was re-elected to a second term as president. Earlier in 1984, his re-election was at best uncertain. The first term was tough: the nation was in a deep recession and Federal Reserve Board Chairman Paul Volcker had dramatically raised interest rates to attack inflation. The nation's economy fought through it, and the recovery came just in time for the November 1984 election. Validation from the American people came with a landslide victory over former Vice President Walter Mondale. Reagan won 49 states and missed taking Mondale's home state of Minnesota by just 3,200 votes. I wasn't a part of the campaign. Either you were a part of the campaign or you were on the White House staff, and I had plenty to do in my role. I took vacation time to work at the Republican National Convention in Dallas in August of 1984. I remain proud to have been part of President Reagan's successful first term.

At that point, I had been in the White House for three years, and I decided it would be time for me to leave in January of 1985. My timing had to do with the turnover that comes with staffing for the next administration; if you stayed past January in an election year and then left before the November election, you were considered a virtual traitor. I had stayed through the 1984 campaign. After Reagan's victory, I went to M.B. Oglesby, who had replaced Ken Duberstein as Assistant to the President for Legislative Affairs, to let him know I would leave in January and that I was interviewing for a new position. "That's great, good luck," he said.

About three days later he called me and said, "You get a job yet?"

I answered, "No, not yet." A pause. He said, "Well, let me know when you do because I have a great guy to replace you and I don't want to lose him." Ah, had I made a mistake by telling my boss? Perhaps, but he was just doing his job to keep the office humming as the White House prepared for its second term.

When I left, you'd think there would have been no end of jobs waiting for a young attorney like me fresh out of the White House. In fact, I had a difficult time finding a job I wanted to take. Did my sexual orientation have anything to do with the lack of offers? I think not, except in one instance when I interviewed with a headhunter for a position at a tobacco company. Noting my age of 38 and unmarried, he made it clear his client was only interested in heterosexual men and women. He was quite skillful in phrasing it, but the point came through loud and clear. I didn't want to work for a tobacco company, but I considered the interview as valuable practice. Various mentors had advised me to speak with anyone who had a job and offered an interview. That's what I did.

I had difficulty finding the right fit. The world of lobbying had not yet reached the major law firms in D.C. The old line, prestigious law firms didn't know what to do with someone like me who had deep knowledge of the legislative process and politics at a high level but no portable clients. Consequently, many firms didn't have a feel for where someone with my background would fit into the law firm hierarchy. An early mentor in Washington, the father of a Denison classmate, was a senior partner in a major D.C. firm. When I met with him after deciding to leave the White House, his first piece of advice was to forget large law firms like his. At the time, the larger, established firms looked down on lobbying as not practicing "real" law and below their dignity. That changed over the next decade when, often at the insistence of their clients, firms began offering government affairs services. While large law firms changed their view on lobbying, it didn't happen in time for my transition out of the White House.

After more than twenty interviews with law firms, consulting firms, trade associations, and corporate government affairs offices, I finally signed on with a law firm headed by the man who became one of the strongest influences in my professional life, Chuck Manatt. It's quite ironic that a dyed-in-the-wool Democrat like Manatt would mentor a lifelong Republican. The more I got to know him, the more I respected his remarkable intelligence on a variety of levels, including his talent for leading people and organizations. Chuck Manatt had been Chairman of the Democratic National Committee from 1981 to 1985, so he was our direct competition during the 1984 campaign. He was a founder of the law firm Manatt, Phelps, and Phillips LLP, which had a major presence in Los Angeles and a small office in D.C. that had been opened to service L.A.-based clients in Washington before Congress and the Executive branch. As I recall, I was the seventh lawyer hired in the D.C. office, and it became my professional home for more than fifteen years. I was hired to be the first Republican lawyer/lobbyist to counterbalance another young lawyer named Tim Furlong, a wonderfully engaging Democratic lawyer from Dallas who had worked for Senator Lloyd Bentsen. Tim was handsome, funny, hardworking, and gay. I knew Tim a bit socially and often saw him at the downtown YMCA where we both worked out.

The D.C. office was looking for a recognizable Republican to join its small legislative practice and I fit the bill. Tim was the designated D and I was the R. At the firm, Tim and I worked together as partners starting in 1985, focusing on the legislation that would eventually become the 1986 Tax Reform Act. In time, I developed a close bond with Chuck Manatt, but it took him a while to get used to having a Republican on the team. In Los Angeles, there were a few known Republicans at the firm. Chuck used to poke me by saying, "Bob, you know most of the partners in Los Angeles voted for Reagan. They'll never tell YOU that, but they did." It took a while for Chuck to warm up to me because he was so angry after Reagan won his landslide victory over Walter Mondale. He also had scars from his own fight to remain DNC Chairman when Mondale tried to replace him during the Democratic National Convention in San Francisco during the summer of 1984. He often would pass me in the hallway and growl the old Reagan campaign slogan. "Morning in America, Bob. Morning in America."

I remember the first time I met Chuck. Tim, who had been assigned the task of guiding me through the firm's interview process, told me to meet him and Manatt at an art gallery reception in Washington that was showing an exhibition of political cartoons. Tim introduced me to Chuck who took a long look at me and said, "Well, at least you are wearing tassel loafers." I still don't know what that meant, but if it made him happy, I was for it. In a few days, I had lunch with Chuck and Tim at the Manatt offices and got Chuck's approval to go to Los Angeles for more interviews. I was in Los Angeles for several days of back-to-back meetings, including a lunch with two young lawyers from the firm, who took me to the poolside restaurant at the Beverly Hills Hotel. I was mesmerized; here I was at the Beverly Hills Hotel with beautiful women modeling clothes around the pool for the enjoyment of the lunch guests. I felt like everything was going my way when one of the lawyers, a tall, rangy associate with a heavy New Jersey accent and a reputation as a rising star litigator, leaned over to ask me an "honest question." I said, "Sure, ask away."

He leans over to me and says: "So, tell me, is Reagan as stupid as he looks?" Suppressing laughter and the lunch I had just finished, I replied, "No, actually not." Rising star? Right.

Later, during my round of L.A. interviews, I met Alan Rothenberg, a partner in the firm and a powerhouse in law and sports who eventually would be elected president of the California Bar Association. Alan also was known for operating and personally bankrolling USA Soccer and for running soccer during the 1984 Olympics in L.A. I thought it couldn't get any worse than the New Jersey guy's question, when Rothenberg offers, "You know, I think that guy Ed Meese is really a Nazi." A longtime Reagan confidante, Meese had been counselor to the president during the first term before becoming attorney general in early 1985. After the Nazi comment, I realized I was in a different universe than the White House, and I simply smiled. As Senator Lugar advised early on, some things are best left unsaid.

One of the kindest people I met in the Los Angeles office was Lee Phillips, one of the most important music lawyers in the country with a stellar list of clients including Barbra Streisand, Michael Jackson, Cher, and many others. Since firms at that time rarely hired attorneys in their mid-thirties without portable business, Lee asked, "Bob, just what do you expect to do on your first day?" I broke out in a cold sweat. While I had thought about that question for some time, I didn't have a prepared answer and was a bit embarrassed. But he let it go, and I eventually received a job offer which I quickly accepted. After I started, I found that Rothenberg and the rest of the firm were happy to walk across the bridges of opportunity I could make for them with the Republican Party and Reagan White House.

The term lobbyist usually brings negative thoughts of phony back slapping, pay-to-play, and sometimes worse. In fact, it's a noble and important profession. Over my 30-year law and lobbying career, I represented a wide range of clients on a variety of issues. It's interesting and, from my point of view, important to note the several types of lobbyists. Some lobbyists specialize in opening doors by raising a lot of money for members of Congress. Others are subject experts. Then there are those who try to do both. I viewed myself as a subject matter expert-type lobbyist working for law firms with substantial political fundraising capabilities. I didn't enjoy having drinks after work with other lobbyists and members of Congress and their staffs. I was much more interested in the nuts and bolts of policy. Nevertheless, I did attend my share of congressional fundraisers over the years. I found these were useful events to find out valuable information and relay my clients' views on their key issues. The rules governing lobbying were tightened several times during my career. Under the current rules, it is virtually impossible to take members or staff for as much as a cup of coffee, much less to dinner or a baseball game. And that's probably for the best even if it seems absurd at times.

When I joined the Manatt firm in January of 1985, Congress had begun hearings on what would become the 1986 Tax Reform Act promoted by President Reagan and supported by a broad bipartisan coalition. My Masters of Law in taxation from Georgetown Law School was a helpful credential to have during that period. I was part of a small team of lobbyists at the firm representing several clients as this tax legislation took shape. My first client was the American Bankers Association (ABA). I had worked with the ABA staff for many years on the Hill and on occasion in the White House. Due to that long-term relationship with the ABA, I was retained by the organization's head of government affairs to represent them on certain esoteric loan loss reserve tax issues. Other clients on the 1986 Tax Reform Act were primarily real estate interests trying to protect various tax preferences. We were less successful in this area as Senate Finance Committee Chairman Bob Packwood, an Oregon Republican, was determined to lower income tax rates substantially by repealing many tax deductions and credits, particularly in real estate. Packwood succeeded, and the impact on some aspects of the real estate industry was dramatic, leading to bankruptcies and the demise in a few years of many banks and thrifts that were engaged in unsound real estate lending.

After the 1986 Tax Reform Act was enacted, lobbying on tax issues in Congress almost disappeared, not just for me, but every other tax lobbyist in D.C. When I was taking evening classes towards my LLM in the late '70s, I decided I had no interest in working the regulatory side of tax issues at the IRS and Department of Treasury. I enjoyed the policy aspect of tax legislation, but implementation by the Executive Branch agencies held no interest for me. The idea of working on detailed regulations, private letter rulings, and other tax regulatory minutia was suffocating. I preferred tax policy.

So I had to find other areas where I could focus my time and energy. And to make a living. My experience working for Senator Lugar on the Senate Banking Committee allowed me to develop clients in the financial services industry. That work became my focus. Two long-time clients included the small business and student lending subsidiaries of The Money Store, best known for developing the second mortgage industry, and a coalition of merchant banking subsidiaries of several major commercial bank holding companies. I worked directly with the CEO of The Money Store to make certain the complex formula that determined the extent of government guarantees in these two programs was sufficiently funded to meet growing market demands for their financial products.

On the merchant banking coalition, I worked with the CEOs of seven merchant banking holding company subsidiaries to expand their authority to match other nonbank merchant banks. Our legislative language became part of what ended up as the Gramm-Leach-Bliley Act, enacted in 1999. We then worked extensively with the Federal Reserve Board on regulatory implementation. The initial proposed regulations were so tough they would have shut down most of the clients' activities. We went back to Congress to pressure the Federal Reserve to loosen its initial regulations. After more than ten years representing these clients, the seven coalition members had been reduced to three because of mergers and acquisitions.The reduction of coalition members was a microcosm of the consolidation in the financial service industry.

During the Clinton administration, I represented the City of Hope National Medical Center which had joined with other cancer centers not affiliated with universities to lobby on what was known as Hillarycare. These cancer centers had been inadvertently omitted from a key funding formula for major health facilities. We worked extensively with Senators Feinstein and Barbara Boxer and several California House members on the House Ways and Means Committee. Fortunately, after much time and effort, Hillarycare collapsed from its own weight with only one committee voting on it in the House.

During my many year of lobbying, I worked with both Republicans and Democrats on behalf of clients. Always, it was the end result that counted. More often than not, the issues I worked on were improved by engaging bipartisan support for whatever the issue might be. Over the course of my career, I represented other types of businesses, including airlines. The Manatt firm served as the outside General Counsel to Flying Tigers, at the time the largest all-cargo airline. The leadership at Flying Tigers hired me because they wanted a Republican lobbyist to help their team in Washington. Our initial assignment was to keep the Japanese carrier, ANA, out of Chicago O'Hare Airport over fear of unfair competition from the behemoth carrier. Eventually, Flying Tigers was bought by Federal Express, which took an entirely different approach to competition. The executive team that ran Flying Tigers went to United Airlines and later to US Airways to lead those airlines. The general counsel hired me to work with their team on a variety of critical issues for both airlines. There's a lesson here; if you do a good job for clients, they'll remember you down the road, even as they move to other companies. Competence and hard work leave an impression on people.

Among the more fun and interesting clients were those involving international trade policy. The Manatt firm had an active international trade law practice involving antidumping, countervailing duty and customs. Some of these clients needed lobbying assistance on policy issues impacting their businesses.

A favorite client was the Colombian Flower Growers Association, Asocolflores. The U.S. had helped Colombia develop a fresh cut flower industry as an alternative to illegal drugs like cocaine. At the time, 70% of all cut flowers sold in the U.S. came from Colombia. After U.S. Customs discovered cocaine smuggled into the U.S. in boxes of flowers, Asocolflores agreed to track all flowers from the time they were picked and transported in locked trucks until they arrived in the Port of Miami.

Our goal was to make certain that if Congress imposed penalties on Colombian products as punishment for not adequately dealing with the illegal drug trade, the flower industry would be exempted. At the time, the flower farms were owned by Colombian families; that has changed a bit over time as some flower farms are owned by large corporations such as Dole Foods. This lobbying work also occurred before changes in gift rules were imposed, so we could send roses on behalf of the client to any congressional office. That delightful practice ended when Congress put additional restrictions on gifts to members and their staffs.

I owe a lot to Tim Furlong's shepherding me through the hiring process, and while both of us were there, we made an effective team for clients and became good friends. When I started interviewing at the firm in late 1984, I mentioned to some friends that Tim was helping me through the interview process. Someone told me he had AIDS, but I thought it was just a rumor until a year or so later when he started developing symptoms. Soon catastrophic infections spread throughout his body. With no medicines available at that time, his fight was painful to watch. Little by little he became sicker and sicker. He left the firm a year after I joined, in part because he didn't want his colleagues to see him waste away. During the early '80s, Tim spent many of his summer weekends at a group house on Fire Island, New York, where thousands of gay men, primarily from New York City, went in the summer. Everyone with a share in Tim's house tragically died early in the AIDS crisis. When Tim told me directly that he had AIDS, he said, "Bob, I was just unlucky." And he was. He was correct; it easily could have been me.

Tim died at age 42 in November of 1988, right after George H.W. Bush was elected president. It hurt very much when he died. There was a hugely attended Mass for him at his local parish church in Washington and then a funeral in his hometown of Dallas. I attended both. Tim had not been out to his parents. He eventually told his dad he had cancer but wasn't specific about it. When he was dying in a hospital, his mother came to visit. She told us she had just learned her son was gay and dying. It was so sad.

Tim's funeral was one of many I attended for friends who died of AIDS. I remember Matt Scocozza's memorial service. Matt was my good friend for several years. He had a history of cancer and then got HIV and eventually AIDS. He was working for Transportation Secretary Elizabeth Dole as an assistant secretary when he became sick and died. Dole spoke movingly at his funeral. Another memorial service that remains in my mind was for a handsome, athletic young guy that Joe had shared a Rehoboth Beach house with a few years earlier. We didn't know him well but wanted to attend his memorial service. He had converted to a Christian Scientist. The service was unusual in that the man who presided talked about how "they had not yet figured out how to cure this disease." Something about that really confused me. I wasn't sure what he had died of but learned after the service that he was another AIDS victim. I should have known, but it was early in the AIDS crisis and I had not yet become familiar with the signals surrounding an AIDS death.

Other than grandparents, my friends who died of AIDS were the first people I knew to die. It was a chilling reminder of how fragile life can be. As more people got sick and died, my coping mechanism was to try to ignore it the best I could. I put all my energy into my work. My brother Greg and I talked often about the AIDS epidemic. He lost several friends in Chicago. I was relieved when Greg became involved in a long-term relationship that lasted several years. Neither he nor my parents liked Joe, but they were pleased we had each other and the home life we had made for each other.

The mid-to-late '80s started the period when people realized, "Hey, I do know gay people" because they had friends or relatives who were dying of AIDS. On Fridays, one of the first things Joe and I would do would be to look at the weekly local LGBT newspaper, the *Washington Blade*, to check the obituaries. Almost every week there would be one or more obituaries of men we knew who had died the previous week. Often it would be someone we had not seen for a while and were not aware was sick.

Our friend Axel who lived in New York was an early AIDS victim. Joe and I often stayed at his apartment in Chelsea. He was a wonderful guy with an amazing history; his parents were from Hungary and emigrated to Argentina to avoid Hitler's wrath. Axel grew up in Argentina but moved to New York City where he worked as a trader for Citibank. He became a consummate New Yorker, always active. He was among the first to die; he went into a hospital and never came out. Another early AIDS death among my New York friends was a man named Henry who was head of government affairs for Avon Corporation.

It was a frightening time for every gay man, including Joe and me. It made my relationship with Joe stronger, at least for a while. We had each other and did our best to help our friends who became sick and died. Looking back, I feel like my relationship with Joe may have saved my life. I was fortunate to have a partner during the period when the AIDS epidemic developed and intensified. A few years before I met Joe, I had spent a week or two on Fire Island two years in a row. I didn't like the Fire Island lifestyle, so I didn't go back and after Joe and I met, it never occurred to me to go back. Early in our relationship we had shares in a beach house in Rehoboth Beach, Delaware and took an annual vacation to Provincetown and stayed to ourselves. Many couples I knew back then are still alive and many are still together.

Shortly after I left the Reagan White House, a friend asked if I would join a small group of gay Republicans to meet with the executive director of AIDS Action Council, an organization that had been created to work with Congress and the administration to fund research on HIV/AIDS and medical care for AIDS patients. I gladly agreed as it was a way for me to use my expertise and contacts to help make progress on these issues. This small group of gay Republicans met every few months at the Seagram's penthouse apartment at Washington Harbor in Georgetown. A Seagram's executive was an openly gay man who was senior enough to stay at the penthouse when he was in town and could host the meetings. The executive director of AIDS Action and I became good friends. The small group of Republicans helped "educate" her and her staff on how to talk to Republicans. That may sound funny, but there are different ways to talk to Republicans and to Democrats to effectively persuade them to help. I was proud that, except for a few notable exceptions, most Republicans members of Congress wanted to help. By this time all members, Republicans and Democrats, had constituents who were dying of AIDS, and by and large their hearts were in the right place.

There were exceptions to this rule. Senator Jesse Helms, Republican from North Carolina, was the number one homophobe in the Senate during his five terms in office from 1973 until

2003. He vocally opposed HIV/AIDS funding and related legislation, including the Ryan White Care Act named after a young heterosexual hemophiliac who contracted HIV through a blood transfusion. Helms was responsible for adding HIV to the "excludable diseases" list for travel or immigration to the U.S. We were the last industrialized country to maintain that policy. It was repealed in 2010. I often wondered if he knew he had gay men working on his staff. Helms and a few other Members of Congress like him were reason enough for gays and lesbians working on the Hill or in the administration to remain quiet if not deeply closeted about their sexuality. Toward the end of his life, he said one of his regrets was in opposing AIDS funding. Fortunately, more reasonable and caring members of Congress prevailed over his opposition.

My advisory role helping AIDS Action continued for several years. I recall a few years later, at a fundraiser for AIDS Action, the then executive director introduced me to his development director as one of their Republican friends. The development director quickly responded, "Well, that's too bad." He was fired shortly thereafter; I hope for having the bad manners and judgment to insult a long-time supporter and advisor to his boss. When I first moved to D.C., the AIDS epidemic had not yet begun to devastate people's lives. The health issue most gay men worried about was contracting a venereal disease such as gonorrhea or syphilis. Whitman-Walker Clinic was founded in 1973 as the Gay Men's VD Clinic in the basement of the Georgetown Lutheran Church with an all-volunteer staff. After complaints from church members, it moved to a rented space on 17th Street NW and hired its first full-time staff member. As the AIDS epidemic grew in the early '80s, Whitman-Walker Clinic took on a greater role in providing up-to-date information, counseling, and direct services such as HIV testing and care to a patient class predominantly consisting of gay men.

At that time, Whitman-Walker and similar clinics in other cities provided services that some private sector health professionals refused to offer. Some medical doctors and dentists refused to treat patients with HIV/AIDS. The stigma surrounding the disease was rampant in the early years due to lack of knowledge of how the disease was spread and, of course, the lack of treatment for the virus, the contraction of which was considered a death sentence. As the crisis escalated, the needs of the HIV/AIDS patient population grew and clinics such as Whitman-Walker began offering more and more services. Eventually, it offered housing, transportation, and nutrition services that were costly and drained the clinic's limited budget. Whitman-Walker, like many other HIV/AIDS facilities in major cities across the country, had a series of financial crises, often brought on by their seemingly ever-expanding mission and the well-intentioned but inexperienced people leading them. Whitman-Walker bounced from one financial crisis to another, often being bailed out by the D.C. government and the passage of federal programs, most notably the Ryan White Care Act that provided much needed financial assistance for treatments. Some, including myself, referred to this collection of services as AIDS Inc. People had begun making a business out of treating patients with HIV/AIDS. Log Cabin often was at odds with these entities as we fought for expedited drug approval authority and expanded funding to get new medications directly into the hands of patients whose lives depended on it and downplay other ancillary services.

As a member of the Washington gay community, I volunteered to help raise funds for Whitman-Walker including co-chairing one year what was then the organization's annual fund-raising gala at the Mayflower Hotel. That evening was particularly festive as three aging divas took the stage to perform. Unsurprisingly, Bea Arthur, Dixie Carter, and Elaine Stritch were huge hits with the largely LGBT crowd. The gala event eventually was phased out but the need for fundraising never stops for such organizations.

Today, most of the larger HIV/AIDS clinics survived by transforming themselves into community health centers. Whitman-Walker

Clinic is now called Whitman-Walker Health. Since 2006, it has been led by a professional manager, Don Blanchon, a straight, married man whose younger brother died of AIDS early in the epidemic. He and other professional managers like him steered their organizations away from AIDS Inc. to a more sustainable model that changes as the delivery and funding of health care changes.

The AIDS epidemic brought gays, lesbians, and many heterosexual people together. Several cities continue to host AIDS Walks each year to raise money for HIV/AIDS and other illnesses. Gay activist Cleve Jones in San Francisco started the AIDS Memorial Quilt in 1985 to commemorate those who died of the disease with 3' by 6' memorial cloth panels. Each one is hand sewn and is unique to the life of individual AIDS victims. Today the quilt consists of more than 50,000 individual panels. The quilt was first displayed on the National Mall on October 11, 1987, during the National March on Washington for Lesbian and Gay Rights. It covered a space larger than a football field and included 1,920 panels. Hundreds of thousands of people, including me, visited the Quilt that weekend. The last time the entire quilt was displayed was in 1996, again on the National Mall. The AIDS Memorial Quilt project continues and is a vivid reminder of those who died. About 700,000 Americans have died of AIDS since the beginning of the crisis. Fortunately, the death rate has slowed dramatically since the FDA approved effective antiretroviral medications in 1996. HIV has become a manageable disease for those who get tested and continue recommended treatments. In the early '90s, I went through my address book and took out whole pages of names of friends and acquaintances who died of AIDS. Doing so was another chilling reminder of how horrendous those years were and how fragile life can be.

One of the highlights of my White House tenure was working at the 1984 Republican National Convention in Dallas. After President Reagan's huge re-election win, I decided to move to the private sector. I was surprised how difficult it was to find a new job.

This is a photo with some of my colleagues from Manatt. I was fortunate to work with many capable and interesting people.

I spent sixteen years at Manatt. After a major tax reform bill became law in 1986, I diversified my lobbying expertise beyond tax policy. For the remainder of my career, I focused extensively on financial services.

After leaving the White House, I remained active in Republican politics. This is a 1990 photo with Vice President Dan Quayle, his wife Marilyn (second from left) and Gayle Wilson, the wife of California Governor Pete Wilson.

CHAPTER 16

Building the Log Cabin

THE NATIONAL PRESENCE OF LOG CABIN REPUBLICANS GREW out of the 1992 presidential campaign. Incumbent President George H.W. Bush faced a surprisingly strong Republican primary challenge from Patrick Buchanan, the pugnacious cable TV host and former aide to Presidents Nixon and Reagan. Buchanan took advantage of a sluggish economy and Bush's apparent indifference to the economic challenges confronting millions of Americans. Aside from focusing on economic populism, Buchanan made his social conservatism a focus of his upstart campaign. He ended up garnering more than three million votes during the Republican primary campaign, mainly from conservative Christians. In exchange for supporting Bush in the general election, Buchanan demanded a prime time speaking slot at the Republican National Convention in Houston.

A poorly run convention was symptomatic of Bush's incompetent campaign. The convention's highlight was supposed to be the last GOP convention speech by former President Reagan. He had not yet publicly announced his Alzheimer's disease, but it was clear this would be his last national convention speech. Buchanan spoke much longer than expected so he pushed Reagan's speech out of prime time. And that wasn't the worst part about Buchanan's speech.

Incredibly, his speech wasn't vetted by the Bush campaign. Buchanan ended up overshadowing not only Reagan but also Bush when he spoke later in the convention. In fact, Buchanan dominated the GOP convention, and not in a good way. He sounded nasty and intolerant. In his most strident voice, he bellowed, "There is a religious war going on in this country. It's a cultural war, as critical to the kind of nation we shall be as was the Cold War itself, for this war is for the soul of America." He also proclaimed "Yes, we disagreed with President Bush, but...we stand with him against the amoral idea that gay and lesbian couples should have the same standing in law as married men and women."

A young gay conservative from Massachusetts stood on the floor of the Astrodome that mid-August night, listening in disbelief to Buchanan's angry rhetoric. Rich Tafel was there as the head of what was then known as the Log Cabin Federation, the coalition of the Log Cabin Republican chapters that had sprung up across the country. He proved to be an articulate spokesman against Buchanan's hate-filled speech and would soon launch a nationwide fundraising drive to open a Washington office for Log Cabin Republicans.

I also was in the audience in my role as a Republican partner at the Manatt firm. I was appalled both at Buchanan's rhetoric and at the roar of approval from many in the convention hall that summer night. I knew this was a pivotal moment for gay Republicans and those who support a more inclusive Republican party. While Buchanan's speech targeted gay and lesbian Americans, other minority groups took notice too, knowing they could be next in line for attack. The meanness and divisiveness of Buchanan's speech ended up hurting President Bush in November when he lost to little-known Arkansas Governor Bill Clinton. Many voters turned away from the GOP in response to this ferocious negativity towards an increasingly visible part of America, LGBT individuals.

Rich and I did not meet during the convention, but our paths crossed soon thereafter. It became clear that night gay and lesbian Republicans had to have a formalized presence in the nation's capital. This effort would bond us and other gay Republicans in a common cause to represent the interests of the LGBT community inside the GOP.

I got connected with Rich and Log Cabin thanks to Denison University of all places. In Washington, I benefited from the area's alumni network by connecting with older graduates who mentored me early in my career. One such alum was Joe McMahon, who encouraged me to become involved in LGBT issues. In late 1992, McMahon invited me to a small gathering at his home one Sunday afternoon to meet Rich Tafel and Marvin Collins, a wealthy Texan who was funding their weekend travels to several cities to meet prospective supporters. Like everyone at the gathering, I was impressed with Rich and his message. All of us had been deeply impacted by the divisive GOP convention a few months before. It was clear that the religious right had become an ingrained foundation in the party. Like a lot of others, I felt helpless about how to confront the religious right other than quietly helping individual lawmakers I knew and admired. It was not until this meeting that I saw a more constructive way to address my frustrations with the state of the GOP. It was time for gay and lesbian Republicans like me to step forward and fight for our party.

Eventually, I learned Rich would have been a compelling figure regardless of what he was championing. He is smart, articulate, and calm, all of which helped him make a great advocate for Log Cabin. Rich graduated from Harvard Divinity School, giving him the ability to debate the Bible-quoting leaders of the religious right. His knowledge of biblical scripture allowed him to go toe to toe with these demagogues, countering their arguments verse for verse. At the event, I wrote Rich a large check, at least by my standards, and said, "Let me know how it goes." As far as I was concerned, that was it. I was going full bore at my law firm and didn't want nor anticipate any long-term commitment to the organization.

Months later I got a call from Rich asking me to be a founding member of Log Cabin's national board of directors. I accepted. Six months after that, he asked me to serve as chairman of the board because Marvin Collins insisted on stepping aside from that role. At the time, I was the only Washington-based board member; all the other members were from other parts of the country. When I was asked to be chairman, I instinctively went to Chuck Manatt for his advice and, hopefully, his blessing. By that time, he had become a close friend and mentor, so I sought his advice and counsel about the new role I had been asked to assume. When I asked what he thought, Chuck quickly replied, "Bob, I would be proud to have the chairman of the Log Cabin Republicans as one of my law partners." That moment remains one of the highlights of my professional and political life.

The initial Log Cabin office staff included Rich as executive director, Kevin Ivers as the political and communications director, and an office assistant. Both Rich and Kevin were smart and had incisive political minds capable of sizing up a situation and knowing the appropriate response. With my experience working in politics and navigating the corridors of power in Washington added to the equation, we made an effective team. Aside from anything else, I had a D.C. rolodex that we used to help Log Cabin. Rich and Kevin had remarkable political instincts. And they had the ability to set a political goal and to maintain laser focus on achieving it, something rather rare in today's political world. I largely stayed out of the news media, but Rich and, to a lesser extent, Kevin, were out front and subject to attacks from all sides, including the LGBT community. They both had thick skin and resiliency, much needed attributes for the arrows fired in their direction on an almost daily basis. They relished their role and quickly grew to be effective in outreach to congressional Republicans and other national GOP organizations.

In the early days as board chairman, I focused mainly on raising money, as it should have been. While I was behind the scenes most of the time in Log Cabin, there was a point where I became more publicly visible, joining Rich on occasion as spokespeople for the organization and its causes. When I was quoted in the *Washington Post*, it marked the first time that many people I had known for years in D.C. may have realized I was gay. I asked a long-time female friend of mine if she was surprised to learn of my sexual orientation. "No, indeed," she said, "women know when a man is interested in women or not." What she was really saying was, "If you weren't interested in me, you MUST be gay!"

We had humble offices, subletting space from organizations such as PFLAG (Parents and Friends of Lesbians and Gays) before eventually moving into a small office of our own on 17th Street NW, near Dupont Circle. At that time, the area was moderately priced and the center of gay life in Washington, so placing our office in that location was motivated in equal parts by our desire to make a political statement in D.C.'s LGBT community and a keen awareness of our bank statement. We used to describe it as the perfect Republican organization, because it was austere, with a small staff and a humble office. We grew slowly and deliberately, only as our budget allowed. By comparison, groups such as the Human Rights Campaign had dozens on staff as opposed to our three. But we matched them in media attention and, more importantly, in impact with our target audience, Republicans in Washington. We quickly began punching above our weight with significant attention in the national media.

We had some thin times, including more instances than I like to remember of barely having enough to make our small payroll and pay the rent. Not long after becoming board chairman, Rich called me to the office and told me the organization had been the victim of mismanagement, theft, or both. Rich, Kevin, and I were concentrated on the political fortunes of the organization and the board member tasked with responsibility for the group's finances had botched the job to the point where we literally had no money. I knew right away that the only course of action would be a direct appeal to our board. The national board was made up primarily of individuals who were successful businesspeople or professionals. As board members, they had already committed to donate or raise at least $5,000 each year. I called the board members and explained the situation as openly and as honestly as I could; they responded with the funds we needed to carry forward.

I met with Rich, Kevin, and the junior staffer we employed at the time. I told them the board had stepped forward to provide enough funding to keep the doors open, at least in the short term. We would get more time to raise additional dollars from new supporters. I have heard Rich and Kevin tell the story, and when they do, they make me out to be a hero of sorts. For me, it wasn't a heroic act; it was about trying to do the right thing to get out of a difficult financial situation and to convince others to follow suit. We focused mainly on developing and then cultivating a major donor base that was national in scope. Rich and others regularly travelled around the country to raise money. Financially speaking, we were far behind other LGBT political organizations. But we were able to reshape the thinking of the GOP and others on our issues because we were competent and passionate. Having passion, a moral vision, and the ability to articulate that vision allowed us to overcome our financial challenges. It also helped that we had the ability to attract national media coverage. Reporters thought we were an anomaly. They found the existence of gay and lesbian Republicans as a surprise, so they gave us coverage, lots of it.

One of the fundraising errors we made in those early days was to ignore the social component of the organization. We had to find ways to make being a Log Cabin supporter more fun. We learned we couldn't just inform and educate our constituency. We had to entertain them as well. And we had to facilitate social connections between our members from around the nation. Our members wanted to feel good about themselves and the causes they supported. They also wanted to meet like-minded people. Throwing a good party is a time-tested way to do that. HRC excelled at black tie events and other fun outings for their members. We needed to find our own ways to throw a party. Our solution was to showcase the nation's capital. We began holding an annual Washington fly-in for major donors that included meetings with their members of Congress and a formal dinner, giving our major supporters the opportunity to network, talk shop, and just have a good time.

At these fly-ins, we reserved a room in one of the House office buildings and invited GOP members of Congress to address our group. The first year we had just a few members speak, but within a few years we had to turn members away, as this part of our program was overbooked. At our first fly-in, we hosted a reception in the Eisenhower Lounge on the first floor of the National Republican Club close to the Capitol. We invited Republican members of Congress to join us at the reception and a surprisingly large number attended.

In the evenings, we hosted a dinner with well-known keynote speakers. An early speaker was Chris Matthews. Matthews loved the fact that our politics went beyond LGBT issues into areas such as defense, economics, and education. He thought our group was well informed and sophisticated, so much so that he invited Rich, then Board Chairman Bob Stears, and me to come on his show *Hardball*. During another annual fly-in, conservative commentator Bill Kristol addressed our major donor dinner. He seemed uncomfortable at first but warmed to the audience when he realized he was among like-minded conservatives.

At our national convention banquet in 1998, the keynote speaker was then-conservative pundit and commentator Andrew Sullivan. He gave one of the first speeches I had heard advocating marriage equality.

I was particularly struck by his statement that heterosexual prisoners on death row had a right to marry before their execution, but gays and lesbians did not have that same right under any circumstances.

When Senator Lugar learned I was chairman of Log Cabin, he was extremely supportive. Ever the forward thinker, Lugar was the first senator to sit down with Log Cabin's leadership. And I didn't even have to request the meeting. His chief of staff reached out to Rich to ask for a meeting. After Rich met with the senator, his chief of staff told me that Lugar was fascinated by the idea of Log Cabin. "He can't stop talking about the meeting. He is fascinated that a gay person would consider voting for a Republican." In fact, *The New York Times* exit polls show that in presidential elections about 25% of the LGBT community typically votes Republican.

The mission of Log Cabin Republicans is to advocate among fellow Republicans for liberty and equality for LGBT Americans. The GOP is the party of Lincoln who liberated the slaves and tried to give them the same freedoms as other Americans. Liberty and equality are at the heart of being a Republican and no Republican group addresses those issues for LGBT Americans better than Log Cabin.

Log Cabin now has dozens of chapters in more than half the states, with multiple chapters in larger states such as California, Texas, Florida, and New York. The organization sprang up from humble beginnings. The movement started as a series of local clubs, the first of which formed in San Francisco in 1977. The impetus for the formation of the club was the Briggs Initiative, which, as I mentioned, would have banned gays and lesbians from teaching in California public schools. Orange County GOP State Senator John Briggs introduced Proposition 6 after being inspired by Anita Bryant, the ex-beauty queen who had found a second career championing social conservative causes in her adopted home of Dade County, Florida.

After the historic victory defeating the Briggs Initiative in 1978, the group of Bay Area gay and lesbian Republicans that had dubbed themselves the Log Cabin Club kept up their efforts.The small band of GOP stalwarts worked to oppose other misguided legislation and make an inclusive case for gay people in the GOP. In short order, other Log Cabin Clubs sprung up elsewhere in California and around the country, including Washington, D.C. Most were organized independently and focused almost exclusively on local issues, but they were aware of each other's existence and drew on the manpower and expertise of neighboring chapters.

Members of these Log Cabin Republican Clubs were determined and tenacious people.You had to have those characteristics as an out gay or lesbian Republican in 1978 and into the 1980s. Most of the original Log Cabin members were business and professional people who wanted to protect and advance their rights as Americans. Many would have been happy being labeled libertarians. Most of the original members are long deceased, including many victims of the AIDS epidemic which took so many people long before their time. In fact, the first effort to form a cohesive national organization started during the 1987 national gay rights march in Washington. Log Cabin leaders from around the country met after the rally to map out plans for a national group. Within two years, the effort floundered after nearly the entire original five-member national board died of AIDS.

Eventually, the various city and state clubs found it helpful to coordinate through what became known as the Log Cabin Federation. Not long after the national office opened, the Federation and Log Cabin Republicans merged into one national organization known since as Log Cabin Republicans.We are all part of the same movement to advance freedom and liberty for LGBT Americans.

Log Cabin became the go-to LGBT organization for Republican lawmakers, many of whom found other LGBT organizations such as

HRC unreliable. For many years, HRC had token Republican board members they touted to GOP Members of Congress, but it was rare for HRC to endorse a Republican over any Democrat. When it became clear HRC had become an arm of the Democratic National Committee, Republicans shunned them.

The mission of our national office in those early days was to be a resource to GOP members of Congress, the White House, and Executive Branch agencies after George W. Bush became president. We focused on issues that would have the most impact on our community. In the mid-1990s, the AIDS epidemic was in full swing with thousands of gay men and increasing numbers of heterosexual African American and Hispanic men and women dying every year. Effective drugs had not yet been developed and the process for drug approval was painfully slow at a time when we urgently needed faster and more dramatic action. We worked with key members of Congress and the Bush administration to expedite drug approvals and to fund programs such as the Ryan White Care Act which provided funding for antiretroviral drugs to those who could not afford them. Eventually we worked with the Bush White House and key Congressional leaders to pass the President's Emergency Plan for AIDS Relief (PEPFAR) that continues to help save millions of HIV-infected patients in Africa and parts of Asia.

For more than twenty-five years, I have been involved with Log Cabin Republicans. After serving several years as chairman of the group's national board of directors, I then chaired the Liberty Education Forum, the nonpartisan foundation affiliated with Log Cabin. I resigned from both boards to run for chairman of the D.C. Republican Party. My years of experience with Log Cabin effectively prepared me for the trials of running a minority political party in Washington. In fact, it was my reputation for fundraising and ability to deal with different personalities in a constructive way that persuaded several D.C. Republican Committee members to vote for me over my opponent who had no fundraising experience. I know from firsthand experience that it takes money to run a political party or a political organization of any kind.

Being part of Log Cabin has been one of the most important and rewarding experiences of my life, both politically and personally, as I have formed lifelong friendships with some people I met along the way. It has given me a platform to address issues within the Republican Party such as the rise of the Christian right and more recently the Tea Party movement.

As gay and lesbian Republicans, one of our most difficult challenges has been dealing with others in the LGBT community. We have been called a variety of names including "Jews for Hitler." A long-time friend included in his dating profile this warning: "Republicans need not apply." That sentiment has been more common than not among gays and lesbians in Washington. It is somewhat better now, especially among those in the community who are familiar with the work Log Cabin has done over the years. However, early on it was common for gay Republicans to be verbally attacked in bars and other public places. The height of this treatment was during Senator Jesse Helms' years in the U.S. Senate. When I became active in Log Cabin Republicans, some gay men I knew avoided me. Despite the occasional discomfort of this situation, it didn't particularly bother me. If someone didn't want to talk to me or invite me to a party or event because I was a Republican, I viewed it as their loss for being so narrow-minded.

Most gay and lesbian Republicans will tell you it was easier to come out as gay to their straight friends and family than Republican to their gay and lesbian friends. This negative attitude from fellow gays caused many of us to band together as gay Republican brothers and sisters. It was even more difficult for lesbians to come out as Republicans in the lesbian community. Over the years many LGBT Republicans have dropped out of the GOP, especially after President George W. Bush endorsed a constitutional amendment defining marriage as between one man and one woman, and then when Donald Trump became the GOP nominee and elected president. Most former Republicans became independents rather than Democrats. I felt it was my obligation to stay and fight for the kind of Republican Party I've believed in for decades. I also believed it was important to set an example for younger LGBT conservatives to stand by their political views and stand up for a Republican Party that supports equality for all. One can be a more effective fighting for change inside the tent than agitating for change outside it.

I became involved in Log Cabin Republicans after the divisive 1992 presidential campaign. Social conservatives had taken over the party, so Log Cabin opened a national office in D.C. to fight back. This photo is from a D.C. gathering where Log Cabin members from all over the country came together to meet with Members of Congress and for socializing.

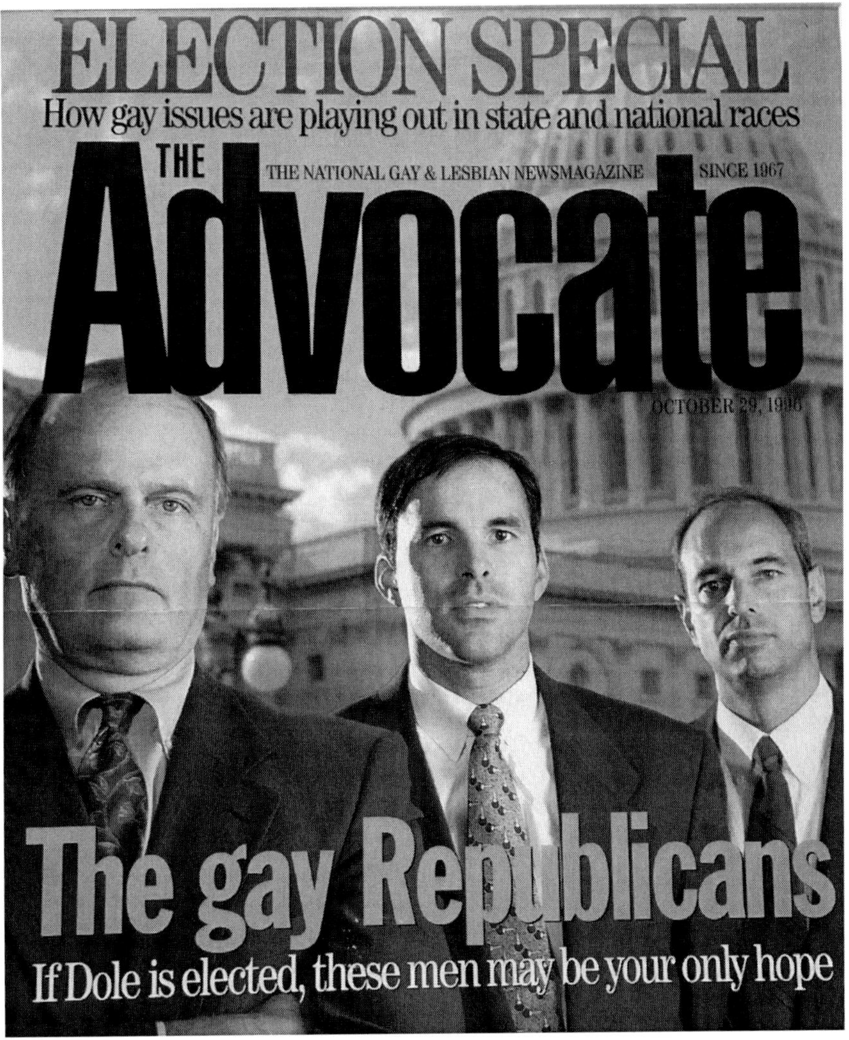

The Advocate is a national LGBT news magazine. I graced the cover just before the 1996 presidential election, along with Carl Schmid (right), and Rich Tafel, my close friend and Log Cabin's first executive director.

This historic 1999 photo is from Log Cabin's meeting with Arizona Senator John McCain during his first presidential campaign. Social conservatives used the meeting to attack McCain later in the campaign.

CHAPTER 17

The Good Fight

DURING PRESIDENT CLINTON'S FIRST TERM, PUBLIC OUTCRY over the prospect of Hillarycare and other big government programs swept Newt Gingrich and the Republicans to the majority in the House of Representatives in the 1994 midterm elections for the first time since the 1950s. The leadership at Log Cabin's Washington office had an incredible opportunity, but our work would be cut out for us. We were now dealing with Republicans as the majority party in the House and the Senate. It meant meetings with committee chairs and other power brokers who would have policy and budgetary power. It was, as the saying goes, showtime.

With newfound power and influence during the mid-'90s, Log Cabin prioritized our goals for policy and funding initiatives. The four pillars of our efforts included promoting HIV/AIDS research funding, fast-tracking FDA approval for drugs, the repeal of "Don't Ask Don't Tell" (DADT), and the legalization of marriage for gay and lesbian couples. Also, there was a desire to see the Employment Non-Discrimination Act (ENDA) enacted but it was not at the top of our list. Many of us thought the marketplace would take care of most employment discrimination as employers compete for qualified workers. The top priority was AIDS research and funding, which made perfect sense, as gay men, and increasingly others, were dying from a disease that had no cure or effective long-term treatment. What good would other rights and protections be if no one was alive to enjoy them?

Some Republican lawmakers refused to work with other LGBT organizations that were relentlessly critical of them but saw a friendly approach by LCR. Log Cabin worked with congressional Republicans to authorize and fund the Ryan White Comprehensive AIDS Resources Emergency (CARE) Act, which was the largest federally funded program for people living with HIV/AIDS. It aimed to improve the availability of care for people with AIDS and their families who were poor, uninsured, or both. The program also promoted the development of antiretroviral drugs by pharmaceutical companies, both in encouraging them to produce the drugs and trying to streamline the regulatory approval process. The law was named in honor of Ryan White, an Indiana teenager who contracted HIV through a tainted blood transfusion. White faced terrible hatred and discrimination from some in his community who tried to keep him from going to school. With quiet dignity, this young boy showed the world that AIDS was not a plague brought by God to smite homosexuals. It was a frightening, insidious illness putting people at risk from all walks of life. The pharmaceutical companies began funding virtually every AIDS advocacy group out there, including Log Cabin, and we used the money to good effect. Due largely to our efforts, the Republican-controlled Congress approved more funding for AIDS research than the Clinton administration recommended in its budgets.

Republicans such as Senator Arlen Specter of Pennsylvania and Congressman John Porter of Illinois were instrumental in the successful effort to increase funding for AIDS research and treatment. They went up against a small but determined minority in the GOP caucus led by Senator Jesse Helms of North Carolina. Helms was among the worst members of Congress with whom we dealt. We always thought it peculiar that Helms had gay men working on his staff. I don't know if he knew it or not, but we did. He wasn't alone; Rick Santorum, while good on HIV/AIDS issues but otherwise homophobic, had gays on his staff too. As noted earlier, few Republicans wanted to work with the Human Rights Campaign or other LGBT groups; no matter what they did, HRC and others would not give them credit or support the candidacy of a Republican. We were the right group in the right place at the right time.

During the early years of the epidemic, there were no known drugs to treat HIV/AIDS but that eventually changed. The first drug was AZT which had been developed as a cancer treatment. It caused severe nausea, and some thought it was in fact doing more harm than good. Other drugs came along but often were difficult to use, had terrible side effects, and/or cost a fortune. Finally, in 1996, a combination of three drugs, known as HAART, was introduced and became a highly effective treatment. Log Cabin was involved in streamlining the government approval process.

"Big Pharma" has a terrible reputation among many people, but tens of millions of people with HIV are alive today because of these companies. They have spent enormous amounts of money to develop effective antiretroviral drugs. Many in the AIDS community vilify "Big Pharma" for the prices they charge. It is true that patients in the U.S. pay for the research and development of new drugs through high prices. Much of the rest of the world benefits from this reality. Eventually, generics were approved, the costs started to be reduced and the federal government established programs such as the Ryan White Care Act to provide free or reduced cost drugs to millions of patients. The U.S. government was key in doing research to isolate the virus that causes HIV/AIDS and to some extent in the development of antiretroviral drugs, but it was "Big Pharma" that discovered key breakthroughs and actually developed the drugs. Today, these companies are working to improve existing drugs, develop new ones, and create a vaccine to prevent HIV.

In the mid-'90s, Rich Tafel was scheduled to appear on the same television show as Patrick Buchanan. They were both in the green room, the waiting area for guests before they go on the air. Buchanan walked over to Rich and said, "You guys should thank me; I raised a lot of money for you!" They both got a professional laugh from it. Over the years, Buchanan has never softened his opposition to LGBT equality.

The summer of 1996 brought Log Cabin unprecedented national media attention, thanks to Bob Dole's presidential campaign. As noted earlier, the Log Cabin organization was comprised of two arms, the national office and board and the federation of Log Cabin clubs around the country. It became clear that there was a need to formally integrate the organizations, for the sake of efficiency, effectiveness, and economics.

In 1996, that integration happened at a meeting of Log Cabin members from across the country in my hometown of Cincinnati. We had the opening reception downtown in the garden of the Taft Museum. I thought the main drama over the course of the meetings would be internal. I was wrong. A few weeks before the Cincinnati convention, Rich had engaged in discussions with the Dole presidential campaign which led to the donation of $1,000 to the campaign from Log Cabin's PAC. But at the opening reception, Rich announced the check had been returned by the Dole campaign. It was more proof about the importance of having a strong presence in Washington. The return of the Dole check garnered intense national media attention for Log Cabin. Over several weeks, high profile news stories chronicled the Dole campaign's defense of its decision to return the check. It was almost comical to watch the Sunday morning political shows as various commentators talked about their "discovery" of Log Cabin. About a month after the incident on a Sunday talk show interview, Dole was again asked about the controversy. He said, "Well, if they had asked me, I would have said keep it." His position was very much like that of Ronald Reagan: If someone agreed with him on most of the issues, why not accept their support?

This was a classic example of how Bob Dole's campaign assured his loss in November. As with Mitt Romney in 2012, if Dole had just been himself, he would have done much better. But, the highly paid political consultants around him kept his humorous and human side hidden from the American electorate.

Another example of the importance of Log Cabin and its foundation, Liberty Education Forum (LEF), was our work to preserve the 1998 Clinton executive order prohibiting discrimination based on sexual orientation within the civilian government workforce. ("Don't Ask, Don't Tell" or DADT had been enacted as the official policy in the military). After George W. Bush was elected President in 2000, some conservatives pushed Bush to repeal the Clinton executive order. In response, LEF retained a former Republican chairman of the Federal Election Commission to prepare a white paper opposing the repeal. On January 20, 2001, we delivered the LEF white paper to White House staff who we knew could have an impact on what we expected to be a hot internal debate. We also provided a copy of the white paper to Attorney General John Ashcroft, who Log Cabin had helped during his Senate confirmation. Ashcroft had been accused by Democrats of discriminating against gays and lesbians when he was the governor of Missouri. We checked out the allegations and concluded they were false, so we quietly helped him win enough votes to be confirmed. During our meeting with him, he quickly confirmed that he agreed with us and had no intention of advocating repeal of the Clinton executive order. As it turned out, repeal of the Clinton executive order was not even given serious consideration by the newly installed Bush White House. The efforts by certain conservative think tanks such as Heritage Foundation had failed to turn back the clock on these protections for gays and lesbian federal employees. That was worth celebrating.

In 2004, my last year as LEF board chair, Log Cabin filed a lawsuit challenging the constitutionality of DADT.This lawsuit was unique among several lawsuits filed to overturn DADT because it was brought on behalf of gay Log Cabin Republican members who had been discharged from the military, thereby addressing the fundamental legal issue of standing.The case was taken on a pro bono basis by the prestigious "white shoe" law firm of White & Case. Marty Meekins, a Log Cabin board member who was an associate in the firm's Los Angeles office, persuaded White & Case to take the case. Over nearly eight years, White & Case and Log Cabin doggedly pursued the case

The Log Cabin lawsuit languished in a Federal District Court in California for several years. That is not uncommon, in both state and federal courts. Log Cabin filed our lawsuit in 2004. Several other LGBT organizations filed similar suits around the same time in other parts of the country. The Department of Justice aggressively worked to defeat all these cases. They succeeded in every case except Log Cabin's lawsuit. A typical litigation tactic is to file motions to delay and/or dismiss the case. The original federal district court judge assigned to our case delayed scheduling hearings on the White & Case motions. When the judge retired (thankfully), the Log Cabin case was assigned to another judge who was more interested in the litigation and began scheduling hearings. That was when the lawsuit began to move. Aside from the White & Case attorneys, Craig Engle, Log Cabin's outside counsel who had a successful election law practice at another firm, was instrumental in pushing the case forward.

The case ended up with District Court Judge Virginia Phillips who started hearings on the lawsuit. The political team in the Obama administration certainly started paying attention after the judge knocked down every DOJ motion to delay or dismiss the case. Judge Phillips made it clear the trial would move forward. It was set for July of 2010. What followed was a remarkable period where the Obama Justice Department advocated a position that conflicted with the views of President Obama. Even though he advocated for an end to DADT, his Justice Department fought to preserve the discriminatory law. With the 2012 re-election campaign not far off, Obama was in a difficult position. The lawsuit forced his hand. Secretary of Defense Robert Gates had said repeatedly he wanted to control the transition to a post-DADT military, not the courts. Once Log Cabin won our lawsuit at the District Court level in the late summer of 2010, the Obama White House and DOD aggressively pushed repeal legislation in Congress. In late 2010, the House of Representatives voted first to repeal the law with support from fifteen House Republicans. The bill looked headed for defeat in the Senate until Senators Susan Collins (R-ME) and Joe Lieberman (I-CT) used their many years of experience to get the legislation passed with strong bipartisan support. The pressure from Log Cabin's lawsuit had forced action in Congress.

I was delighted to be invited to the presidential signing ceremony. It was a great day when, for the first time, gay men and lesbian women could serve openly in our nation's military. As a former Army officer, I remember what it was like to worry about being found out and suffer the humiliation of being dismissed from the military because of my sexual orientation. While I never saw combat during my service, I was proud to have served my country as an Army officer and to be a part of the successful effort to bring justice for those gay men and lesbians who serve now and in the future.

Regardless of how successful we felt we had become in political circles, Log Cabin would never match the size and fundraising prowess of other LGBT organizations. Foremost among the other organizations is the Human Rights Campaign. Founded in 1980, 12 years prior to LCR, and known by its initials and its ubiquitous logo featuring a yellow equal sign on a blue background, HRC is the largest LGBT civil rights organization in the U.S., with about 1.5 million members and supporters. HRC has three parts: a lobbying arm that promotes and advocates for LGBT issues to government officials, a political action arm that raises money to assist candidates who support HRC's agenda, and a foundation that focuses research and education. HRC has always been the best-funded LGBT organization in Washington. In fact, HRC is an amazing fundraising machine, raising millions of dollars with a huge staff and its own building in downtown Washington. HRC's annual black-tie dinners outgrew every venue they tried and now is held in the cavernous Washington convention center.

Many people past and present wonder what the need is for the Log Cabin Republicans when there are other organizations like HRC that hold themselves out as bipartisan and are in theory advocating for the exact same things. The answer is quite simple; HRC is an unofficial arm of the Democratic Party. HRC rarely, if ever, endorses a Republican. If there was a Democrat and a Republican running with the same stand on LGBT issues, they would reliably support the Democrat. At its heart, HRC and other left leaning LGBT organizations have been more interested in advancing the goals of the Democratic Party than the gay community.

Eventually, I got tired of the strident partisanship of most other LGBT organizations. I quit buying tickets to most LGBT events after a pair of particularly toxic fundraising dinners for HRC and GLAAD. The HRC dinner was at least fifteen years ago. David Catania, the gay Republican member of D.C. Council whose campaign I chaired twice, was booed after being introduced. That was rude and nasty but also typical in an LGBT community, at least at that time, which disrespected anything not meeting their approval. Later that year, several gay Republican friends and I attended the annual dinner of GLAAD, an organization formed to fight defamation against LGBT people in the media. During the dinner, some unknown (at least to me) starlet said during her award acceptance speech, "As I was preparing to come here, I told my parents about the organization and my father asked me if any of 'those people' would be there. I said, 'Of course there will be gay people, Dad. How could you even ask that?' He said,

'Not them. I meant do you think there will be any Republicans?'"The room collectively groaned, including the 30 or so Republicans who had paid a hefty price to be the butt of a bad joke by a half-witted starlet. Afterward, I told GLAAD's executive director, "I'm done. I won't pay money to be insulted." I never went back.

While marriage equality is the political and cultural issue that HRC claims credit for changing, it was the Log Cabin Republicans that came out in support of marriage equality long before HRC and other liberal LGBT organizations. For years, HRC opposed promoting the freedom to marry. They thought it was "too far, too fast and would promote a political backlash that would set back the equality movement for decades. Instead, HRC wanted to focus on the Employment Non-Discrimination Act. Because of state legislative and court victories and, more importantly, the U.S. Supreme Court's decision to legalize same-sex marriage, it is the law of the United States; meanwhile the ENDA has still not been enacted.

At one Log Cabin board meeting, we were debating what our level of involvement should be regarding the Employment Non-Discrimination Act. I asked the room for a show of hands of anyone who had been fired or not hired because they were gay. Nearly every hand in the room was raised, including mine. I favor the passage of ENDA, and it probably would pass both houses if the leadership would allow it to come to a vote. Early in the debate about ENDA, many congressional Republicans opposed it because they said it would add an additional legal burden on small businesses, including the potential for costly litigation. However, ENDA and similar legislation exempts small businesses. And corporate America is nearly in unanimous support of legislation to prevent workplace discrimination against LGBT people. Big business, broadly speaking, has done an excellent job protecting LGBT employees. Market forces drove some of this, as did the American sense of fairness. The big tech companies and banking industries began more than twenty years ago to implement policies that abolished discrimination based on sexual orientation, and much of the private sector has followed suit. Today, most big businesses have adopted the principles embodied in the legislation on their own, though non-discrimination laws in nearly 20 states helped move the needle as well. Sure, there are outliers, and it will be the stubborn resistance of those companies that may require legislation like ENDA to be enacted when common sense and civility ought to be enough.

There isn't a lot of nuanced discussion about party politics in the LGBT community. The loudest voices among gay Americans have always been liberals. For them, there was no room for differing opinions on LGBT issues and tactics. You were either with them or against them. Not surprisingly, the hard right operated the same way. There is one basic premise underlying the mission of Log Cabin; if you don't understand why our organization is key to advancing equality issues, then you simply do not understand politics. Politics is about making a difference, and Log Cabin was created to change the hearts and minds of those in the Republican Party whose hearts and minds need changing. No civil rights movement in our nation's history has succeeded with support from only one party. Democrats alone won't be enough to provide full equality for LGBT people. We saw that with "Don't Ask, Don't Tell." It wouldn't have been repealed without sufficient support from Republican members of the Senate. We don't have a parliamentary system, so a bipartisan strategy is essential for success.

It's important to note that the whole party does not need changing. In fact, it is no longer political suicide for Republicans to be gay-friendly. Ronald Reagan is the perfect example, coming out against the Briggs Initiative. Many of his staff thought it was the wrong thing to do politically, but Reagan thought that it was a moral injustice and must be treated as such. Reagan had courage, and one of the things Log Cabin does well is to promote that kind of courage. The issues of concern to the LGBT community in recent years are different than when Reagan was in office. Debates about marriage equality and employment protections were years away, and the AIDS epidemic was just beginning.

HRC, with all its shortcomings, was there first with events such as National Coming Out Day and other initiatives such as its Workplace Equality Index, which scores corporate America on its LGBT inclusion. The index has helped make corporate America strong advocates for LGBT equality. Companies don't want to get a poor score in the index because they would turn off customers and potential employees. The index incentivizes better behavior. Several years ago, I was with a group of fellow Log Cabin Republicans and someone complained that all HRC does is have big black-tie fundraisers and not much more. Another person in the group responded, "That may be true, but they were out and doing good work in the gay community while I was still trying to find the closet door."

I met a lot of politicians over the years, especially in my leadership role at Log Cabin Republicans. This 2005 photo is with then California Governor Arnold Schwarzenegger.

Republican former Senator Al D'Amato from New York (second from left) made quite a mark in public office. This photo is from a 2005 Log Cabin Republicans event. My close friend Craig Engle (left) arranged D'Amato's appearance. Log Cabin's president at the time, Patrick Guerriero, is on the right.

CHAPTER 18

Pink Elephants

I CALLED LOG CABIN MY "SECOND FULL-TIME JOB" AND IT WAS not an exaggeration. I resigned my post from the LCR and LEF boards in 2004 after 10 years doing both. I decided to resign from them when I ran for Chairman of the D.C. Republican Party. There would not have been enough hours in the day to do both and maintain my private practice. Also, I promised people in the local party that I would not be directly involved in an advocacy group that, to some at least, might appear to pose a conflict of interest.

While I enjoyed my work and it provided a comfortable living, over time it became a little too routine and the spirit of the Manatt firm changed. Chuck Manatt was no longer running the firm, and the new regime had fostered a less collegial atmosphere than when I arrived. I decided to look for another professional home. I eventually returned to my Midwestern roots by joining Baker & Daniels in January 2002. The firm later merged with Faegre & Benson to form Faegre Baker Daniels and FaegreBD Consulting. I needed to practice in a friendlier atmosphere.

During my years at Faegre, among other things, I led the team representing the state-based insurance guaranty systems in Washington. In short, these two state-based systems, one for life and health and the other for property casualty, were the FDIC system for the state regulated insurance industry. We worked to protect the funds that were there to make insurance policy holders whole if their insurance company ever became insolvent. I enjoyed working with the presidents of the two organizations. Our busiest time for this client was the year leading up to the enactment of the Dodd-Frank Act and then its initial regulatory implementation period.

During the second term of George W. Bush, I served on the Presidential Advisory Commission on HIV/AIDS (PACHA). PACHA provides advice, information, and recommendations to the Secretary of Health and Human Services regarding programs, policies, and research to promote effective treatment and prevention of HIV/AIDS. I served on the international committee which focused primarily on the soon to be expiring PEPFAR program. PEPFAR was the program started by President George W. Bush to confront the HIV/AIDS epidemic in Africa. PACHA offered a series of recommendations to the administration for what should be included in the program's renewal. I met a lot of interesting and dedicated people, including several doctors who had been involved in HIV/AIDS work from the beginning of the epidemic. It was satisfying to put my expertise to work on this committee.

During this period, I participated in a congressional delegation trip to Mexico, Brazil, and Jamaica to explore ways to invest a portion of PEPFAR money to prevent the spread of HIV in South America and the Caribbean. We met with patient groups, local advocates, and the business sector. In Brazil, the American Chamber of Commerce sponsored a reception for our delegation.

Two interesting clients resulted from that trip. For both clients, I teamed up with my friend and former Log Cabin Executive Director Rich Tafel and another friend I met through Log Cabin, Abner Mason. Our group received a grant from the U.S. Agency for International Development (USAID) to build corporate membership councils in

Mexico and Jamaica to do workplace education on HIV/AIDS and encourage testing and treatment, if necessary. We called this initiative the Stigma Reduction Program. My role in developing these councils was to work with corporate government relations offices and other U.S. corporate offices to secure meetings in Mexico and Jamaica for our team on the ground building the councils. I also traveled several times over a two-year period to meet with corporate leaders to persuade them to join the council. The Mexico council became very successful and was viewed by many corporate members as a status symbol to have our logo on their front door.

During our meetings in Mexico, some corporate executives suggested we develop a corporate-based council on chronic illnesses such as diabetes, obesity, and cardiovascular diseases. Five years later, my partners and I launched the Workplace Wellness Council of Mexico which has become a leader in the field of corporate wellness in Mexico.

The Brazil trip also resulted in my representation of the Brazilian American Chamber of Commerce in Washington. My job was to extend and limit changes to Brazil's participation in the Generalized System of Preferences (GSP) which was up for reauthorization during the Bush administration. GSP laws were enacted after World War II to help underdeveloped countries improve their economies through exports to developed nations such as the U.S. and European countries. Many in Congress and the administration viewed Brazil as a difficult trading partner because of how difficult it was to resolve trade disputes. There was some truth to this contention. In fact, the U.S. and Brazil have never signed a single bilateral trade agreement despite an active trade relationship between these two large nations. The chamber brought delegations of corporate leaders to Washington to make the case for preserving Brazil's involvement in the GSP system. Brazil is a major producer of automobile parts. U.S. auto manufacturers imported auto parts duty free from Brazil to use in U.S. built vehicles. Bringing in the products duty-free allowed U.S. auto producers to build their vehicles at a much lower price. We argued that closing the door to Brazil by adding a tariff would open a huge opportunity for China. This argument proved effective and we succeeded in reauthorizing GSP and keeping Brazil in it.

I retired from Faegre in the summer of 2016. The firm hosted a retirement party for me in September of 2016 at the Metropolitan Club in Washington. Attendees included firm clients, my colleagues, and friends. I also sent invitations to RNC Chairman Reince Priebus and Co-Chair Sharon Day but didn't expect them to attend. To my surprise and delight, both attended, and Reince asked if he could make a short speech. He and Sharon had become my friends and allies on so many issues. Reince offered a positive and kind assessment of my role at the RNC and the many battles we had fought together. Both he and Sharon stayed for the entire program. The reception was a wonderful sendoff made even more special by the attendance of my RNC colleagues. Having come to Washington as a young lawyer 40 years before, trying to navigate the nation's capital as a gay Republican, this was quite a symbolic sendoff to my retirement. I sure had come a long way. So had the country.

Aside from my legal work, I was very proud of what we accomplished with Log Cabin Republicans. There was always one lingering internal question among the organization's membership: were we gay first or Republicans first? When President George W. Bush endorsed a constitutional amendment to prohibit same-sex marriage in early 2004, he made the decision for us. We had to be gay first, as a matter of self-preservation. The amendment also was a violation of core conservative principles. His support for the constitutional amendment was further evidence of how the definitions of Republican and conservative have shifted over time, just like the definitions of liberal and progressive. Liberal used to mean those who wanted freedom from government until William Buckley helped redefine those people as conservatives.

While I am most certainly a Republican, I am conservative on fiscal, defense, and foreign policy issues and libertarian on social issues. Many Log Cabin Republicans view themselves as libertarians. While many of our views may be libertarian, we recognize that the way to make a difference nationally is to make a difference in the Republican Party, not to bring the libertarians in from the cold. Again, the impetus for the founding of LCR was the hijacking of the Republican Party by the Christian right. I viewed it as their hijacking of MY party, not me infringing on their party. Log Cabin was created to meet a practical need. We filled the role no other LGBT organization could fill, and we did it boldly and tirelessly.

Some gay Republicans feel bitterness toward gay Democrats. I don't. The level of rhetoric has toned down somewhat over the years. There has been a lot of progress on LGBT issues, and both parties can take part of the credit. With Log Cabin's lawsuit playing a key role in the repeal of the "Don't Ask Don't Tell," it's clear we have made bipartisan progress. But still liberal Democrats and LGBT Democrats try to define the entire Republican Party by its extremes such as Texas Senator Ted Cruz. They won't say "Rob Portman is a great guy" or "Susan Collins and Lisa Murkowski are stand up senators."

The GOP needs the traditional establishment Republican Party. Observers have seen how states such as Kansas and Iowa were gradually infiltrated and taken over by the religious right. When moderate Republicans were forced out of the party in Kansas, they became Democrats and won elections. True politicians are some of the most practical people on the planet. They understand they cannot do anything if they are not elected, so the practicalities of winning elections can often overshadow all other priorities including consistency and morality. It might sound cynical, but there is reality and then there is political reality, and those who are best able to synthesize the two are the ones able to endure and actually enact their public policy priorities.

There is a misconception that the Democratic Party doesn't have any homophobes in it. That simply is not true; I have known Dems who publicly "accept" gay people because it is politically correct, while in private they are just as dismissive as anyone in the GOP. That fact is not a surprise if one understands the history of how FDR constructed the modern Democratic Party. It was a loose coalition of socially conservative Southern Democrats and liberal pro-union northern Democrats. There is still a residue of prejudice in the party to this day, although those who feel that way have enough guile to conceal it. The FDR coalition goes back to the time when the urban Democratic political machines were being built in northern cities. There was plenty of homophobia in place then, but the party leaders realized that gay people often lived in urban environments, voted and contributed to campaigns, and they could help them win elections. The acceptance of LGBT people into the Democratic Party was both a practical and essential step toward their domination of urban elections. This reality was accurately and elegantly depicted in the movie *Milk* about gay activist and path-breaking politician Harvey Milk, who was a Republican his entire adult life until deciding to run for public office in San Francisco as a Democrat in the early '70s.

Richard Nixon's Southern Strategy of the late '60s and early '70s that welcomed former Southern Democrats of all stripes into the party was the other side of the coin. Most Southern GOP politicians of today are not homophobic. In my role on the RNC, I regularly meet and work with Southern Republicans. Of course, that was not the case when North Carolina GOP Senator Jesse Helms and his ilk defined the party's hostile stance to gay rights. But that position evolved over time and Helms himself admitted towards the end of his career that one of his biggest mistakes was his opposition to AIDS funding.

Another Republican from that generation was Senator Strom Thurmond from South Carolina. His weaknesses and failures have been well-documented. He was a notorious womanizer, even when he was well into his 80s. Even though he built his career on racism and segregation, he fathered a child with his African American maid and kept it a secret. But I always thought he was a fascinating character study because of his ability to change with the times. He switched from Dixiecrat to Republican, and he mellowed his stance over time on a range of issues from civil rights to school busing to AIDS funding. By the end of his career, he was a man of advanced age but also a modern politician. Many of the generation of politicians that have succeeded him in South Carolina and other states may have learned from him. Former Republican Governor Nikki Haley and Republican Senator Tim Scott, both of South Carolina, are among the most forward-looking and thoughtful Republicans in the country. Add to that South Carolina's Republican national committeeman is African American, and it becomes clear South Carolina is much different than it was in the Nixon era.

Thurmond died before the gay marriage issue dominated political debates. It has been on the political radar since the passage of the Defense of Marriage Act in 1996. As the issue gained in notoriety and favor, social conservatives used the issue as a tool to raise passions and, more importantly from their perspective, money. Televangelist and one-time GOP Presidential candidate Pat Robertson was so successful raising money with phone banks and direct mail on the gay marriage issue that he once said, "If gays didn't exist, we'd have to invent them."

At many Log Cabin events, most attendees are young people in their twenties and thirties. Many of them have been out from a young age. Their attitude is "This is me: gay and Republican. I have nothing to apologize for." They have no thought about reprisals or recriminations from anyone, including LGBT Democrats and especially those in their age group.

I rejoined the Log Cabin board a few years ago and again am serving as chairman. I thought this was an important time to rejoin Log

Cabin's efforts to continue to make progress for the LGBT Americans. Also, after retirement, I had more time to devote to the effort. In the summer of 2019, Log Cabin's board voted to endorse President Trump for re-election. Our decision has been both controversial and rewarding. After going through the endorsement process outlined in our by-laws, including surveying our chapters throughout the country, the board overwhelmingly voted to endorse President Trump. Those members most unhappy with President Trump left the organization and party after the 2016 elections. The overwhelming number of current Log Cabin members supported the president and pushed for the board to endorse his re-election. After the board's decision, we lost a few board members but also gained several capable new board members as a result.

Our endorsement has provided us with the opportunity to work with the Trump administration on key initiatives of interest to our community, specifically the Trump initiative on HIV/AIDS that targets communities with high infection rates and his effort through the United Nations led by openly gay U.S. Ambassador to Germany Ric Grenell and our country's UN Ambassador Kelly Kraft to address laws that discriminate against LGBT people in countries around the world. In both of these initiatives, other LGBT organizations will never praise him. For them, no matter what he does, it's never enough.

There still are gay people who are closeted both as gay and Republican. On occasion, I will meet someone who shares with me that they aren't out. I have been there and done that with more than one partner. Joe, the partner I was with for the longest period, never wanted to admit he was gay, a notion most people around him found odd and disconnected from reality. I won't avoid someone because they are closeted. Many people believe they have good reasons for staying closeted. I know middle-aged men who have not come out to their families because they believe they would pay a high price. I don't judge them; it's a personal decision. But I made my decision long ago and am at peace. Our nation has progressed on LGBT equality mainly because more people are out now. Average Americans changed their views on LGBT issues when they learned family members and friends are part of this community.

There has been advancement on many issues of great importance to the LGBT community. HIV has become a manageable chronic disease for those who get tested and have access to life-saving medication. There's even a once-a-day pill that's almost 100% in preventing someone from contracting HIV. Additionally, the freedom to marry exists across the nation. And corporate America has done a remarkable job providing workplace protections for LGBT employees even as federal legislation on the issue remains stalled. The progress in corporate America is partly the result of changing public opinions on equality. Corporations know being LGBT supportive is the right thing to do, and it's good for the bottom line. More Americans support freedom and fairness for all Americans. The fact that the situation is so much better makes me proud of my country and in the political arena where I have spent my life.

I left Manatt at the end of 2001 and joined another firm, what eventually became Faegre Baker Daniels. I retired from that firm in 2016. This photo is from the retirement reception the firm hosted for me.

President George W. Bush was very impressive during personal interactions. He is quite warm and engaging. That didn't always come across on camera to the public.

Over the years, I have remained closely connected to my alma mater, Denison University. I was honored to serve on the school's Board of Trustees from 2005-2011. This photo is from a Denison capital campaign kickoff event in the early 2000s.

CHAPTER 19

The Long Haul for the Freedom to Marry

ON A COOL MORNING IN THE EARLY SPRING OF 2013, I STOOD ON the steps of the U.S. Supreme Court facing hundreds of people rallying in support of equality for LGBT people. I was representing Log Cabin Republicans at a rally in support of the plaintiff, Edith Windsor, in Windsor v. United States. The court was scheduled to hear oral arguments in her case which sought to have Section 3 of the Defense of Marriage Act (DOMA) ruled unconstitutional. Edith Windsor and Thea Spyer were legally married in Canada in 2007, and their marriage was recognized by the state of New York in 2008. Thea Spyer died of cancer in 2009 and left her estate to Windsor who sought to claim the spousal estate tax exemption, a provision in the tax code that allows a surviving spouse to avoid paying estate taxes on his or her inheritance. The Internal Revenue Service took the position that Section 3 of DOMA, signed into law by President Clinton, prohibited same-sex couples from claiming the exemption. As a result, Windsor was forced to pay more than $350,000 in estate taxes. She filed for a refund claiming that Section 3 of DOMA was unconstitutional.

When I took the podium and looked out at the large crowd gathered to hear speeches about the freedom to marry, I was humbled and proud. I talked about my experience as a gay Republican who had worked for two Republican senators and in the Reagan White House. I explained how I had done my best to live an open, honest life. I emphasized the importance of providing equal treatment before the law to loving and committed couples. It was a memorable and historic day, especially having the opportunity to represent Log Cabin Republicans, an organization that has been a major focus of my life for more than 25 years. Almost three months after oral arguments, the Supreme Court ruled that Section 3 of DOMA was unconstitutional under the equal protection guarantees of the Fifth Amendment. The ruling in favor of Edith Windsor was a major victory for LGBT Americans. She had approached several gay advocacy groups to represent her, but they all declined. Eventually, she found Roberta Kaplan, an attorney at Paul, Weiss, an old-line New York law firm to represent her. The ACLU joined in filing the case in the Federal District Court for the Southern District of New York. Edith Windsor was a courageous and determined woman. We are indebted to her for pursuing this case.

In the months after the Windsor decision, plaintiffs around the nation filed federal lawsuits in several jurisdictions arguing that state constitutional amendments banning same sex marriage violated the federal constitution. Eventually four Federal Circuit Courts of Appeal ruled such prohibitions unconstitutional. When the Sixth Circuit upheld a state statute prohibiting same-sex marriage, the Supreme Court was almost mandated to hear the case given the conflicting opinions among the circuits. Two years to the day after the Windsor decision, the Supreme Court went further in Obergefell v. Hodges by deciding the U.S. Constitution provided a fundamental right to marry for LGBT couples. As with the Windsor case, Justice Anthony Kennedy, a Reagan appointee, provided the swing vote and wrote the majority opinion. "In forming a marital union, two people become something greater than once they were," wrote Kennedy. "As some of the petitioners in these cases demonstrate, marriage embodies a love that may endure even past death. It would misunderstand these men and women to say they disrespect the idea of marriage. Their plea is that they do respect it, respect it so deeply that they seek to find its fulfillment for themselves. Their hope is not to be condemned to live in loneliness, excluded from one of civilization's oldest institutions. They ask for equal dignity in the eyes of the law. The Constitution grants them that right."

I never would have predicted the speed with which the freedom to marry became a nationwide right in our country. In hindsight, it's nothing short of breath taking. The Court's embrace of marriage equality would not have happened nearly so fast without increasing public support for same-sex marriage. Year after year, polling showed increasing support for the freedom to marry among various demographic groups, most notably among younger American who often grew up knowing LGBT people. The power of being out as a gay person was making a difference. Also, it was hard to deny same gender couples the right to marriage when so many heterosexuals were getting divorced and having kids out of wedlock. The institution of marriage was struggling, but that had nothing to do with gay and lesbian people. In 1950, 78% of American households were married; today it is less than 50%. It became harder to prevent a loving couple of the same gender from making a lifelong commitment through marriage.

Attitudes about the freedom to marry changed lightning fast not only for straight people, but also for LGBT people. When the movement for gay liberation, as it was then called, began in the late 1960s, few gays and lesbians favored marriage. Many were outright hostile to the notion, viewing it as a middle-class patriarchal institution that produced homophobes. Many gay liberation activists were mainly focused on securing sexual freedom. They didn't want to fit into heterosexual society and institutions like marriage, they wanted to be liberated from it. Early activism focused on getting the police to avoid hassling gay people at bars, clubs, and bathhouses. The controversy over closing gay bath houses during the AIDS crisis in the '80s is further evidence that many gay people of my generation were focused on sexual freedom not fitting in. However, AIDS eventually changed everything. As thousands of men were dying, their loved ones often didn't know they were gay until they were terminally ill. Issues such as visitation rights were the first compelling issue for gay men as their partners lay dying in a hospital. I know of too many sad stories during the early days of the AIDS crisis when gay men involved in long term relationships were denied hospital visitation rights to see their dying partner either by his family or hospital staff. Some even lost their homes having been kicked out by their partner's family. Gay and lesbian people saw firsthand that same-sex couples would benefit from the protections and benefits that come with government recognition of same-sex partnerships.

I witnessed several instances where a gay partner was denied hospital visitation rights and even told they were not welcome at the funeral. It's tragic enough to lose a partner, but it's unimaginable to be kept away from their deathbed and funeral. When my personal assistant at my law firm died, he was buried in a family plot near his birthplace in Kentucky. His partner, a D.C. fireman, was told he and other gay friends were not welcome at the funeral. Instead, his partner and other friends hosted their own Celebration of Life. These ceremonies were common for years during the height of the AIDS epidemic. The need for certain family rights became apparent and eventually LGBT organizations began advocating for them. Couples who had spent years together became interested in some official recognition of their relationships. This effort took various forms, including domestic partnerships that might include visitation rights and health care benefits among other things. Eventually, same-sex couples challenged the system through the courts. Supreme Court rulings like the Windsor and

Obergefell cases were the ultimate result of the four-decade effort to seek equality for LGBT families.

The push for the freedom to marry in the United States began almost 40 years ago with little progress to show for it. Hawaii put gay marriage on the national map in 1991 when three same-sex couples challenged state law regarding marriage in Baehr v. Lewin. A victory in the state Supreme Court was overturned after the adoption of a state constitutional amendment that provided the Hawaii legislature with the authority to deny marriage licenses to same-sex couples. Reacting to the Hawaii Supreme Court decision, Congress enacted the Defense of Marriage Act (DOMA) in 1996 which prohibited the federal government from recognizing same-sex marriages and permitted states to deny recognition of same-sex unions performed in other states. DOMA was passed with a substantial bipartisan coalition. President Clinton signed the legislation and highlighted his support for it in radio ads in conservative areas during his 1996 re-election campaign.

The following year, the fight shifted to Vermont where three gay and lesbian couples sued the state after being denied marriage licenses. Eventually, Vermont's Supreme Court ruled in favor of the couples in a late 1999 decision which said the state constitution entitles gay and lesbian couples with "the same benefits and protections afforded by Vermont law to married opposite-sex couples." To satisfy the ruling, state legislators in Vermont passed a law to provide civil unions for gay couples.

In 2003, Massachusetts became the first state to recognize same-sex marriage after a decision by the state's high court. There was an intense and concerted campaign to overturn the Massachusetts decision, which lasted several years. Even though the Bay State's legislature is dominated by Democrats, it took Republican support to defeat efforts that would have rolled back the freedom to marry. It was a huge turning point.

The Massachusetts case and similar efforts in other states to legalize the freedom to marry led President George W. Bush to use same-sex marriage as a wedge issue during his 2004 re-election campaign. Top political advisors, led by Karl Rove, worked with social conservative groups to place anti-gay marriage referenda and constitutional amendments on as many state ballots as possible. Rove hoped anti-marriage ballot initiatives would increase turnout among evangelical voters and other social conservatives. Because of that 2004 effort, fourteen states amended their constitutions to ban recognition of same-sex marriages and some even banned civil unions. In the years following the Massachusetts marriage decision, twenty-eight states passed similar state constitutional amendments.

In 2004, President Bush also endorsed a federal constitutional amendment that would have banned the freedom to marry nationwide. As a result, Log Cabin Republicans declined to endorse Bush's re-election, reversing its 2000 endorsement. As noted earlier, Log Cabin had been a supporter of marriage equality years earlier than any other LGBT organization. Bush's action in 2004 forced Log Cabin to stand up against a president of our own party, showing we were a gay organization first and a Republican organization second. Log Cabin spent more than $1 million in an effort to defeat the proposed constitutional amendment in the Senate. The effort was successful when the amendment failed even to get 50 votes in the United States Senate, well below the two-thirds threshold needed for constitutional amendments.

Key supporters of LGBT rights, including marriage equality, have been political liberals and libertarians. In fact, libertarians have been leaders on many LGBT issues over the years, including the freedom to marry. Key opponents have been political and religious conservatives. Numerous national organizations took up the anti-gay marriage cause including the Family Research Council, Focus on the Family, the Catholic Church, the Mormon Church, the Republican Party, and others. Some of these groups had principled reasons for their opposition, but some of them used the issue to raise money.

As with most movements, support builds gradually. Log Cabin played an early and continuing role in the push for marriage equality. The most important organization in this fight was Freedom to Marry, which was founded and led by Evan Wolfson. He formed the group in 2001 after he left the Lambda Legal Defense and Education Fund to focus exclusively on the freedom to marry. While extremely liberal, Wolfson understood the importance of making the campaign for marriage truly bipartisan. To his credit, that's what he did. He knew victory would be impossible to achieve without support from people across the ideological spectrum. Aside from a legal strategy, the movement for marriage succeeded by making progress in the court of public opinion. Without growing support for marriage among average voters, the U.S. Supreme Court would not have ruled for nationwide freedom to marry nearly as fast.

The debate over religious liberty began soon after the Supreme Court case. Of course, freedom of religion is a fundamental right guaranteed by the Bill of Rights. Religious conservatives quickly pivoted to freedom of religion arguments to counter the newly granted right to marriage. An early test of this was in Indiana where then Governor Mike Pence worked with conservative religious groups to craft a bill that was immediately attacked as being transparently anti-gay. The backlash to this legislation was immediate and ferocious. An organized effort to modify or repeal it was led by the Indiana business community which was concerned the law would scare away investment from the state. The backlash to the Indiana law bodes well in helping deter similar legislation in other states.

Kim Davis, the Kentucky county clerk charged with issuing marriage licenses, refused to do so due to personal religious objections. As a result, she spent time in jail when she disobeyed a Federal

Court judge's ruling to begin issuing marriage licenses to same sex couples. She became an immediate hero to some Christian conservatives. Clearly, she had the right to object and resign her position, but she refused and stood her ground while receiving a paycheck. She worked out an accommodation that calls for other officials in her office to issue the marriage certificates. The good news for the LGBT community is that key players including local business associations, mainstream churches, and the federal judiciary are there to help protect our rights.

Religious liberty is the next battlefront in the fight for LGBT equality. That's the issue in an important case that faced Supreme Court justices, the first LGBT-related case to reach the high court since 2015's Obergefell ruling. Masterpiece Cakeshop v. Colorado Civil Rights Commission is a troubling case. Jack Phillips, a talented baker, refused to make a cake for a gay couple's nuptials. He also refused to make cakes for other events that conflicted with his religious beliefs such as Halloween. The gay couple who had been denied service said they felt humiliated by his refusal to make a cake, even though they found another baker to make their wedding cake and Colorado did not yet recognize same-sex marriages. The couple filed a complaint with the Colorado Civil Rights Commission under the state's public accommodations law. Phillips had offered to sell them anything in his shop so long as it didn't reference a gay wedding. The commission ruled for the plaintiffs and mandated that the bakery change its policies and provide comprehensive staff training regarding public accommodation discrimination. The commission also said Phillips must provide quarterly reports for the next two years regarding the steps the store had taken and whether it had turned away any prospective customers. Phillips refused and decided to challenge the commission's ruling. His lawyers knew precedent would prevent him from using religious liberty to challenge the ruling, so they decided to make this a First Amendment case. His attorneys argued that his cake-making amounts to free speech, and he couldn't be compelled to engage in speech with which he disagreed.

There were several difficult issues for the court to resolve. It troubles me how quickly some in the LGBT community allege "discrimination" when someone denies service because of deeply held religious convictions. The oral argument before the Supreme Court was lengthier than usual and brought a number of challenging questions from justices about what should be a reasonable definition exception for artistic discretion.

In a 7-2 decision, the court held for the baker. On behalf of the majority, Justice Anthony Kennedy wrote that "the record here demonstrates that the commission's consideration of Phillips' case was neither tolerant nor respectful of his religious beliefs" protected under the U.S. Constitution. While the court ruled in favor of the baker in this case, this decision has not settled the law in this important area. Other cases will be brought.

There is a reasonable middle ground on these issues that respects both LGBT people and those with a religious concern about equality. Utah, for example, passed a bipartisan bill in 2015 that provided non-discrimination protections for LGBT people and people of faith. Even the Mormon Church supported the legislation. More issues like the Colorado case will come up in the years ahead and hopefully common sense will prevail.

I believe more conservatives will come to support marriage equality in the future because they will come to understand it's a conservative institution that benefits both the couple and society. When Britain's Conservative Party decided to support marriage equality in the fall of 2011, then Prime Minister David Cameron told party members, "It's about equality, but it's also about something else: commitment. Conservatives believe in the ties that bind us; that society is stronger when we make vows to each other and support each other.

So I don't support gay marriage in spite of being a Conservative. I support gay marriage because I am a conservative."

Cameron's eloquent statement succinctly states the conservative case for marriage equality. Marriage can be good for couples regardless of their circumstances. One of the reason LGBT people want the right to marry is they see the value of the institution. It provides stability and protection, especially for those raising children. To deny marriage to a whole class of individuals reduces their standing in society and weakens the institution of marriage.

Some deeply religious people, especially evangelicals and Catholics, may always have an issue with same-sex marriage. Most cite Biblical verses to support their contention, particularly the idea of Adam and Eve and specific passages in the Old Testament that often are misused and misinterpreted to demean gay and lesbian people. In recent centuries, the Bible also was misused to justify slavery, segregation, and the oppression of women.

Opponents of marriage equality always forget to mention how the institution of marriage has changed throughout history. The marriage we know today only came into being during the 16th century. Before that, and still in some societies, polygamy was the prevalent form of marriage. As society has evolved to become better educated and more tolerant, the traditions and acceptable definitions of marriage have changed. If marriage had not changed throughout human history, an adult man would be allowed to marry a 13-year-old girl, kids could be forced into an arranged marriage, a person would not be allowed to marry someone of a different race, religion or economic class, men could treat their wives as property, a husband would be allowed to have concubines in addition to his wife, and it would be impossible to divorce, no matter the reason. Marriage is a constantly changing institution so it makes sense that it should have evolved to include LGBT people.

As a member of the Republican National Committee, a short-term objective is to address the marriage issue differently during development of the 2020 GOP platform. In 2016, the Trump campaign turned the platform process, at least on social issues, over to social conservatives to write whatever they wanted. The 2016 platform repeatedly calls for reversal of the Windsor and Obergefell decisions either by the court or constitutional amendment. It also takes a strong stand against LGBT civil rights in any form. In 2016, there was a concerted effort to limit the GOP platform to a set of principles without turning it into a Christmas tree for special interest groups to add their pet language. Unfortunately, this effort fell short of the votes needed to adopt it. In 2020, a similar effort to limit the platform to a short set of principles is underway and reportedly has the support of President Trump. I anticipate the 2020 platform will be silent on many issues that had been mentioned in previous platforms, including those targeted against LGBT equality.

As a young gay man in a conservative Nashville during the early '70s, I would never have imagined living in a world where gay couples can marry. The change has been rapid and positive, so much so that we already look back and wonder what all the fuss was about. Giving LGBT people access to marriage hasn't weakened society, it has strengthened the institution of marriage for everyone.

I was honored to represent Log Cabin Republicans at a 2013 rally for the freedom to marry. This event happened in front of the United States Supreme Court.

President George W. Bush's top advisor, Karl Rove, was the architect of the 2004 Bush re-election strategy to use gay marriage as a wedge issue to energize social conservatives. That strategy is a stain on the legacies of Bush and Rove. This photo is from a fundraiser during the second term of President Bush for the District of Columbia Republican Party.

Mary Cheney is the lesbian daughter of former Vice President Dick Cheney. She became a campaign issue in the 2004 election when Sen. Joe Lieberman brought up her name during a question about LGBT rights in the vice presidential debate. Her father famously said, "Freedom means freedom for everyone." This photo is from a Log Cabin Republicans Spirit of Lincoln dinner when Mary Cheney was the keynote speaker.

CHAPTER 20

D.C. Republicans: Worth the Effort

IN LATE 1999, MY FRIEND AND MENTOR CHUCK MANATT SUGgested I run for Republican National Committeeman in the District of Columbia. I thought it was a crazy idea until I attended a few DCGOP meetings and saw firsthand the organization's ineffectiveness. I had met Julie Finley, the then chair, during my involvement in a couple local Republican campaigns. I liked her very much. When I told Julie of my interest in running, she said I should become actively involved in the local party first. After attending a few meetings, I saw the inactivity of the incumbent committeeman. I had worked on his congressional campaign a few years earlier, but now I decided the party needed a fresh face, me, to shake things up. While I saw a moribund local political party, I also could see lots of potential based on my experience working with a pair of Republican politicians in D.C.

When I announced that I was running, two things quickly happened: the incumbent committeeman announced he would not seek re-election and I became the "skunk at the picnic" because I dared to "jump rank" and run against a longtime party favorite. D.C. is divided into eight wards and I won six of them, but that wasn't enough to win.

The longtime favorite won Ward 3 which at the time was the most Republican ward. The only other one I lost was Ward 4 where the third candidate lived. I finished a respectable second place.

My interest and involvement in the D.C. GOP is consistent with a lifelong effort to make a difference in tough situations. What could be more of a challenge than becoming a leader of an urban political party with less than seven percent of registered voters, as it is in the District of Columbia? Part of the reason for my interest was the challenge itself. Also, I recognized the damage being done by one-party Democratic rule, in virtually all the nation's urban areas.

My involvement in the D.C. GOP traces back to my work with Log Cabin Republicans. I had volunteered on the campaigns of two D.C. Republican City Council members: first for Carol Schwartz whose campaigns had been run by local Log Cabin chapter volunteers and subsequently David Catania whom I met after he won a special election to fill an open seat on D.C. Council. David's first re-election was less than a year after his successful special election. He attended an annual Log Cabin Republican fundraiser at my home and took me aside to ask if I would chair his re-election campaign. He was honest to say he needed to raise money from gay Republicans nationally to have the necessary funds to run a competitive re-election campaign. He had not been in office long enough to raise dollars from the local D.C. business community as most local council members did. Add to that, his election was considered a fluke by most who gave him little chance of winning a full term.

In the special election, David defeated Arrington Dixon, a former City Council Chairman, who took the special election for granted and lost to David, an openly gay, young lawyer whose political experience amounted to one-term as an Area Neighborhood Commissioner (ANC) in the upscale neighborhood of Sheridan-Kalorama. ANCs are located throughout the city to provide grassroots input on zoning and neighborhood issues. David came from a politically active family in St. Louis. His godfather had been the Missouri Republican Party chair. David inherited his political savvy and instincts from his mother who had died of cancer some years earlier.

We raised enough money for David to run a successful campaign that November. He turned out to be a tireless and smart candidate. He won re-election easily and almost immediately became a highly successful fundraiser. From the get-go, David was an outspoken member of D.C. Council and an annoyance to just about anyone who came before him. When his political career ended in early 2015, he had burned many bridges. Instead of running for another term as an At-Large member of the council, David ran for Mayor as an independent. *The Washington Post* and other news organization highlighted David's abrasive personality and his penchant for political brawls. He lost to Democratic candidate Muriel Bowser by almost 20 points.

Carol Schwartz also asked me to chair one of her re-election campaigns, and I did so happily. She served one term on council in the '80s after first being elected to the D.C. School Board in 1974 while her three children attended the city's public schools. After her husband, a successful lawyer, committed suicide in 1988, she dropped out of politics until 1994. Carol reentered politics to run for mayor. Convicted criminal Marion Barry, the self-proclaimed Mayor for Life, defeated unpopular incumbent Sharon Pratt Kelly in the Democratic primary and Carol won the GOP nomination. While Barry won, Carol got 42%, far more than any other GOP candidate for mayor had gotten before or since.

Carol ran for an at-large council seat in 1996 and continued to be re-elected until she was defeated in the GOP primary in 2008 by Patrick Mara. He was a young former Congressional staffer who went door-to-door convincing D.C. Republicans to oust Carol in the primary and nominate him. Patrick Mara lost the election in November, losing the at-large seat to former longtime Democratic consultant turned D.C. "Independent" Michael Brown, who later pleaded guilty to corruption in office and resigned. The DCGOP challenged Brown's election on the grounds he was a Democrat who changed his registration to run as an Independent. This had become a common occurrence in recent years where Democrats changed their registrations to Independent for the sole purpose of running for the at-large seats reserved for non-majority party candidates. That provision was part of the Home Rule Act of 1973, a law passed by Congress and approved by D.C. voters, that gave more autonomy and local control to the District of Columbia.

Brown's election as an "Independent" was so egregious in its audacity that the DCGOP devoted some of its scarce resources to challenge Brown's election, first at the D.C. Board of Elections and Ethics and then in the courts. During the campaign, Brown's website described him as a Democratic political consultant and commentator. The Board of Elections took the position that it didn't have the legal authority to look behind the registration of candidates. A change to the D.C. statute would be required to permit them to do so. The courts concurred. We made our point even though we lost.

Carol was smart and a tireless worker. She seemed to be everywhere at the same time. For many years, she was the most popular local political figure and had a high level of support east of the Anacostia River in heavily African American Wards 7 and 8. Both David and Carol were strong, effective members of D.C. Council and they helped put the local GOP on the map. They had a falling out some years later but for a long time, they made an effective team on Council. Having even two Republicans on D.C. Council deterred most unethical behavior. Without them as watchdogs, there were several instances of unethical behavior by other council members (which I will discuss later.)

After my second-place finish for Republican national committeeman, I didn't lick my wounds for long. Betsy Werronen, the likely candidate to replace Julie Finley as chairman, asked me to run on her ticket as one of three vice chairs. I agreed and eventually won in a tight race. My assignment was to work with the ward chairs and help with fundraising. I did well enough at both and my reputation from my Log Cabin days as a seasoned fundraiser served me well when I ran for the chairman's position in 2004. A longtime member of the DCGOP ran against me, but I won with more than 60% of the vote. I won re-election two years later by the same margin and then was unopposed during the next two elections. Fortunately, I was term limited in that role. When asked, I always comment that only an insane person would serve eight years as Chairman of the DCGOP. Making the GOP more inclusive on LGBT issues was easy compared with trying to make D.C. friendlier to Republican ideas and candidates.

During my eight years leading the party, we had a small but highly active local GOP. During that period, Carol Schwartz lost in a GOP primary and then David left the Republican Party to become an independent because of President Bush's endorsement of a federal constitutional amendment to ban same sex marriage. That was David's stated reason, but he had told me previously that to run citywide for mayor or city council chair, he would need to become an independent in order to have a chance of winning. To Carol's credit, she never changed her party affiliation. With both Carol off the council and David no longer a Republican, the local GOP began to take stands on local issues that differentiated us from the incumbent Democratic mayor and D.C. Council. We highlighted issues that neither Carol nor David would have wanted us to address. These policy positions helped the party develop its own identity, separate from them.

Over the decades, one-party rule has taken its toll on many D.C. residents, particularly minority populations who remained and sent their children to the city's public schools and struggled to make a decent living. The District spends more money per student than almost any other school district in the country, nearly $20,000 per pupil. Despite piles of money, D.C. students have among the worst results in the nation, with nearly half not graduating from high school. D.C. schools are failing its students as most kids end up being woefully unprepared for the local workforce. In recent years, reform efforts have produced some gains, but much work remains to be done.

It is extraordinarily difficult for businesses to succeed in D.C., especially small and medium size companies. The largest employers in the District are the federal and local governments, four major universities, and Fannie Mae, the mortgage giant. All other large businesses in the region are headquartered in Maryland or Virginia. Small and medium size businesses encounter a complex and stifling regulatory maze. Despite occasional lip service about the need to curb regulatory overreach, no sincere or effective effort has ever been undertaken by the mayor or council. A Republican mayor or majority on D.C. council would streamline and rationalize regulatory requirements, allowing business to grow and thrive. Additionally, Republican stewardship of D.C. would create an education system that prepares young people to compete and succeed in our modern economy.

During my eight years as chairman, the local party was actively involved in helping weed out corruption in D.C. politics, including helping to uncover the corruption of three incumbent council members, including the chair. The scope of their corruption was breathtaking. Ward 5 Councilmember Harry Thomas Jr. was the most egregious. He had city council appropriate funds for after-school programs in his ward, focusing specifically on what he termed "swing" sports like baseball. But his was a corrupt plan that he barely tried to cover up. Most of the funds went directly into his bank account to purchase custom made suits, an SUV, a motorcycle, and expensive golf trips, just to name a few things. In 2012, he got sentenced to 38 months in federal prison for stealing $350,000 in city funds.

Also in 2014, City Council Chair Kwame Brown pleaded guilty to a federal felony charge of loan fraud and for violating D.C. campaign laws for failing to disclose certain payments outside of his official campaign. In addition to resigning as city council chair, Brown was sentenced to one day of confinement and six months of home detention.

As noted earlier, so-called Independent Council Member Michael Brown was convicted of accepting illegal campaign contributions and bribes from undercover FBI agents. He was sentenced to 39 months in federal prison. Brown is the son of the late Ron Brown, a former chair of the Democratic National Committee and commerce secretary during the Clinton administration. While we regularly ran candidates for council without success, our efforts at disclosing and weeding out corruption led to D.C. Council passing some minimal anti-corruption reforms and a more active United States attorney paying attention to corruption in D.C. politics.

As my last term was coming to an end, I tried to recruit qualified candidates to run for chairman. I should have started earlier to focus on this important task. The small group of qualified candidates didn't work out for various reasons; they were too busy with their careers, suddenly moved out of town, or had family obligations. This vacuum left an opening for an opportunist to come along and he did. At an early membership meeting in 2011, we brought on new members, including Ron Phillips, someone I had never met before. At the end of the meeting, Ron introduced himself to me and said he was off to visit clients for a few weeks but wanted to meet for coffee when he returned. I told him I would be happy to but was on guard after checking into his background.

At our first one-on-one meeting, he told me he had not seen a local GOP without an heir apparent to the retiring chairman. That was all I needed to hear to understand his objective was to run for chairman. After our third meeting, he announced he was running and began mounting the most aggressive and ugly campaign I have ever seen. The more I learned about his behavior as chairman of a county Republican Party in Florida some years earlier, the more I became concerned about his intentions for the DCGOP.

Phillips started a full press campaign to gather support from DCGOP committee members who elect the officers. At the time, central committee had a little more than 100 members and to his credit he did his best to meet with all of them to discuss his plans. In early April of 2012, I was elected National Committeeman on the D.C. primary ballot. My term as committeeman was to begin the day after the RNC ended. Ron immediately started insisting I resign the chairmanship as soon as I was sworn in as committeeman. If I had resigned, the senior vice chair, a good friend and reliable colleague, Margaret Melady, would have become chair under our bylaws.

After consulting with other committee officers, I decided to remain as chairman through the November election less than two months away. Nevertheless, the hounding from Phillips never ceased. Because of my decision, committee meetings became battlegrounds. It was a classic case of us versus them. Given how ugly Ron and his supporters were, no one wanted to run against him knowing how he would personally attack them. To put it in perspective, we are talking about the D.C. Republican Party, not the RNC or even a large state GOP, but the Republican Party of Washington, D.C. Rather than recruiting candidates and raising funds, all of that stopped for the sole purpose of electing Ron and discrediting the "old guard." Having challenged the status quo several years earlier by running for national committeeman in 2000 to try to bring life back to a moribund political party, I was now the "old guard."

After Ron's election in January of 2013, he alienated nearly everyone who had worked hard to build the party and instead brought in new people whose only qualification was their pledge to support Ron.

Most executive committee meetings ended up being a shouting match often with Jill Homan, the national committeewoman, and myself taking the brunt of angry criticism for not helping raise money, among other charges. Fundraising dropped off dramatically. Members stopped attending and got tossed out of the party under newly passed bylaws that included absurdly strict attendance requirements. That happened to several local members, some of whom subsequently returned, and others have not. With limited funds, Phillips asked RNC Chairman Reince Priebus to use office space for the DCGOP. He kindly agreed but with the understanding it would be only for a few months.

It was painful to watch a party I had helped build come apart. It's hard enough being a Republican in D.C. To be effective, party members must effectively work together to advance our priorities. Ron divided our small group and went to war with good and loyal people. An already hard job became even more difficult.

After much effort, a terrific leader, José Cunningham, stepped forward and defeated Ron by a margin of two to one in January of 2015. Ron and his supporters had exhausted everyone. Those two years were draining and a total waste of time and energy. After Ron's departure, an audit of the party's books determined that his hand-picked Executive Director had stolen funds from the party. He set up two accounts with similar names. One of them was the legitimate state party account and the other went directly into his bank account. That person ended up pleading guilty to one count of felony theft. Ron Phillips was censured by the executive committee for gross mismanagement.

These were the two most trying years for me during my lengthy career in politics. But diligence and tenacity paid off as people stepped forward to right the ship and get back to the challenging work of building a viable, effective alternative political party in our nation's capital. The challenge continues.

I served 20 years in various leadership roles at the D.C. Republican Party. This is a campaign flyer from my last election in 2016 to be Republican national committeeman for D.C.

This is a photo from the 2008 Republican National Convention. Tony Parker (left) was the Republican national committeeman for D.C. at the time and Betsy Werronen was the national committeewoman.

To Bob
Best Wishes,

As chairman of the D.C. Republican Party from 2004 through 2012, I had the occasion to meet President and Mrs. Bush several times.

CHAPTER 21

The Obama Years

BY 2008, THE LGBT COMMUNITY HAD EXPERIENCED INCREDIBLE progress both in the court of law and the court of public opinion. Five years before, the U.S. Supreme Court had struck down anti-sodomy laws, and that same fall the Massachusetts Supreme Court ruled that same-sex couples could not be denied marriage licenses. Meanwhile, HIV/AIDS had become a manageable disease for many, but the level of new infections in certain populations remained stubbornly high. Average Americans were showing more favorable views toward gays and lesbians. The Democratic Party welcomed members of the LGBT community while many in the GOP continued to resist efforts by Log Cabin Republicans and others for more acceptance.

Barack Obama was elected president on a campaign of hope and change. He aggressively ran against the record of President George W. Bush and, on virtually every issue, tied Senator John McCain to the Bush record. With the nation in a deep economic crisis, a seemingly endless war in Iraq, and close to a financial meltdown, he easily won the presidency. In this environment and after eight years of a Republican president, his election was all but guaranteed once he survived the long primary campaign against Senator Hillary Clinton, a well-known politician and former first lady. The Democratic primary was long and tough. The Obama team outsmarted a Clinton campaign that couldn't get its act together, in part because of internal feuding.

By any standard, President Obama is an historic phenomenon. He brilliantly offered Americans an optimistic vision for the future, promising a less partisan atmosphere in Washington and a more civil approach both in politics and society. He also offered a fresh approach to fix the ailing economy where GDP was shrinking and millions of people were out of work. Obama defeated the Clinton political machine by running a flawless campaign and repeatedly bringing up her votes in favor of the Iraq War and other unpopular topics with Democrats. He was the dove to her hawkishness, and it played well in the Democratic primaries, especially five years into the Iraq War. He also played on the fear that with Hillary we would get Bill again at a time when his reputation was still damaged, even among Democrats who didn't seem interested in creating a Democratic dynasty like the Republican Bush dynasty.

Before the 2008 primary season started, I remember discussions with Senator Lugar about Obama. He was very impressed with the junior Senator from Illinois. He said that if Obama won the presidency, he would expect to work well with him on a range of issues, especially those that would come before the Senate Foreign Relations Committee, typically considered one of the Senate's least political committees. After all, as the saying goes or at least used to go, all politics stop at the water's edge. Those comments coming from the man I admired most in the United States Senate went a long way with me. I also liked the elegant sophistication of Barack Obama in his style and the cool, collected way he carried himself. While I thought Obama might one day become president, I didn't expect he would be catapulted into the White House in 2008, when so many others were in line ahead of him on both sides of the aisle, in particular Senator Hillary Clinton, who I had begrudgingly grown to admire for her solid performance as a senator. Many will find these comments odd coming from a life-long Republican, but they result from years of observing politics and, especially, the U. S. Senate, one of the most important political institutions in our country with a rich history of great men and women serving in it.

Obama sold himself as the ultimate conciliator, able to bridge gaps between all opposing factions in Washington. I readily admit that as his term started, I thought perhaps someone like him, totally different and new, might be able to successfully end the gridlock that had settled over politics for the past decade.

I had watched the political atmosphere become more strident and divisive during the late '90s and early 2000s. I didn't just dislike the toxic atmosphere, I hated it. The Washington I matured in during the '70s and '80s was always intensely competitive but at the same time cooperative. Politicians had strong differences of opinion but understood the country must move forward to address important issues. Thinking back to 1975 when I arrived in Washington, Big Labor controlled much of Congress, especially the Senate. The U.S. Chamber of Commerce, National Federation of Independent Businesses (NFIB), and other business organizations were well represented on the other side. Even with these two diametrically opposed philosophies backing each side of the aisle, through arduous work, determination, and difficult compromise, legislation got passed. And through it all, presidents of both parties were part of the process, including their use of the veto pen. That pen has all but disappeared in recent presidencies.

By 2008, I was not an admirer of Senator John McCain. Despite his well-earned stature as a war hero and serious legislator, the McCain I had observed for many years had a hair-trigger temper that I had personally witnessed. No doubt he is a solid conservative with a remarkable personal background of service and sacrifice for his country, but temperament matters, especially with our commander in chief. I had concerns about McCain that simply did not go away. I will always admire him for meeting with members of the national board of Log Cabin Republicans during his run for president in 2000, against the advice of his campaign staff. The Bush campaign used this meeting against him in the pivotal South Carolina primary. McCain was very cordial in the meeting and responded directly to our questions. When one board member asked for his support in repealing the "Don't Ask Don't Tell" policy, he quickly replied that repeal would happen only after General Colin Powell favored repeal.

Running an uphill campaign in 2008, things got worse after McCain added Alaska Governor Sarah Palin as his running mate. In my role as the D.C. GOP Chairman, I was a delegate for McCain/Palin in 2008 and voted for the ticket in November. I was on the convention floor in Minneapolis in early September of that year when Palin made her enthusiastic acceptance speech. I was as wowed by her as everyone else. That late summer night in Minnesota was the high point of the McCain campaign and Palin's political career. Within days of her speech, Palin started unraveling as the nation watched. It was sad and frustrating. In bumbling media interviews, it became clear she was grossly unqualified to be vice president or, God forbid, president. Given McCain's age and prior health problems, questions about Palin's fitness for the office were more important than ever. I understood McCain wanted someone fresh as his running made to shake up the campaign as it entered the final weeks, but his bet backfired.

Even though I voted for Senator McCain, at some level I had bought into the promise of hope and change that candidate Obama offered. Along with most people, I was tired of the strident partisanship and gridlock in Washington. I was fooling myself. Washington is an extremely complex place with many layers and subtleties. A president not only needs direct understanding of issues that comes with years of work, he must have people around him who can help him work his way through "the maze." Dick Lugar used to talk about "navigating the rocks and shoals" of Washington. It is a wonderful expression about how to survive in the nation's capital. It takes time and experience to understand how to navigate the swift currents, safe passages, and places to avoid.

President Obama is an extraordinarily gifted man, but his arrogance has proven to be a problem for him and the nation. Obama believed, even with minimal experience and virtually no meaningful relationships with the people who understood the workings of the federal government, he could not only navigate the Potomac, but single-handedly change its course. In hindsight, it is a preposterous notion, and it was an utter failure as a practical matter during his first term.

I became disappointed with President Obama almost as soon as he took office in January of 2009. He quickly made clear in policy statements and actions that he was a committed liberal who was going to impose his views on the country regardless of the cost. That fact should not have come as a surprise given his voting record, albeit a short one, in the U.S. Senate. We had elected a liberal as president and a liberal Democratic majority in both houses of Congress.

Obama's top priority was to address the economic debacle he inherited. His hands-off approach to the Democratic Congress was apparent in the stimulus package he proposed, and Congress enacted. While he made some attempts to bring GOP members into the discussions, Speaker Pelosi, Majority Leader Harry Reid, and Democratic committee chairmen would have none of that, telling the new president that Democrats were in control and they would call the shots on Capitol Hill. The Democrats in Congress knew they were dealing with an inexperienced politician. They were delighted he was elected president since most power in Washington emanates directly out of the White House, but they knew they could run circles around him in the business of legislating. And they did.

Rather than having a laser focus on the economy, President Obama shifted focus to health care reform after passing the trillion-dollar stimulus package. Many Americans were unemployed, many others had watched their retirement savings dwindle because of a tanking stock market and millions of people were losing their homes to foreclosure. Rather than working to get the economy on a faster recovery track, he pressed relentlessly for a vast rewrite of the nation's health care laws, which represents almost 15% of the economy. He was playing with fire. Pushing adoption through the Congress with no Republican votes further divided the nation and helped propel the rise of the Tea Party movement and the return of Republican control to the House in the 2010 midterm elections. Speaker Pelosi said it best when she proclaimed that Congress had to pass the health care bill to find out what was in it. Her senseless statement epitomized the view many Americans had of their new president and his Democratic colleagues in the Congress: they were determined to remake America to fit their liberal view instead of focusing on the issues they cared about.

My opinion of Barack Obama was complete: we had elected an unabashed liberal who was also a political amateur. We had been sold a bill of goods and we bought it, only to quickly have buyer's remorse. President Obama had no executive experience and his administration suffered as a result. Also, he did not recruit business executives to any key cabinet or senior White House staff positions. He would have benefitted from spending time as chief executive or other senior elected executive of a state. As much as I disagreed with President Clinton, he at least had the benefit of his time as governor of Arkansas to give him practical experience as an executive. He knew how to execute and brought in experienced executives to his administration. President Reagan was of course the consummate pro who honed his skills as governor of California. George W. Bush was governor of Texas for six years, and no matter which way you fall on his presidency, there can be no doubt that his experience was a valuable asset.

Mitt Romney, while an accomplished man and a former governor, was not my idea of a strong candidate. I, like a lot of people, thought we could have done better. Some of the heavyweights didn't enter the race. Mitch Daniels, my former colleague and the governor of Indiana at the time, was my first choice to be the GOP candidate in 2012 and again in 2016. I was disappointed when Daniels didn't run, and I think he was as well. He ultimately decided not to for the sake of family. Some marital issues that had long since been resolved would have been exhumed in a most public and painful way if he ran for president.

Former Florida Governor Jeb Bush also would have been a formidable candidate in 2012, although there was strong sentiment in the GOP against nominating a third Bush for President. I also liked Jon Huntsman, the former governor of Utah, who was appointed ambassador to China by President Obama. Being ambassador hindered Huntsman from the outset. He was still ambassador when he started putting together his campaign, which made it difficult to get his campaign off the ground. He turned out to be a mediocre campaigner. He is an erudite man and a sophisticated thinker, but on the campaign trail he came off as elitist and aloof. Like Romney, the patina of success shone just a little too brightly on Huntsman and his handsome family for today's populist campaigning styles. When it comes to presidential candidates, the Republicans have a history of nominating the "next in line." Candidates such as Bob Dole, John McCain, and even Romney were perceived to be the guy whose "turn" it was. That is not to say they were handed the nomination, far from it. Candidates faced grueling primaries that toughened them up, but at the same time they exposed vulnerabilities that were exploited in the general election.

During the 2012 campaign, Romney sold himself as a problem solver, and I thought he did so effectively. He had been a successful businessman for years, the kind of person who has the innate ability to size up an issue, build consensus, develop a strategy, and get all the stakeholders to buy into his strategy. He ran a flawed campaign and, again, Obama ran a flawless campaign. Romney's infamous 47%

comment at a private fundraiser was one of many mistakes that made him look out of touch. He seemed to be writing off vast segments of voters. Whether it was true or not doesn't matter in the final analysis. The damage was done.

The 2012 campaign was a prime example of how damaging a long primary season could be for the nominee. The seemingly interminable season and the more than twenty debates resulted in a miserable slog for all the candidates. And then there was the media propensity to choose "flavor of the week" candidates as a frontrunner whether that candidate had even the slightest chance to win the nomination. There is no doubt about a liberal bias in the mainstream media; there are surveys showing members of the press voting more than eighty percent for Democrats. Proof of that is the fact that businessman Herman Cain and Congresswoman Michele Bachmann were held up as mainstream Republicans, while similarly radical politicians on the left were not portrayed as mainstream Democrats. Cain and Bachmann were touted as leading in the primary contest but then quickly receded into the pack as their obvious weaknesses were exposed. Portraying candidates such as these as potential winners made the Republican Party look silly and worthy of suspicion.

President Obama altered his sales pitch when running for re-election in 2012. Rather than optimistic platitudes about uniting Red America and Blue America, he decided to divide and conquer; pitting rich against poor, white against Latino and man against woman. His campaign was largely based on fear; scaring voters about what Mitt Romney would do as president. There were still hints of the optimistic rhetoric from 2008, but his campaign essentially came down to this message: "You might not love me, but the other guy would be worse."

Obama certainly was not perfect in the 2012 campaign. At one point, he used the phrase "you didn't build that..." when referring to successful businesspeople. He denigrated entrepreneurs, main street businesspeople, and all the others who worked hard, succeeded, and, most importantly, created most new jobs. As the son of a small business family, I know first-hand how much work it takes to achieve sustained success with a business. I feel the same way in my own career; first in my family to graduate college and law school, worked hard in the U.S. Senate, recruited to work at the Reagan White House, built a successful law and lobbying career and chaired boards only to be told "I didn't do that"? How insulting! One could make the case that he was just trying to say people have help along the way, including government help in building roads and so forth. That premise is true, but the tone he used was dismissive and insulting. And it came from a man who never had a private sector job, except for a couple years at a big law firm.

In addition to my differences with President Obama on domestic issues, his management of foreign affairs was devastating to America's stature in the world. Here again, he tried to reshape our foreign affairs to fit his worldview, one with which I strongly disagree. While presidents should be cautious in getting us involved in international disputes, America has a key role to play in maintaining stable alliances and working directly and indirectly to resolve international disputes. Our friends and allies look to the U.S. for leadership, but Obama was unwilling or simply not interested in providing it.

Early in his presidency, his international "apology tour" angered many Americans and rightly so. No other president has traveled the world and talked about our country as Obama did. I never thought I would witness a U.S. president question American exceptionalism, but he did. For all our faults and mistakes, the U.S. has been a force for good in the world and should not shrink from the role we have played well since emerging as a world power after World War II until today when we are the only remaining true superpower. Obama thought that making a speech, as he did early on in Egypt, would be sufficient to make that part of the world feel better about the U.S. It did just the opposite; it made us seem weak and leaderless and in the eyes of our Middle East allies, unreliable.

Time after time, Obama made misjudgments and missteps that damaged our international relationships. His failure to achieve a status of forces agreement with Iraq left a void that was filled by ISIS. President Bush had made a politically unpopular decision to implement the "surge" in Iraq in early 2007. His risky move paid off as the extra troops and improved strategy helped stabilize the country. If Obama had left in place even 10,000 American troops, ISIS never would have risen to destabilize Iraq. President Trump has turned the tide against ISIS, but it remains an on-going threat around the world. President Obama also badly mishandled his response to the Syrian civil war. He drew a "red line" against Syrian President Assad if chemical weapons were used. When that happened, Obama retreated from his red line and destroyed our nation's credibility.

It became clear that reaching an agreement with Iran regarding their nuclear program was his single most important foreign policy objective during his second term. He seemed willing to agree to almost anything Iran wanted just to conclude an agreement. Finalizing a deal seemed to matter more than what was actually in the agreement. The inspection regime is so weak it allows the Iranians to "inspect" sensitive facilities themselves and send samples to the United Nations. The deal also has a sunset horizon that seemingly allows Iran to complete its path to a nuclear weapon when the agreement expires. Additionally, it doesn't mention any of Iran's troublemaking around the region. And it doesn't constrain the regime from continuing to develop ballistic missile technology. All this and Iran gets $150 billion in cash that had been impounded in the U.S. since the Shah left power in the late '70s. Obama knew the deal was so bad that there was no point submitting it to the Senate for approval as a treaty. Instead, it's more like an informal agreement. Because it wasn't a treaty, President Trump was able to drop out of the agreement in the spring of 2018 after failing to get

European allies to press Iran for radical changes to the deal. Obama might consider this agreement a great foreign policy accomplishment, but it's one of the biggest mistakes he made as president.

Almost no American president has had a worse relationship with Israel, our most important Middle East ally. As with his domestic policy, Obama has tried to shape his foreign policy to his campaign promises and personal worldview. Obama has been criticized by former senior administration officials such as former Defense Secretary Robert Gates for lacking a clear vision and for his policy of leading from behind in international conflicts.

As his presidency continued, American voters grew weary and looked for an alternative. During the 2014 midterm elections, the GOP won a larger majority in the House and regained a majority in the Senate. Several factors contributed to the 2014 midterm success for the Republicans. First, and probably most importantly, Republicans did an excellent job managing candidate recruitment, particularly in Senate races but also in House and governorship elections.

Recent elections have featured GOP candidates with backgrounds that would be more appropriate for a TV reality show than a seat in Congress. But the new crop of governors and House and Senate members is impressive for their backgrounds and the largely problem-solving tone they set during their campaigns. Most of these new members are expected to work with their respective leadership or legislatures to address key public policy issues. Most state parties came together after the primaries to support the winning candidates. Candidates also stayed on message, focusing on key economic issues and opposing President Obama on high profile issues such as Obamacare, immigration, and energy. Candidates also avoided the embarrassing campaign mistakes that Republican candidates made in 2012. Successful debate strategies were used to address pseudo issues like the Democrats' drumbeat about the so-called war on women.

After the electoral debacle of 2012, GOP leaders were wise to run on positive agendas and avoid the negative tones of many Tea Party members. An excellent example is Republican Larry Hogan, who pulled off one of the biggest upsets in decades by beating Democratic Lieutenant Governor Anthony Brown for governor of Maryland, a state that rarely elects Republicans. Hogan ran a focused and disciplined campaign emphasizing the need to change unpopular and harmful tax and spending policies of outgoing Governor Martin O'Malley and Brown. Another key factor was that the Tea Party's typical shenanigans were largely ignored. There is a bully factor to many in the Tea Party movement, a sense that it's their way or the highway. Most bullies back down when their targets fight back or simply ignore them and for this election cycle the "grown-ups" took over from the petulant kids.

Having Republican majorities in both houses of Congress was an opportunity for President Obama to have a legacy of accomplishments in his last two years, just as Presidents Reagan and Clinton did when they had to work with a Congress controlled by the opposing party. Both wisely decided to compromise on key issues and that strategy worked well for them but, more importantly, it worked for the country. In 1983, Reagan worked with Democrat House Speaker Tip O'Neill to address the looming insolvency of Social Security by gradually raising the retirement age from 65 to 67. That was followed a few years later by the bipartisan development and passage of the Tax Reform Act of 1986 that lowered the top marginal tax rate from 70% to 28% and consolidated 14 tax rates into two tax brackets. It was revenue neutral by reducing or eliminating many tax preferences. Passage of this important reform resulted in extended economic expansion.

President Clinton faced a Republican Congress from 1994 through the end of his Presidency. During these six years, he worked with Congress to enact bipartisan federal welfare reform in 1996 and the Balanced Budget Act in 1997. None of these bipartisan accomplishments were easily achieved. There were significant differences to overcome in all of them but in the end, each was a compromise that was good for the country and established both presidents as real leaders.

Immediately after the November 2014 election, incoming Senate Majority Leader Mitch McConnell and House Speaker John Boehner talked about working collaboratively with President Obama on a series of issues, including passage of trade legislation that would facilitate the conclusion of two major international trade agreements, one with the EU and the other with Asian countries. Trade agreements are never easy to negotiate and even harder to get approved by Congress. It takes a bipartisan coalition to get the job done. Part of Obama's natural base, organized labor, stridently opposes these trade agreements and many Republican Congressmen represent districts that also oppose them. The North American Free Trade Agreement was ratified when Democrats controlled both houses of Congress, but more Republicans than Democrats voted for it. President Obama and the Republican Congress could have achieved a similar success. Sadly, from my perspective, the two pending multilateral trade agreements, in particular the Trans-Pacific Partnership (TPP), was opposed by both presidential candidates in 2016. Soon after taking office, President Trump unwisely pulled out of the trade pact, rather than concluding the negotiations and submitting it to the Senate for ratification.

President Obama's legacy remains uncertain. Undoubtedly, he was an historical figure who presided over the nation with dignity. However, he was an ineffective leader and his foreign policy was naive and destructive to American interests around the world. He seemed to like running for president a lot more than being president. Presidents Reagan and Clinton enjoyed the sausage making of government. Obama seemed to disdain that part of the job. He looked down on the process of building compromise. He didn't even bother building relationships with leaders of his own party. It became a big story after the GOP took control of the Senate in 2014 when he had dinner with a group of Republican senators. I was surprised he hadn't been doing this throughout his presidency. It wasn't just Republicans he ignored in Congress. He didn't even know members of his own party. One example: Obama played 333 rounds of golf during his two terms in office, but he almost never played with members of Congress, even his own party. Anyone who has golfed knows it's one of the most social sports you can play. My father's devotion to it turned me off from the sport, but I understand it's a fantastic way to build friendships. I don't begrudge Obama for playing a lot of golf as president (as is President Trump), but I criticize him for not using those rounds of golf to help him become a more effective deal maker. What does golf have to do with being a good president? Fundamentally, being a good president depends on being able to forge compromise. If you don't have any friends on Capitol Hill who know and trust you, cutting a deal becomes nearly impossible.

One other note about President Obama. He amplified divisions in this country. That was partly based on his decision to run a divisive 2012 re-election campaign that pitted one American against another. That was part of a broader tendency he had to question the motives of his political opponents. In the 1980s, House Speaker Tip O'Neill and President Reagan vehemently disagreed on a range of issues. So, too, did Speaker Newt Gingrich and President Clinton in the 1990s. However, all four of these men believed their opponents wanted what they did for our nation: a strong country that provides help for those in need and prosperity for everyone. The parties disagree on how to achieve those goals, but for the most part we share common goals for the nation. President Obama didn't seem to share this view about the GOP. He blasted the motives of his political opponents as if Republicans wanted sick kids, dirty air, and starving poor people. Instead of uniting the country, his style caused further polarization. And that helped lead to the rise of Donald Trump.

Jill Homan served as the Republican national committeewoman for D.C. from 2012 through 2020. I very much enjoyed working closely with her to advance the GOP in Washington.

This photo is from inside the D.C. GOP office which was open from 2003-2013. It was called the Edward Brooke Leadership Center. In 1966, Brooke, a D.C. native, became the first African American man elected to the U.S. Senate since Reconstruction. The Massachusetts Republican served two terms in the Senate, including part of the time I worked on Capitol Hill.

CHAPTER 22

The View From Here

I AM NOT A JOURNALIST, PUNDIT, OR COMMENTATOR. I HAVE always been skeptical of my qualification to do broad political analysis, especially for public consumption. But the process of writing this book has bolstered awareness of my abilities in this area. Before writing this book, I mentioned to a friend I didn't think my political opinions were particularly noteworthy because I hadn't been in the highest of positions. My friend responded, "You may think there were a lot of people above you, but I assure you there were far more people below. You have observed the workings of the government for a generation from a privileged perch. It may not have been the summit, but it sure wasn't base camp!" With that perspective in mind, I now feel that examining the recent history of the Republican Party from my point of view could yield useful ideas about how it can become the inclusive majority party I have long envisioned.

The image of the national Republican Party began to change with what became known as Richard Nixon's Southern Strategy. Through the 1960s and into the early 1980s, the Democratic Party held onto the Southern states, along with the vestiges of the old Confederacy and the legacy that carried. At that time, the national Democratic Party was an odd coalition of Dixiecrat conservative Southerners from the old Confederacy (e.g., Strom Thurmond, Trent Lott and others who eventually switched their party affiliation) and Northern liberals from states above the Mason-Dixon line. There were also a lot of ex-hippies, former communists, and socialists held over from earlier years. It was an odd urban/southern combination that made for a peculiar mix in Congress.

Republicans were the party of Lincoln. Most African Americans were Republican until Franklin Roosevelt's New Deal. During the '30s, the Roosevelt-led Democratic Party began shifting its focus to urban and labor constituencies, away from rural voters. In the '50s and '60s, Northern Democrats, seeing moral and political benefit, embraced the civil rights movement, which was anathema to whites in the segregated South. Even as the Democrats did more to court black voters, Republican presidential candidates still attracted solid support from African Americans. President Eisenhower received nearly 40% of the black vote in his two elections. Richard Nixon got a third of the African American vote in his failed 1960 campaign.

Arizona Senator Barry Goldwater's opposition to the 1964 Civil Rights Act, which was supported by many of his GOP Senate colleagues, seriously damaged the Republican Party with African Americans. Goldwater objected on libertarian grounds (he believed it was an overreach by the Federal Government) not because he believed in racial segregation; however, the reason for his opposition didn't matter to Southern voters who liked his stand against the 1964 Act or African Americans who vehemently opposed his position. His opposition to the law drove black voters in droves to the Democratic Party. As the 1964 GOP nominee, he received only 6% of the black vote and created an enormous challenge for Republican candidates for decades to come. The 1964 presidential election and the growing civil rights movement brought most African Americans into the Democratic party and left white conservative Southern Democrats feeling they didn't have a political home.

Nixon's Southern Strategy aimed to convert disaffected Dixiecrats into Republicans. He believed these voters could be courted using fiscal conservatism and a hawkish foreign policy that already existed in the Republican Party, while at the same time taking a sympathetic view of their grievances regarding race, gender, and other cultural issues. This began to work as more and more of the South began to vote Republican. Slowly, elected Southern Democrats started breaking away from their party. Thurmond and others started switching to a newly configured Republican Party. Nixon effectively used the Southern Strategy to gain the White House.

In the mid-twentieth century, Republicans were strong in the Northeast, in the Western states, and in parts of the Midwest. But Nixon wanted to break into the Southern states, so he decided to use cultural issues to gain a foothold. His issues were Vietnam and the hippie movement. He ran on a platform of law and order, opposing "radical" ideas that had found a home in the Democratic Party. He then started appealing to the ingrained bigotry of the Southern electorate using code words to gain sympathy without using blatantly racist terms. School busing was a cultural issue that resonated strongly in both parties, and Nixon used it as a wedge to pry loose Southern Democrats and convert them to the GOP. The results were effective; in 1968 Nixon won several former Confederate states such as Tennessee, North Carolina, South Carolina, and Virginia, propelling him to victory over Democratic candidate Hubert Humphrey. It was no cakewalk. Former Alabama Governor George Wallace, running for President as an independent, did well in the deep South, winning 13.5% of the popular vote. Nixon defeated Humphrey in the popular vote by less than one percent (43.4% vs. 42.7%) while winning the all-important Electoral College by 301 to Humphrey's 191 and Wallace's 46.

The evangelical church is now deeply involved in politics at every level, and the percentage of Americans who view themselves as evangelicals has increased dramatically in recent decades. That fact is so familiar to us now, but it is a fairly recent phenomenon. It wasn't Pat Robertson or Billy Graham who brought evangelicals into national politics; it was Jimmy Carter. Carter, a devout Southern Baptist, was one of the first politicians to wear his faith on his sleeve. He went to Falwell, Pat Robertson, and other evangelical leaders and said, "I am one of you. I am a born-again Christian. You should support me." It was a radical thing for a politician to do in what was still a secular America, at least politically speaking. Churches had traditionally stayed out of politics, but once Carter invited them to the political table, they have remained in politics, but not for long with the Democratic Party.

President Eisenhower was the most popular man in the country in the '50s and he never talked about religion. When he ran for president he was advised to "decide" his religious denomination. (He settled on Presbyterian, the most common Protestant denomination at the time.) Ike's matter of fact approach to religion was the rule of thumb for the entire Republican Party and the Democrats, too. Carter's open show of faith was a game-changer. He received the endorsement of Jerry Falwell, Pat Robertson, and many other evangelical ministers. So, contrary to widespread belief, it was the Democrats, not the Republicans, who brought evangelicals into national politics.

Another turning point happened when the leadership of the now politically active Christian right finally told rank-and-file evangelicals it was okay for them to become involved in politics. For a long time, religious conservatives weren't interested in direct involvement in politics. It wasn't that they were not interested in the issues; it was just that they eschewed direct involvement in politics because it wasn't part of their mission. Aside from Carter courting them, the controversial 1973 Roe v. Wade Supreme Court decision galvanized people of faith who were outraged that unelected judges had legalized abortion nationwide.

Ronald Reagan came from what was then the predominantly Republican West and expanded on the new Southern constituency Nixon had established. Reagan was interesting in that he courted the evangelicals even though he was not necessarily on-board with their issues and rigid values. He maintained this fervent base in the Party on the premise that he was as passionate about their issues as they were. But his personal history contradicts that view. He had not lived as a social conservative in his personal life. Reagan had been divorced and remarried, something very rare in the 1940s. He had worked in Hollywood and had many gay friends. He listened to evangelicals without ever fully committing to their agenda. Reagan, in his wisdom, knew that getting too closely aligned with the religious right was a tenuous proposition. One example of that is the pro-life movement, whose leaders Reagan rarely, if ever met in person, though he did get behind their cause. It was a departure from his earlier views. As governor of California, he had signed legislation that increased access to abortion.

Before President Reagan, the GOP was split on abortion. In fact, President Ford had supported the Roe vs. Wade decision. Reagan shifted the party to the right on this issue and created a strong bond with evangelical voters even if he didn't speak much about the issue. Reagan utilized the social conservatives very strategically in the states where they had real political clout. With votes from the Christian right in hand, Republicans completed their takeover of the Southern states. In recent years, a Democrat seldom wins in the South except in densely populated cities such as Atlanta and Houston with large minority voter populations. The converse has also become true; it is difficult for a Republican to win in the urban North and much of the West Coast.

A 2017 Pew Research Poll shows the two parties more polarized than ever, with Republicans polling more conservatively than ever and Democrats more liberal than ever. Thus, we have a tremendous gulf between the ideologies of the two major parties. President Obama was a polarizing president, and President Trump has accelerated that division. Independents have filled the ideological gulf between the two parties. In several states, independents outnumber Republicans and Democrats. Democrats won the House in 2006 with the support of the independent vote, but Republicans took back the House in 2010 in a dramatic defeat for Obama during his first mid-term elections. Republicans maintained control in 2012 and increased their margin in 2014 and 2016 only to lose an enormous number of seats in the 2018 midterm elections. That was a dramatic defeat for President Trump. In each of these elections, independent voters decided the outcome.

Because the parties have become so polarized, the only thing that will moderate their views is the independent middle. For most independents, social issues are not important. Those who have social issues at the top of their list are firmly in the GOP or Democratic camps. Independents are more influenced by day-to-day economic issues such as jobs and the economy. They are turned off by the radicalization of both parties and the fact that both sides cannot get along well enough to produce important legislation.

Even though there are some things I don't like about President Trump, it would be very difficult for me to vote for Democrats because of certain core Democratic Party principles I oppose. The idea of big government intervening on every issue large and small is anathema to me, but it has been a core value for the Democrats beginning with Roosevelt's New Deal. I naturally lean towards the core values of the Republican Party that I grew up with and worked in for many years, values such as a pro-business economic policy, support for small business, limited regulation, fiscal discipline, a strong national defense, and a robust foreign policy. It's not only the way I was raised but why I have always felt more at home within the Republican Party. America remains a center-right country and the traditional center-right Republican Party I grew up with has the winning strategy.

This is a 2019 photo from the White House Christmas Party with Jill Homan and José Cunningham. José served as chairman of the D.C. Republican Party from 2012 until early 2020. I very much enjoyed working with both Jill and José.

GOP Senator Tim Scott from South Carolina (second from left) offers an inclusive vision for the party's future. Jill Homan, José Cunningham (far left), and I met Senator Scott after he spoke to members of the Republican National Committee.

CHAPTER 23

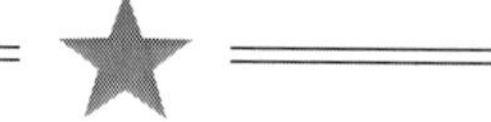

How the Elephant Changed Its Stripes

FOR SEVERAL YEARS AFTER LOG CABIN OPENED ITS WASHINGTON office in 1993, Republican office holders told Log Cabin leaders that on a personal level they were accepting of gay people and many gay issues, but they couldn't say so publicly, or they would risk alienating their base and losing their election. In recent years, there is ample evidence this has changed. LGBT issues are discussed more freely now by Republicans at the local, state, and federal levels. It is a healthy development that an honest dialogue is underway.

In his 2016 GOP convention acceptance speech, Donald Trump vowed to protect the rights of the LGBT community. "As your president, I will do everything in my power to protect our LGBTQ citizens from the violence and oppression of a hateful foreign ideology," he said.

I was surprised and thrilled with his simple declarative statement. Trump's background and businesses brought him into contact with LGBT people over many years, especially living in New York. The response from the delegates was heartwarming too. There were delegates who were taken aback by his statement, but as a delegate myself,

I witnessed firsthand the loud applause he received for this statement. In fact, Trump deviated from his prepared remarks as he heard the applause. "As a Republican, I'm so happy to hear you cheering for what I just said."

As President, Trump has been the target of relentless criticism from the gay left that control most LGBT media and civil rights organizations. Nothing he can do is enough for them on LGBT issues. In fact, he has followed through on commitments he made during the 2016 campaign. An initial win for our community was keeping in place an Obama administration executive order that prohibits federal government contractors from discriminating against LGBT employees. Additionally, the Justice Department has filed a sexual harassment lawsuit to protect a transgender person. Trump also has nominated openly gay and lesbian people to important posts in the executive and judicial branches of government and has hired others for positions that don't require Senate confirmation. Of note is his selection of Ric Grenell as Ambassador to Germany. Grenell is the openly gay former spokesman for our U.N. ambassadors during the George W. Bush administration. In contrast to just four years earlier when Grenell departed the Romney presidential campaign after a brief stint as its foreign policy spokesman when social conservatives objected, Trump chose him to be ambassador to one of our most important European allies. And earlier this year, Trump promoted Grenell to serve as acting director of the Department of National Intelligence. That makes Grenell the first openly LGBT person ever to serve in a cabinet-level position for any president, Democrat or Republican.

Grenell was sworn in as ambassador to Germany at the State Department by Vice President Pence with Ric's husband holding a family Bible. Symbolic gestures often express something words cannot. Trump was the first Republican president to support the freedom to marry before running for president and the first president to recognize LGBT Pride Month. Last year, he used that opportunity to announce a global campaign to end the criminalization of homosexuality in more than 70 countries. Grenell is leading this effort.

In his 2020 budget proposal, President Trump launched an aggressive program to eradicate HIV/AIDS in the U.S. by 2030. The program targets key geographic areas where infection rates remain high by providing access to PrEP, the prophylactic drug combination that is proven to stop the spread of HIV. In launching this ambitious program, the White House announced deals with national drugstore chains to distribute the drug. None of the gay left media or LGBT organizations, other than Log Cabin Republicans, have given him credit for this forward leaning effort to eradicate HIV/AIDS.

All that being said,Trump and his administration have taken some actions that are harmful to the transgender community. For decades, trans people were barred from serving in the U.S. military.That prohibition ended with a Department of Defense (DOD) directive issued in June of 2016, the last year of President Obama's second term to permit transgender people to serve in our military.The outcry was immediate among many conservative and others who questioned the timing of this directive months before the 2020 presidential election.

In June of 2017, President Trump tweeted his intention to block transgender people from serving in the military even as some served on active duty in combat situations around the world. Senior Pentagon officials seemed surprised by Trump's tweet. The DOD quickly stated that its policy would not change as the result of Trump's tweet because the department was in the middle of examining the status of trans people in the military. That seemed to be borderline insubordination but welcome news to many. Eventually, the Trump administration finalized a policy allowing people who came out as transgender under the Obama administration's policy to continue openly serving. However, anyone who comes out now can only continue serving if they do so in their biological sex. The military services can grant waivers on a case-by-case basis. The Pentagon denies the policy is a ban because of the transgender troops grandfathered in under the previous policy and because transgender people can serve in their biological sex. Legal battles over the policy continue in federal court. I believe anyone physically and mentally capable of serving in our military should be able to do so. During this controversy, it has been heartening to have conservative senators such as Orrin Hatch (R-UT) and Richard Shelby (R-AL) defending the right of transgender Americans to serve in our military. "You ought to treat everybody fairly and give everybody a chance to serve," said Shelby in an interview on CNN.

Other federal departments and agencies are trying to roll back a variety of regulations about transgender issues that were implemented during the Obama administration. Many of these Trump administration initiatives are being challenged in the courts. All of us, including President Trump and his administration, need to show compassion and sympathy for trans people. While I believe we should accept people as they are, I also understand that this is a complicated issue. The American public is far from embracing transgender equality. Hopefully, that will change as more Americans meet trans people and learn about the discrimination they face.

Long before Trump and probably long after him, Republicans and Democrats play cultural word games to send messages to their core constituencies while at the same time working their way towards the political middle. At Log Cabin, we worked with many Republicans who could not support us publicly but agreed to work behind the scenes to tamp down anti-gay language in legislation and in public discourse.

Politicians speak to their base on core issues, but there are cases where saying what people want to hear goes from being practical to pandering. An easy place to look for these cases is the Tea Party movement. Tea Party candidates lean heavily on inflammatory rhetoric intended to set them to the right of mainstream conservative Republican incumbents in the hopes of convincing people of the need to "change for change's sake."

The Tea Party movement started as a response to the profligate spending of the Bush and early Obama years and the massive government bailouts of banks and big auto during the 2008 economic collapse. The grassroots movement included conservatives disgusted with government overreach and liberals incensed by the failure of the Obama administration to prosecute the bankers who had abused the system. The passage of a huge stimulus bill and the move towards the passage of Obamacare in late 2009 ignited the powder keg. Various Tea Party organizations offered millions of people a platform to express their displeasure. Over time, the Tea Party was co-opted by organizations such as Freedom Works, which used the Tea Party's money and enthusiasm for its own purposes. In the same way that the Christian Coalition would openly acknowledge that the "gay agenda" was "great for business," the Tea Party came to rely on the demonization of a group or issue as much as it does the promotion of its original principles.

My friend and mentor, Senator Lugar (R-IN), got caught in the Tea Party wave. Over the course of his Senate career, Lugar often had primary challenges from his right flank where some Hoosiers thought he was vulnerable. Richard Mourdock, the Tea Party-backed candidate running against Lugar in the 2012 GOP primary, ran on issues that fired up the conservative right enough to defeat Lugar. Mourdock's extreme positions made him vulnerable in a general election and he was soundly defeated by a Democrat who almost certainly would have lost to Lugar. In 2012, Mitt Romney won Indiana by 9 percentage points, but Mourdock lost the Senate race by 6 points, a whopping 15-point spread! I was pleased that the seat Senator Lugar held was reclaimed in 2018 by Republican Mike Braun, a businessman with no prior political experience.

The issue of race in American politics has been avoided by many given its potentially explosive nature. Most white people I know strive to avoid discussing racial issues, especially those in the public arena. They're concerned that putting one or two words in the wrong place during a discussion about race could lead to staggering consequences. That's why I usually stay away from those conversations, not because I don't have confidence in my convictions, rather because I am not always a perfect orator and might say something that could be misconstrued or twisted beyond what I meant.

However, recent events mandate a change in that posture. The white supremacy rally in Charlottesville, Virginia in August of 2017 was a pivotal event for many Americans, but especially Republicans. Perhaps naively, I was astonished to learn about the level of hate that still remains among some people in our country. It was deeply disturbing to see so many young white men filled with hatred, marching against people different from themselves, including vile rhetoric and actions against people of color and Jews. One young white supremacist sped his car into a group of counter protesters killing a young woman.

President Trump initially responded that there was "hatred, bigotry, and violence on many sides." After a firestorm, he changed his tune, but the impression remained that he blamed both sides, although protesters were there peaceably while the white supremacists were there to cause trouble. At a minimum, Trump's initial comments showed a lack of compassion and racial insensitivity. Some of his own cabinet members including then Secretary of State Rex Tillerson publicly chastised him for his comments, especially for his failure to immediately condemn the white nationalists.

The Charlottesville protests happened at a time of growing racial discord. Race relations had been souring near the end of the Obama administration driven largely by a spate of questionable shooting deaths of black men by white police officers. In 2015, riots erupted in Ferguson, Missouri after the police shooting of unarmed 18-year-old Michael Brown. From those riots, the Black Lives Matter movement developed across the nation. The Brown shooting turned out to be justified, but that was not the case in other killings across the country. I disagree with the tactics of the Black Lives Matters movement, such as shutting down freeways and intense anger aimed at police officers, but they have succeeded in raising an important level of awareness about how black people often are mistreated by officers of all colors. In 2017, black males accounted for a disproportionate percentage of killings by police of unarmed people, 22%, while they make up only 6% of the population. In the wake of nationwide protests, many police departments wisely reexamined their procedures and training of officers. However, more must be done. The number of unarmed police killings initially dropped from 94 in 2015 to 51 in 2016 but then it went back up to 86 in 2017.

I supported the bipartisan criminal justice reform bill signed into law by President Trump in late 2018. The First Step Act aims to reduce recidivism and refines sentencing laws and harsh penalties. It's a good start because the GOP must take a more honest look at racial issues. The Party of Lincoln must offer practical solutions to address problems facing minority communities. I initially thought President Trump's blustery rhetoric would alienate people of color and leave many Americans wondering if he is racist. He won just 8 percent of African American votes. But decades of Democratic Party policies have failed to end poverty among populations of color. Recognizing decades of neglect and failure by Democratic politicians, in 2016, Trump bluntly asked African Americans, "What the hell do you have to lose?" The economic boom that followed his election resulted in historically low unemployment rates for both African Americans and Hispanics. Trump's blustery ways are still often cringeworthy, but the results he has produced provide Republicans with the opportunity to make inroads into African American and Hispanic voters. It's uncertain what impact COVID-19 will have on our politics, including the racial make-up of various voting coalitions.

No matter what happens in November, GOP candidates are well positioned to provide both the truths and the solutions. And our party's best advocates are people of color such as Senator Tim Scott from South Carolina. A black man, he represents a state with a painful history of racism and oppression. Party leaders now use much more inclusive language on issues of race. The Republican Party does not get credit for the progress it has made on racial issues. A prime example of that was in late 2002 when then Senate Majority Leader Trent Lott (R-MS) commented at Senator Strom Thurmond's (R-SC) 100th birthday party that Thurmond "would have made a good president." The implied racism of the statement was enough to exile him from the party leadership. The pressure was so intense he declined to run again for Majority Leader in the next Congress. And if someone in the Party were to use the n-word, that person would be a pariah. Senator Ted Cruz of Texas, one of the most outspoken Tea Party conservatives, was quick to blast Donald Sterling for his despicable remarks about African Americans while he was the owner of the Los Angeles Clippers NBA franchise.

Like many others, I thought Barack Obama was going to be a transformational figure when it came to race, but he did not take advantage of the opportunity to have an honest conversation about race. It is wonderful our country progressed enough on racial issues to elect a person of color to lead the nation, but that person needed to be president of the whole country, not just those who voted for him. He ran on the promise of uniting the country and building bridges. Unfortunately, Obama quickly left the bridge and retreated to the safety and comfort of standard liberal Democratic ideology. An opportunity was lost.

If the Republican Party is to remain a viable party nationally, it must resolve some divisive internal problems. A big part of that involves taking stances on race as well as social issues that attract independent voters rather than repel them. Meaningful, thoughtful policy is needed, not just a change in rhetoric.

The demographics of America are changing rapidly with Hispanics now outnumbering African Americans and becoming a significant force in several states such as California and Texas. Every four years the percentage of white voters shrinks. It is essential for Republicans to make concerted efforts to appeal, in particular, to Hispanic, Asian, and African American voters. Some Republicans have done an excellent job. Republicans in Texas do well with Hispanic voters. George W. Bush received solid support from Hispanic voters in both of his gubernatorial elections and two presidential elections. Again, in Texas, former Senator Kay Bailey Hutchison and sitting Senator John Cornyn both have done well attracting Hispanic voters. Karl Rove, former Deputy Chief of Staff to President George W. Bush, says that Texas Republicans do well among Hispanics because they campaign throughout the state and the Texas GOP makes a strong effort to recruit Hispanic candidates. Other states should replicate the Texas model.

In his acceptance speech at the 1996 Republican National Convention, Senator Bob Dole said, "The Republican Party is broad and inclusive ... It represents many streams of opinion and many points of view. But if there's anyone who has mistakenly attached themselves to our party in the belief that we are not open to citizens of every race and religion, then let me remind you, tonight this hall belongs to the Party of Lincoln. And the exits which are clearly marked are for you to walk out of as I stand this ground without compromise." The GOP needs more men and women with Bob Dole's inclusive vision and the fortitude to discuss race in such a way. We are above all else the Party of Lincoln.

Over the last 25 years, LGBT rights, including the freedom to marry, were a defining social issue in much the same way as race a generation before. It inspires passionate responses from the left and right, though it's quickly becoming less of an issue as younger, more inclusive Republicans come of age. Debates about these issues are much different from a generation ago, especially within the Republican Party. I have been asked whether I would rather have a Democratic president who favors LGBT rights or a Republican president who opposes them. This question gets to the core of the decisions I and other LGBT Republicans must make on a regular basis. I would never support a truly homophobic Republican presidential candidate who was working to roll back LGBT rights such as the freedom to marry. I doubt the GOP will ever nominate a candidate for president who advocates rolling back rights for any group.

George W. Bush posed a difficult choice for me. In his personal life, it's clear he has no bias against LGBT people. For example, he attended a gathering in his honor early in his presidency hosted by a gay neighbor of mine in Washington. But he also raised my suspicions. During the 2000 Republican primaries, John McCain met with the board of the Log Cabin Republicans against the advice of his staff. During the South Carolina primary campaign, the Bush campaign used that meeting like a cudgel against McCain. South Carolina was peppered with robo calls and flyers decrying McCain as a "fag lover."

During an appearance on *Meet the Press*, Bush was asked if he would meet with Log Cabin Republicans, his answer was "probably not." True to his word, when Bush finally secured the nomination. he met with a group of gay Republicans, none of whom were connected to Log Cabin. The nominal purpose of the meeting was to show the campaign was not homophobic and to smooth out some of the damage that had been done during the primaries. As the 2000 convention was commencing in Philadelphia, Bush's campaign finally met with Log Cabin. They literally threatened to destroy LCR if we persisted in criticizing their candidate. Of course, we did not back down; rather we submitted a list of demands of our own, including the appointment of a Log Cabin board member to a senior post in the administration. We wanted someone in the Office of National AIDS Policy. In short, we engaged in real politick. We got some of what we wanted, and we endorsed Bush in 2000. We ultimately had a very positive experience during the first three years of the Bush administration. However, Bush's endorsement in 2004 of a constitutional amendment to ban gay marriage changed all of that. What had been a productive but sometimes awkward relationship quickly became an adversarial one. Log Cabin's board voted not to endorse Bush for re-election in 2004.

Just as with LGBT issues, when things got tough in the GOP, I have stayed to fight. Some LGBT Republicans left the party after Bush's 2004 campaign. I stayed to be a counterweight to that effort and work internally for change. I am glad I did because it has paid off. When it came to Trump, some Republicans decided to leave the party rather than stay and fight for their values. That's a mistake. I have no intention of leaving the party because of Trump. Although I disagree with him on some fundamental issues, I agree with him on many issues, especially his positions on the economy and defense. Most people who left the party did so more because of Trump's style and rhetoric, rather than differences on policy. For me though, it's best to stay and fight for the party's future.

In recent years, the Democratic Party has moved dramatically left. The strident far left views of political figures such as Senator Bernie Sanders (I-VT), Congresswoman Alexandria Ocasio-Cortez (D-NY), and others are downright scary. Whether it's the economy, immigration, the environment, or a host of other issues, the new loony left wants to drastically expand the role of government and erode personal and economic freedom. This faction is now the most powerful in the Democratic Party. This was made clear in the 2020 Democratic presidential primary debates when virtually all candidates agreed with even the most strident positions of Sanders and Ocasio-Cortez. Vice President Biden ultimately won the nomination, but the party is much closer to the views of Senator Sanders and others like him.

The 2018 midterm elections resulted in Nancy Pelosi (D-CA) again becoming Speaker of the House. The democrats wisely recruited mainstream candidates to run in GOP-held districts that had been won by President Trump. Many of these candidates downplayed attacks on President Trump and focused on mainstream kitchen table issues. Once they got to Washington, these new members of Congress reverted to the liberal playbook and followed the herd to the left - even voting to impeach President Trump in late 2019. Even Pelosi - who had supported the mainstream congressional candidates in 2018 is pushing her party left. Like others in her party, she seems blinded by rage against President Trump. Nothing better exemplified that reality than Pelosi tearing up President Trump's 2020 State of the Union speech. It was something I never thought I would witness. A disgusting display of disrespect for the office of the President of the United States from the individual second in the line of succession to the presidency. Again, symbolism often speaks louder than words.

Those who are outside the political process and the party structures often do not have an accurate understanding of how and why change is enacted within the party. As an example, controversial former Michigan GOP committeeman Dave Agema posted on his Facebook page in 2013 that Russian President Vladimir Putin is on the right track with his oppressive policies against the LGBT community. Agema previously had made disparaging comments about gays, Muslims, and other groups. There was an outcry from people outside the party wondering when the national RNC would "do something" about the committeeman. There is no impeachment process for committee members and no tribunals for those who violate party orthodoxy. The only people who can act are the Republican Party members in Michigan in this instance; and that's the way it should be. The

Republican governor and Republican members of the Michigan congressional delegation urged Agema to resign his committeeman seat but to no avail. Although the RNC had no power to remove him, Agema was censured at the 2015 RNC national winter meeting by the executive committee. Agema declined to run for re-election in 2016 and has been replaced by Dr. Robert Steele, who was elected at the 2016 Michigan GOP Convention. It took nearly four years, but Dave Agema more than wore out his welcome. He became an albatross around the neck of the Michigan GOP, and they succeeded in purging him.

Occasionally, even those within the party misunderstand the process. Several years ago, a Log Cabin board member quit because of an incident in Washington State where he lived. He is a Jewish gay man who felt he was being discriminated against by fellow members of the state GOP. He came to me as a member of the Republican National Committee and to the Log Cabin executive director demanding to know what we were going to do about the Washington State GOP. My response was, "What are YOU going to do about it?" He needed to take responsibility for making change happen in his state instead of looking for someone to do it for him. It's not the RNC's job to take care of the problems that exist within the Washington State Party or any other state party; it has neither the responsibility nor the authority to do so.

Perhaps it's my Midwestern upbringing again, but I firmly believe in the principle of self-reliance. People must begin to embrace the authority and responsibility they possess within their own lives and situations. We should foster a spirit of motivated action, not one of petulant entitlement. That goes for the left, the right, and everyone in between. And it certainly goes for those within the Republican Party. Change within the party happens with action, persistence, and patience, as exemplified by the work done by Log Cabin.

But change can also come through attrition. Several years ago, at one of my first D.C. Republican meetings we were about to elect new members when a member stood up and asked, "I wonder how many gays are in the group being recommended to us? We seem to pay attention to how many blacks we have, how many Hispanics, how many women? So now how many gays are a part of this new group?"

I was shocked, but it was the straight people in the room who went ballistic. One older straight white male member made it clear that we should be concerned with the quality of the individual members, not their race, sexual orientation, or cultural background. It was a powerful moment, one that made me proud of our local GOP in the nation's capital. As for the offender, he soon quit attending meetings.

At the 2013 Hollywood RNC meeting where I made my statement about my sexual orientation, there was a promising moment at the event's closing breakfast. In his closing remarks, RNC Chairman Reince Priebus made an impassioned speech. He said that as long as he was RNC chairman, everybody was welcome in the GOP. It was a direct reference to me and to the events that occurred earlier in the week. It also was meant to be a general declaration of where the party needs to be.

My tactics always lean towards private dialogue rather than public statements. For example, a few years ago I sent a book by Log Cabin board member Dave Lampo titled, *A Fundamental Freedom: Why Republicans, Conservatives, and Libertarians Should Support Gay Rights* to my fellow Republican national committee people. I wanted to share a well-written treatise about LGBT rights with all RNC members in the hope that it would spur conversation, thought, and change. I knew some members would probably reject the subject matter and resent me for sending it. I was right on both counts. I received quite a few positive responses including a comment from RNC Chairman Reince Priebus saying that he intended to read the book as soon as possible. Bruce Ash, Chairman of the RNC Rules committee, sent a note thanking me for sending the book and that he too intended to read it at the first opportunity. In addition to favorable comments, I received notes from a few committee members saying I was a heathen who would end up in hell. As expected, the responses covered a range of opinions. But those who received the book again learned I am not ashamed of who I am, and I am not afraid to express my views even when they might be unpopular. It's not in my nature to call myself courageous, but I try to maintain my intellectual and moral integrity regardless of who I am interacting with. That will continue.

My mother moved from Cincinnati to Florida in 2014 after my father's death. I try to see her as much as possible. She's nearly 100 years old.

Ronna McDaniel (third from right) has led the Republican National Committee since 2017. She has been a great chairwoman and good friend.

Republican Senator Susan Collins from Maine has been a vocal and consistent supporter of LGBT equality and a strong ally of Log Cabin Republicans. This photo is from a Log Cabin Spirit of Lincoln dinner a few years ago.

CHAPTER 24

A More Perfect Union

WHAT HAPPENS NEXT? WHETHER DONALD TRUMP SERVES FOUR years or eight years, it's useful to think about what happens to the nation in general and the Republican Party in particular after he's gone from office. Our nation is in a unique and challenging time, especially the political environment. Whether left, middle, or right, most Americans would agree the U.S. is more divided than any time in recent memory. Not since the late '60s has the country seen such division and disorder. Back then, we emerged from those difficult years stronger than ever. There's no reason the same thing can't happen in the years and decades ahead. I've always been an optimist at heart, and I remain one today. Before mapping out some thoughts on the road ahead, it's helpful to assess how we got to now.

President Donald Trump is a symptom of our toxic political environment, not the cause. He sometimes has amplified the nastiness, but the discord certainly didn't start with him. Even so, the division is at a fever pitch. That is a function of three factors: the dominance of social media, 24-hour cable news, and partisan media outlets. When I was growing up in the 1950s and '60s, the news sources in my hometown were limited to the two daily papers, the *Cincinnati Enquirer* which arrived in the morning and the afternoon *Cincinnati Post*, and the three national television networks. Talk radio did not exist. CBS anchorman Walter Cronkite was the most trusted man in America. Even if you disagreed with your neighbors on one issue or another, we were all getting our news from the same sources, so we could at least agree on the facts. Today, too many Americans live in an information silo where they're never exposed to opinions different than their own. Similarly, their Facebook feed is filled with like-minded friends, they only follow ideologically similar people on Twitter, they watch whatever cable news channel suits their ideology and they peruse news websites whose slant matches their own views. The result is an echo chamber. This has made too many Americans intolerant of people with different opinions. Instead of rationally discussing differences in polite tones, everything is blared in all caps and multiple exclamation points. Quiet dialogue and low-key debate seems impossible. This phenomenon has happened on both the left and right. People on each side are angry with the other side. It's no wonder our society has become more coarse, crude, and cynical.

The root problem of our present national division is a lack of trust in almost every institution; from corporate America to Congress to the presidency to the courts to the military to educational institutions to churches and to Hollywood. Over the last 50 years, Americans have experienced upheaval in many areas, including their churches, their jobs, and their family life.

When I first moved to Washington, the city was filled with people who had strong opinions on just about every public policy issue. Rarely though did people question the motives of their opponents. Not so today where too many people on the left think Republicans are not just wrong on policy, but they're bad people. It's the same on the right. When you question the values and dignity of your political opponents, it's easy to call them names. Or worse, engage in political violence which is what we saw in the spring of 2017 when a deranged Bernie Sanders supporter opened fire on a group of congressional

Republicans practicing for a charity baseball game. Thank God no one was killed, but that may not be the case if something similar happens in the future. Both parties must step back from the brink.

Various organizations have offered ideas to ease partisan tensions and make Washington work better. Among those is the Bipartisan Policy Center (BPC) founded in 2007 by former Senate Majority Leaders Howard Baker, Tom Daschle, Bob Dole, and George Mitchell. Over the years, the BPC has offered suggestions in several areas including governance and specific issue areas such as health, housing, immigration, and others. Its Commission on Political Reform offered a series of specific suggestions to improve public discourse and bring civility back to the public arena. Given my years of working in Congress and the executive branch, I agree with several of their suggestions and offer them and others here. The best thing we can do to improve our political discourse is to elect better people to public office. The environment is so toxic right now that one wonders what person in their right mind would run for Congress, governor or president.

As a starting point, each party should encourage more moderate voices to enter the fray. As parties have gotten more polarized and ideologically "pure," party nominees for House and Senate races are more liberal or conservative. Historically, only party loyalists vote in primaries. That has created a situation where many members of Congress worry only about losing a primary. Therefore, they have no incentive to compromise with the other party. The best remedy for that is having more people participate in the nominating process. Typically, turnout is under 10% in most primaries. Independents and moderates need to get engaged in the process in order to help select more mainstream candidates.

Most states have closed primaries where only registered Republicans or Democrats can vote. As both parties have grown more extreme in recent years, the most extreme voices usually win the nomination of their respective party. It creates a continuous loop which has left Democrats increasingly more liberal and Republicans more conservative.

Some states have gone to open primaries where all registered voters, including independents, can participate in whichever primary they choose. Party leaders often oppose this system because they allege it can lead to mischief. There have been instances where the Republican and Democratic parties have encouraged their voters to cross over to vote for a candidate in the opposing party they view as the weakest general election candidate. As clever as this sounds, it has backfired in some elections, including some states where in 2008 some Republican Party leaders encouraged members to cross over to vote for Barack Obama thinking he would be an easier candidate to defeat than Hillary Clinton. Party leaders also contend that allowing independents and voters registered in the opposing party to vote in their primaries can lead to the nomination of candidates who do not hold the views of rank-and-file party members. Nevertheless, a case can be made that open primaries encourage candidates to soften the hard edges to appeal to independents and voters of the opposing party.

A third alternative primary system is the "modified closed primary," that has been used in California for nearly a decade. Since 2011, as the result of Proposition 14, California primary voters have been allowed to vote for any candidate on the ballot. The top two candidates advance to the general election regardless of party. Presidential elections are exempt as they are contests for convention delegates. In 2016, this system resulted in two Democratic candidates running for the open Senate seat vacated by Senator Barbara Boxer. Similarly, in some recent congressional elections, two Republicans have run against each other and in other congressional districts two Democrats have run against each other. Washington State has a similar process for its primaries. This system, while well intentioned, has not led to a reduction in partisan fervor.

Some states, including Arizona, have open primaries for all offices except president. Louisiana has used a system known as nonpartisan blanket primary since 2008 where all candidates run on the same ballot with candidates needing 50% plus one vote to win; if no one achieves that result, there is a runoff between the top two vote-getters. As a starting point, at least independents should be allowed to vote in whichever primary they prefer.

States should take concerted efforts to increase voter participation in primaries. Primaries are notorious for their limited appeal to voters. Only the most ideologically strident show up to vote for the most strident candidates. Having been deeply involved in the DCGOP for many elections, there are proven ways to encourage voters to participate in primaries and general elections. Doing so takes concerted efforts by state and local parties to educate the electorate on candidates and election day activities by implementing robust get-out-the-vote efforts.

States also should avoid low voter turnout candidate selection methods such as caucuses and conventions that limit the participation rate of registered voters. These systems lead to only the most strident voters showing up to vote. Be vigilant for voter fraud, including comparing state voter lists that can be done electronically, to make certain voters aren't voting in more than one jurisdiction, unless local law permits otherwise.

Aside from flawed candidate selection methods, gerrymandering has led to more extreme candidates for Congress and state legislatures. The decennial census determines how many congressional seats are allocated to each state. After every census, some states lose seats, primarily in the East and Midwest, while others, primarily in the South and West, have gained seats in recent decades. The U.S. Constitution specifically says state legislatures are to draw Congressional districts. The Supreme Court has ruled that each district must have approximately the same number of residents. If the state legislature is controlled by one party, that party works to draw lines that favor its candidates. This may include drawing districts that assure defeat for candidates of the opposing party while enhancing districts that favor their candidates. This is known as gerrymandering. The term comes from Massachusetts Governor Elbridge Gerry who in 1812 signed legislation to draw district lines in Massachusetts to favor his political party. The outline of one Senate district looked like a salamander, thus the term "gerrymander" was coined.

In states where the two parties split control of the chambers, compromise is required to reach a consensus redistricting plan. Redistricting determinations often are challenged in court. In 2018, the Democratic controlled Pennsylvania Supreme Court threw out the maps drawn by the Republican controlled legislature. The move ended up giving Democrats at least three more U.S. House seats. The Pennsylvania Republican Party unsuccessfully challenged the state court ruling to the U.S. Supreme Court. The nation's high court recently decided to stay out of the redistricting fight. They will let states continue to call the shots.

Some states have established independent commissions to determine congressional and state legislative district seats. In 2008, California voters approved the California Citizens Redistricting Commission, a bipartisan commission that determines the districts for state political offices. In 2010, congressional seats were brought into this system. The mission of the California Commission is to try to make political districts more balanced and less calculated to favor one party or another, however subsequent investigative reporting showed that Golden State Democrats manipulated the Commission to create maps more favorable to them. Time will tell if this concept works in practice. It hasn't so far in the California. However, for decades Iowa has been a model of non-partisan redistricting. States should adopt redistricting commissions with bipartisan support. Some states have already taken this approach, but it is too soon to know if it will succeed in bringing credibility to the redistricting process, thereby encouraging more voters to participate in elections. Collectively, these initiatives embrace the democratic process by encouraging more voter participation. Having broader based voter participation will strengthen our system and give the electorate reason to feel better about the system men and women in uniform have fought to protect.

No discussion of contemporary politics can occur without talking about money. Our system is largely influenced by the Bipartisan Campaign Reform Act of 2002, commonly known by the names of its sponsors, Senators John McCain and Russ Feingold. McCain-Feingold took the major party entities out of their power position by setting limits on the amount of money individuals could give to party campaign committees. McCain-Feingold led to a significant unintended consequence: the creation of so-called Super PACs. Since donors could no longer give unlimited amounts to official party campaign committees, Super PACs emerged as legal and efficient ways to indirectly provide money to candidates.

Super PACs answer to no one except the people who run them. One catch though. Super PACs are not allowed to coordinate their activities with candidates. That means a Super PAC might spend millions of dollars on a congressional or senate campaign, but it's not in coordination with the candidate. They often have enormous amounts of money and few guidelines about when and how to spend the money. PACs, run by figures such as the Koch Brothers and Sheldon Adelson on the right and George Soros and Tom Steyer on the left, spend money to support like-minded candidates and ideas. In a controversial 2010 decision, a divided Supreme Court protected campaign spending as a First Amendment freedom. Unfettered political spending has been damaging, especially insofar as it has neutered the authority of the party organizations and their ability to produce effective candidates and campaigns. Only the political parties can legally coordinate directly with candidates and McCain-Feingold seriously damaged their ability to do that job. Super PACs cannot fill that void. Also, Super PAC donations are anonymous, so voters have no idea who is influencing a race. McCain-Feingold had a noble goal to remove the corrupting influence of money in politics, but it hasn't worked. To bring more transparency and accountability to the system, Congress should once again allow campaign committees for each party to receive large donations, requiring disclosure in a meaningful and timely fashion. Doing so would give the parties more control over candidates which will inevitably lead to more mainstream office holders on the left and right. A member of Congress will be more likely to tow the party line if their campaign support hinges on it. Loyalty is a two-way street. Making this change also would decrease the role of Super PACs.

It usually takes millions of dollars to run a congressional or a gubernatorial campaign. Candidates must devote a huge amount of time and energy to raising money. Someone unwilling to do that might as well skip the race altogether. Consequently, many qualified people choose not to run. Who can blame them? It's important to remember that money is no guarantee of victory. Several studies show that the better-funded candidate loses about half the time. There are also numerous cases of wealthy entrepreneurs or uber-rich heirs and heiresses losing races even though they had virtually limitless budgets. That research is encouraging because it debunks the notion that having more money than your opponent is the sole deciding factor. Having sufficient money gets you a ticket to the dance as a serious candidate, but many other factors determine whether you win. President Trump certainly showed that money isn't everything. He was outspent in both the GOP primary and the general election, but he still won the race. Joe Biden showed the same thing in 2020. He won the Democratic nomination in spite of his anemic fund-raising totals.

Getting any campaign finance laws passed in our current political environment will prove difficult, but I hope both parties could agree that transparency should be the consistent rule in campaign contributions whether for individual candidates, PACs, Super PACs, Leadership PACs, or any other vehicle used for contributing political money. As noted above, the McCain-Feingold contribution limits should be lifted for contributions to state parties. The current limitations led to the creation of Super PACs that are prohibited from coordinating with candidates. This development has damaged the credibility of our political system. Only official political parties, whether state or local can work directly with candidates and they should be strengthened. Also, Congressional Leadership PACs should be required to limit expenditures to political activities and not personal use.

One more note about the chase for cash. Members of Congress spend so much time raising money that one wonders when they study policy proposals. Also, they have little time to forge friendships with their colleagues in the House and Senate. When I came to Washington, most lawmakers such as Senator Lugar lived in Washington with their families. Lawmakers weren't dashing to fund-raisers all the time, so they had time to enjoy a meal or cocktail with their colleagues. The friendships that emerged became essential when lawmakers had to craft difficult compromises. Those close relationships are largely missing today. And so are compromises.

The reforms mentioned above should lead to a better crop of public officials in Washington: more mainstream and less beholden to special interests. There are also reforms that should be done to improve how Congress operates, especially the Senate. I'm proud to have worked in that august institution, but the body today is much different than it was in my day. And not in a good way. Hyper-partisanship makes governing nearly impossible, no matter which party controls the Senate. The downward spiral has been a long time coming. The 1987 Supreme Court nomination fight over Robert Bork changed everything. It has worsened through the years, so we're now in a situation where Democrats block routine nominees for the Trump administration. Precious floor time is wasted to clear the roadblock. Democrats argue that during the Obama administration, Republican senators used the same techniques. It's tit for tat.

When Senator Harry Reid and the Democrats controlled the Senate during the first six years of the Obama administration, Republicans were criticized for being the party of "No" because they extensively used the 60-vote requirement on filibusters. The news media rarely pointed out that Harry Reid utilized procedural moves to prevent Republicans from offering amendments on the Senate floor. In fact, Reid's approach led several Republican challengers to attack their Democratic opponents for siding overwhelmingly with the unpopular Obama. They didn't have the opportunity to vote on measures Obama found objectionable. This approach backfired and damaged the Senate as the "greatest deliberative body in the world." Since early 2015, Republican Senator Mitch McConnell has led the Senate. While he allows members of both parties to offer more floor amendments, he should do so more often. However, that's partly the Democrat's fault for slowing Senate business with procedural roadblocks against Trump nominees.

Another way to regain credibility and stability for both parties in Congress is to return to what in Washington is known as "regular order." This means returning to the way Congress traditionally has worked, pursuant to the established rules. A good example of this is passing individual appropriations bills rather than lumping all twelve appropriations bills into one massive omnibus or Continuing Resolution, referred to as the "Chromnibus" at the end of the 113th Congress in 2014. The same thing happened more recently with the massive spending bill passed in March of 2018. Getting back to regular order will require arduous work and discipline from the Republican majority, including meeting deadlines and limiting floor time for debate in the Senate. The last time all twelve individual bills were passed before the beginning of the fiscal year was way back in 1994. Returning to this process will require Congress to focus on its oversight job of reviewing and acting on the President's budget that usually is delivered in mid-to-late January near the time of the president's State of the Union speech. It will take much of the mischief out of a distorted process that results in intense ridicule from many quarters. Congress should get serious about imposing "regular order" in the legislative process. This means having the legislative system work as it was designed, including requiring committee markups, amendments on the House or Senate floor and conference committees for important legislation to iron out difference on critical issues. For many years, very little legislation has gone through this rigorous process. Bringing back regular order would produce better legislation and secure broader support from members of the House and Senate.

For decades, Congress utilized the system of earmarks as a carrot to gain votes for legislation that might otherwise be difficult to pass. Earmarks allowed members of Congress to direct funding of specific projects to his or her district. Often criticized but generally recognized as helpful to the legislative process, earmarks were abandoned in the House when Republicans took control in 2011. New House Speaker Boehner from Ohio had always opposed earmarks and prided himself in never seeking any for his district. In 2005, an earmark by Alaska Republican Congressman Don Young to build a bridge in a remote part of his state became known as "The Bridge to Nowhere." The debate over this earmark became national news and contributed to the end of earmarks. Keep in mind that eliminating earmarks didn't mean less money was spent. It just meant executive department bureaucrats doled out the dollars. In fact, a member of Congress has a better idea than bureaucrats where federal dollars should be spent in their districts. Earmarks accounted for less than one percent of the federal budget, and they helped encourage members to vote for legislation they might not otherwise support. Earmarks greased the skids of Congress and allowed for more bipartisan legislation.

The House and Senate should coordinate their legislative calendars, so they are in Washington at the same time and take recess breaks at the same time. Doing so would assist the legislative process and allow members more time to work together, thereby getting to know one another better. Knowing both chambers will be in recess at the same time may encourage more members to remain in D.C. on weekends where they can get to know each other on a less formal basis. As with most things in life, personal relationships are essential to productivity and general happiness.

Encourage the opportunity for floor amendments to be offered in both houses of Congress. The House and Senate rules differ greatly but both can be adjusted to accommodate this basic rule of civility. Both Republican and Democratic leaders have worked to limit or prevent amendments for members of the minority. Changing this dynamic will produce a better working relationship with both parties. And more importantly, it'll produce better legislation.

Additionally, a biannual budget and appropriations process should be established. The federal government is so massive that a two-year cycle make sense from a process standpoint and for Congressional oversight of programs. In recent years, Congress often has not produced a budget resolution that merely provides guidelines to congressional committees on authorizations and appropriations.

Since arriving in D.C. in 1975, I have seen how politics has gone from being intensely competitive but also respectful and collegial to bitterly divisive and excessively partisan. While politics involves conflict and clear differences, there was a time when legislation got passed with support from bipartisan coalitions and politics always stopped at the border. I hate today's excessive partisan atmosphere, as does almost everyone I know who has lived through this period. Mine is not a yearning for the good old days because many of them were not particularly good, it's more a desire to return to a more civilized and respectful world of politics.

Beyond Washington, it's heartening to see continued progress for the LGBT community. Aside from legislative and judicial victories, the biggest change continues being seen in the hearts and minds of Americans. Having LGBT individuals out in their communities has had a positive impact on the increasing level of acceptance. Even so, much work remains to advance full equality for LGBT Americans. While the Supreme Court has ruled in favor of the freedom to marry, the bitterly divided Court reflects the country's sentiments on this issue. Some will never find same sex marriage acceptable. Others will come around slowly as they get to know married same sex couples and realize their marriage isn't hurting anyone.

Another issue that has made progress but is not fully resolved is workplace discrimination. In most states, it's still legal to fire someone for being LGBT. Despite that fact, many businesses, particularly large corporations, have nondiscrimination policies in place to protect LGBT employees. More states such as Michigan and Pennsylvania are considering LGBT workplace non-discrimination laws with bipartisan support. In too many places, progressive organizations make the perfect the enemy of the good. They refuse to allow reasonable exemptions for religious liberty. Efforts to pass federal legislation are bogged down for the same reason. LGBT advocates have proposed overly broad legislation they know Republicans will oppose. It appears Democrats don't want to enact legislation but instead want to keep the issue alive to rally the base and make Republicans look intolerant. Eventually, a federal employment non-discrimination law will pass Congress, but it's still years away.

I return to the theme I stressed at the Members Only breakfast in Los Angeles. Generational change will mandate essential reforms to the GOP, or it will cease to exist as a viable national party. As younger generations that were raised to accept LGBT friends, neighbors, and family members mature, there will be a time when we will wonder why same sex marriage was ever denied or why any LGBT person lost a job due to his or her sexuality. This time is not that far off.

I am delighted to have had so many opportunities to be involved and to lead at certain junctures in this effort. My involvement has enriched my life with meaning and brought me numerous friends and new colleagues along the way. I am optimistic about the future of the Republican Party and its acceptance of LGBT Americans. While the Trump administration hasn't been perfect on LGBT issues, the president's inclusive rhetoric and recent initiatives on HIV/AIDS and international decriminalization of homosexuality have shown leadership on issues of importance to us.

Donald Trump's strident rhetoric on immigration has alienated millions of Hispanics and other minority groups. The economic gains Hispanics made during his first term before the COVID-19 economic downturn may alter that view, but the rhetoric is there, nonetheless. The country is becoming more diverse. In the decades ahead, white people will no longer be a majority of the population. It's imperative for Republicans in the years ahead to attract these voters. Our economic message and record can help attract these Americans. I believe there's a reasonable compromise on immigration: tighter border controls, permanent status for illegal immigrants, and a rigorous system to keep employers from hiring undocumented immigrants. America is unique in our ability to integrate immigrants from across the planet into one nation with shared values. Despite the hot rhetoric in Washington, we can continue this successful integration. Beyond the divisive social media platforms, Americans have more that unites us than divides us. We must do better talking to our neighbors, rather than staring into our phones.

Going forward, the party can appeal to a broad constituency by advocating these policies:

- Stress the basic framework of a strong national defense and foreign policy, limited government, and free enterprise principles.
- Take it easy on the social issues. Pandering to pro-life groups and anti-LGBT factions will alienate independent voters.
- Stress economic growth through entrepreneurship. The young entrepreneurs in this country want minimal government regulation and pathways for growth and innovation.
- Advocate for limited government in private life. History has shown an all-powerful government will abuse its power. Millennials and other independents are against the idea of federal government agencies having access to every part of their lives. Government needs to be diminished not just in the boardroom and bedroom, but also in cyberspace.
- Improve existing trade agreements and trade adjustment assistance legislation to provide realistic opportunities for the displaced blue and white-collar workers who are impacted by globalization and international trade agreements. These Americans deserve focused attention so their lives and those of their families can be improved.

It takes an optimist to confront a tough situation and believe it can be changed. It's important to continue being involved in political life in America. Only those who show up and participate are heard. I continue working in the political arena because I want to impact our public policy and our society. History teaches us that a small group of people with a big idea grounded in principles can change the world. A carpenter's son has an idea about the nature of love and redemption, twelve men agree with him and there is change. An exhausted African American woman refuses to give up her seat on a bus to a white man, a young preacher in Alabama hears about it and there is change. For all the stress and sacrifice that I and others have had to make as LGBT Republicans, the progress we've seen advancing our just cause makes all of it worthwhile.

My brother Greg and I visited our mother in Florida to celebrate her 99th birthday in 2019. My mother has a great network of friends in Naples who look after one another.

I remain very close to my brother Greg. He joined me for a White House holiday party in 2018.

This is a recent photo at the dedication of a statue in the U.S. Capitol to honor Frederick Douglass, the abolitionist and orator who was the most prominent member of the D.C. Republican Party, which was founded before the Civil War. The D.C. GOP continues to be inspired by his views of equality and freedom.